TO THE
BONE

TO THE BONE

PAUL LIEBRANDT & ANDREW FRIEDMAN

PHOTOGRAPHY BY EVAN SUNG

I dedicate this book to my father, who set me on the road that I am on. Never has there been a wiser word said to me by any man other than you.

Published in the United States by Clarkson Potter/
Publishers, an imprint of the Crown Publishing
Group, a division of Random House, Inc., New York.
www.crownpublishing.com
www.clarksonpotter.com

CLARKSON POTTER is a trademark and POTTER
with colophon is a registered trademark of Random
House, Inc.

Library of Congress Cataloging-in-Publication Data
Liebrandt, Paul, 1976–
    To the bone/Paul Liebrandt and Andrew
Friedman.—First edition.
        pages cm
1. Liebrandt, Paul, 1976–   2. Cooks—United
States—Biography.   3. Cooks—Great Britain—
Biography.   4. Corton (Restaurant)   I. Friedman,
Andrew, 1967–   II. Title.
    TX149.L48A3 2013
    641.5092—dc23
    [B]
2013007785

ISBN 978-0-7704-3416-8
eISBN 978-0-7704-3417-5

Printed in China

Book and jacket design by Stephanie Huntwork
Jacket photography by Evan Sung

10   9   8   7   6   5   4   3   2   1

First Edition

CONT

Canapé		Eggs		Foie Chantilly ✔	
Potatoes croquette					
marshmallows ✔		asparagus royal ✔		Cucumber gelee ✔	
black rice		Parmesan Espuma		pickled egg yolk	
crackers		black garlic jelly H2O ✔		Rubarbe Terrine *cool & slice* ✔	
		smoked maldon		Combawa	
		coffee salt		Pistachio Dentil	
Financier batter				Red Pepper Dentil ✔	
Herb Puree				lemon mayo	
Ricotta yogurt/kombu				Rubarbe paper	
Mornay ✔		**Foie Gras**			
		Devein Foie			
Sea		Cook/pipe Foie ✔			
		Glaze Foie		**Guinea Hen**	
Quail egg		beet/hibiscus glaze		cook / glaze pheasant ✔	
Halibut		glazed apple ✔		cauliflower puree	
yuzu gel ✔		beet gel ✔		pickled cauliflower ✔	
~~seaweed~~2		beet cylinders ✔		pea puree	
pickled cucumber ✔		mustard/huckle mix ✔		rye dentil	
kinome		dry black olives		apple	
		apricot/olive butter		pheasant consomme jelly	
john dory		beet dentil ✔			
john dory terrine *slice* ✔		cooked apples			
black rice		pickled beet			
textured EVO					
tapanade					
lemon confit					
bowl set ✔ II		**pork terrine**			
		smoked anchovie ✔			
		mandarinequat c			
Oysters		ruhbarbe confit		Wh... ...ragus	
Oyster gel		pickled onion			
Mandarin Oil		croquette			
kumquat confit		white oni			
Buckwheat		gribec			
Smoked Maldon					
~~X...~~					
		du			
		her			
Beef		Carr			
tartar		cauliflo			
buckwheat blini		herb c			
grapefruit confit		pickled			
		pickled			
		cockle			
		razor c			
		Razor			

FOREWORD

Although he has made his name at the terrific Corton in New York, Paul Liebrandt is, like me, a London boy. In the opening pages of this captivating book he writes evocatively about a number of experiences I can relate to. Chinatown, Butterkist popcorn, and watching movies in the big West End cinemas were all part of my upbringing, too. Paul tells of how, as a kid, he was fascinated by the hare and grouse hanging in the Berwick Street butchers' windows, marveling at the mechanics of taking an animal and separating it into neat cuts of meat. (His dish, Royale of Hare, is in part inspired by this.) Similarly, I remember well being made to trudge round a West London market on Sundays with my gran, with only the promise of an ice cream at the end of it all to keep me going. Ever since, ice cream has been a special enthusiasm of mine. Such formative influences have a great impact on your creative life.

Paul and I took very different routes up the ladder of our profession. I'm a self-taught chef, whereas he undertook apprenticeships at various establishments—L'Escargot, Marco Pierre White's legendary The Restaurant, Pied à Terre, Le Manoir aux Quat'Saisons, Pierre Gagnaire, Bouley—all of which he memorably describes here. He's good on the crazy nature of restaurant life: the dodgy dorms, drinking binges, sleep deprivation, cama-raderie, and quirky personalities, and the infernal heat in poorly ventilated kitchens that had him periodically tipping an entire bottle of water over himself. He's thoughtful and eloquent on the downsides of culinary life that can make it hard to take: the repetitive drudgery, the pressure of proving yourself day after day, the isolation. Reading these pages, you'll get a good sense of what it's like to be in the kitchen, the highs and the lows.

Although we cut our teeth in different ways, when Paul came to eat at The Fat Duck, I quickly recognized a kindred spirit—someone who, culinarily speaking, speaks my language. For me, good food is ultimately about emotion. Of course, you have to practice, develop, and perfect the necessary techniques (as you'll see, Paul learned how to devein foie gras the hard way), otherwise there are likely to be limits to what you can achieve creatively. But eating is a multisensory experience, and a large part of the deliciousness of food comes from its appeal to the five senses: taste, smell, sight, touch—in terms of our appreciation of different textures—and even sound. (You'd be amazed at how much of our detection of the freshness of, say, an apple, comes from what we hear as we crunch into it.) And this appeal in turn triggers all kinds of memories and associations that can enormously enhance the perception of flavor.

This is something that Paul understands. Early on in his apprenticeship, he says, he realized that in cooking there was "a simple animal attraction to the tasks that appealed to my senses." It's this sensual appreciation that gives his cuisine a strength of character. Thus his dish "The Marine," with its oyster, apple, onion meringue, and shallot cream, grown out of Paul's fondness for the heady saline scent of sea foam. His Smoked Caramel and Pomegranate picks up on the caramel flavor of the Butterkist popcorn he relished at the movies. Many people think that this emotional aspect of cooking doesn't fit well with a technical, scientific approach. To me this attitude never made much sense, and Paul takes a similar viewpoint. Working with pastry in the early days of his apprenticeship showed him the value of precision and consistency and, like me, he saw no reason why that shouldn't apply to savory dishes just as much as sweet ones. This has become part of his signature style. There's a telling moment early on in this book where Paul talks of his youthful enthusiasm for *Star Wars* action figures. "I was most drawn to Darth Vader," he says, "but it wasn't because he was the villain; it was the purity and clean lines of his black-as-night costume." Purity and clean lines—it's a pretty good description of his style of cooking.

It's this approach that leads to the kind of dishes included in this book: Cod Cheek with Smoked Bone Marrow and Black Trumpet; Beet-Hibiscus-Glazed Foie Gras with Trevise; Black Sesame Crème with Purple Potato Ice Cream and Cashew Paste—these are beautiful, precise, well-thought-out plates of food. But from the way Paul talks about his cooking, you can also understand the emotion that has gone into them—how his Rhubarb, Strawberry, and Cucumber Royale is infused with memories of his Sussex boarding school. How the dress-shaped white-beer gel in his Summer Crab Composition reflects Paul's Sundays spent girl-watching in the pub. And how his take on "The Bagel" and the skyscraper shape of his "Gold Bar" dessert both reflect his excitement on first arriving in New York as a twenty-three-year-old looking for work. If you've ever wondered where the heck a modern chef gets his inspiration from, these pages will give you some idea of how it works. You'll get privileged access to one of the most innovative, skillful, and idiosyncratic chefs in America.

Paul calls this book—which is part-memoir, part-cookbook—a literary tasting menu. It's time to dig in and enjoy.

—HESTON BLUMENTHAL

INTRODUCTION

From the time I was old enough to make decisions about such things, my life has been defined by The Food.

I write it that way because that's how I think of it: as the object of an existential quest, to be pursued at the expense of just about anything else. In the name of The Food, at one time or another, I've worked for nothing in faraway lands where I didn't speak the language, lived in meager and unsanitary quarters, commuted to and from work at times and in places that would make any mother fear for her son's safety, and slept on a banquette or the floor in my own restaurant for days on end.

Why would I, or anyone, voluntarily do such things? It might be difficult for those not blessed and burdened by such attachments to understand, but at some level, cooking is an art that relies on the marriage of craft and inspiration. Craft is the easy part: anybody armed with the requisite aptitude and discipline can master the technical part of cooking, though it might take years. Inspiration, on the other hand, is like a demanding lover who flits in and out of your life as she pleases, insisting that you be available for her arrival and ready to act on a moment's notice, lest the opportunity pass you by.

Then, of course, there's the cruel joke perpetrated on chefs by the cosmos. It's not enough to have one perfect idea; it must be realized dozens of times each day, at great expense, with most of the work carried out by people who don't have the benefit of living in your head. There are no Emily Dickinsons in the cooking trade, no chefs who toil anonymously and independently in their family attics, leaving their work to future generations to discover and appreciate. On a daily basis, chefs need a well-equipped place in which to work, cooks to prepare our food, and guests to pay for the privilege of eating it. If you've ever wondered why so many chefs are known to terrorize their staffs, or behave like alcoholics after a night on the line, or burn out and fade away at tragically young ages, much of the answer can be found in the pressures created by that unholy trinity.

Does all of that sound unhealthy? It can be. But in my experience, the highs justify the lows. I discovered The Food as a painfully shy, unhappy boy, and it gave shape and meaning to my life. Hailing from a single-parent household, it offered me an alternate home in which to pass my days and nights. Without a specific ambition, it provided something to strive for; as a child never given to words, it gifted me with a vocabulary of flavors, colors, and textures with which to address and engage the world.

It also became the lens through which I see my life. Where some people have photo albums and journals, I have The Food. The ingredients and techniques I have worked with, and the way they come together in my dishes, are nothing less than snapshots of my life—not only of the kitchens in which I've worked and the influences I took from them, but also of where I was living and what I was thinking and feeling at any given time.

In these pages, I share a bit of my story, along with some dishes that mark the stops along the way—all with the hope that they might give a sense of what it's like to become and to be a chef. I'm too young to consider this a memoir. And there are not enough recipes to qualify it as a cookbook. Think of it, then, as a literary tasting menu, a representation of one chef's life so far, summed up—as all chefs inevitably are—by the dishes cooked and eaten along the way.

—PAUL LIEBRANDT, New York City, Summer 2013

FIRST STIRRINGS

London 1982–1990

The more I think on it, the more I regard The Food in near-religious terms.

Chefs come and go, contributing what we can to the continuum, but we are players in something much larger than ourselves. Moreover, for me and for many who have taken up this pursuit, The Food was our salvation, offering a shape to our lives, a sense of purpose and direction that was lacking before we found our calling.

Kitchens aren't just kitchens: they're insane asylums, penitentiaries, and classrooms all rolled into one. In a way, it's amazing that any cooking actually gets done in them, but then again, cooks have to eat, too.

Cooking has become a more respectable pursuit in the past few decades, so it attracts a broader swath of eager participants than it once did. Not long ago, it was the profession of last resort, the final stop on the way out of society or the first stop on the way back in. Now it promises glitz and glamour, but only to its most famous practitioners. At its heart, it remains a menial endeavor that often demands sweatshop hours and wages, requires one to work on weekends and holidays, and leaves you unable to relate to anyone other than your kitchen brethren.

Whatever attracted me to such a place?

Like so many cooks, I stumbled into it, then realized it was where I belonged. I'm not sure whether to call it fate or luck or a combination of the two, but fortune definitely played a role because I was born into a life bereft of anything resembling fine dining. I didn't grow up in the Hudson River Valley eating ramps or in Paris with fresh bread on every corner. My first and only taste memory from earliest childhood was the occasional strawberry-picking trips my family made to the countryside outside London. I was too young to remember exactly where we found them, but I remember being fascinated by both their vibrant red color and the pleasures unleashed with each bite, qualities about which I ruminated on the drive back to London. Those berries stand out in my memory, bursts of color and flavor against the gray backdrop of my youth, like the flashes of an amnesiac. There were no external signs pointing me to where I am now, but when I look back at those berries and how vividly I recall them, I realize that there was within me the seedling of a chef, a larval being waiting to be nurtured and coaxed into existence.

Were I prone to melodrama or self-pity, I might say that I had the most clichéd of beginnings: the unhappy childhood. I was an only child, and my parents had no extended family. It was just me and them, and they did not get along, separating when I was six years old, then getting back together for one last, ill-fated go at it when I was eleven. Life at home was turbulent and isolating, even though we lived in the center of London, one of the busiest cities in the world. I could look out the window or venture outside into the street, with thousands of people rushing by, yet my enduring memory is one of complete and utter loneliness.

Our living situation was the great silver lining of those years: we resided at 90 Charing Cross Road, a government-subsidized Victorian building in central London. Like many working, middle-class families—my mother was a flight attendant for British Airways, my father a military man—my parents had put themselves on the wait list for such an accommodation. When our number came up, we lucked out with a spacious three-bedroom penthouse flat beyond what I ever could have imagined. The location itself was unconventional, the equivalent to living in New York City's Times Square.

My mother was a passable cook, but for the sake of convenience, we often ate ready-made meals. To her credit, she sought out the very best prepared foods available, such as those sold by Marks & Sparks, the nickname by which we all referred to British retailer Marks & Spencer. My favorite, both for its flavor and presentation, was a perfectly rectangular piece of cod that came packed in a vibrant, green parsley sauce in a vacuum-sealed bag. You boiled the bag (my first introduction to a kind of *sous vide* cooking), then snipped it open and laid the fish out on a plate. My mother served it with *petits pois* and homemade mashed potatoes in our family living room.

Even those dinners were emblematic of my parents'—especially my father's—modus operandi: always making the most of their resources to give me the best things possible within our means. For the same reason, they worked their asses off to get me into a proper school and also to get me out of our odd but luxurious location in central London. And so, there I was at eight, a shy lad arriving at St. Aubyns, a boarding school in Rottingdean, a lovely, quaint little village just down the British coast from Brighton. The school was an exclusive academy with just a dozen or so students per class, and was a far sight better than the overcrowded classrooms of London.

St. Aubyns was populated by the upper crust: classmates' names were preceded by "Lord" and "Lady," "Duke" and "Duchess." Every three weeks, we were allowed to go home for the weekend, but because my parents' schedules often found them in far-flung countries or literally in the air, I wouldn't always have a home to go to. Fortunately, some friends invited me to stay with them, but the dichotomy between their lot and mine was stark. One classmate lived on an estate in Buckinghamshire, an expansive and manicured property that you entered through regal, motorized gates opening up to a private road, at the end of which stood a Georgian-era almost-castle with forty rooms and more staff than family. We rode quads (motorized four-wheel bikes) around the grounds and shot clay pigeons out in the field.

The food at St. Aubyns lacked such grandeur or nobility. Breakfast, served at long, wobbly wooden tables, might be fried eggs swimming in a tray of fat or, in the winter, gigantic bowls of porridge, thick as cement, that'd we'd top with milk and—in the British fashion—mountainous heapings of white sugar. The first day they served it to us, the cooks perpetrated a harmless prank, swapping dishes of salt for the sugar. The other students were scandalized, leaping from their seats and cursing the kitchen staff; however, I couldn't help but chuckle at their malicious sense of humor, perhaps a sign of the cook that lurked inside me.

If you could look past such indignities, there were some sensory pleasures to be had at St. Aubyns. In springtime, the gardens were redolent with cucumber, and wild strawberries and raspberries winked at us from beneath the low-lying bushes like hidden Easter eggs. We students loved nibbling on those berries, but the faculty didn't appreciate it. They thought our snacking showed a lack of discipline, and the picked-over shrubs weren't near as lovely to look at as those in full fruit. And so the faculty dreamed up a myth, perpetuated to dissuade us: "Don't eat the fruit off the tree. You'll get sick." (I hear it in my memory as a variation of the infamous schoolmaster rant in Pink Floyd's *The Wall:* "How can you have any pudding if you don't eat yer meat?")

Did I say that I didn't think much about food as a child? Let me amend that: those berries, forbidden fruit that they were, positively obsessed me. When I was certain nobody was looking, I'd help myself to a few. Their flavor, relative to their size, never failed to put a smile on my face. Like those strawberries I'd picked with my parents, they were among the first delicacies I'd ever tasted. *How could so much bright flavor be contained in those little berries?* I wondered.

If you described the kind of food I cook today to either of my parents at the time, it would have seemed the stuff of high comedy or maybe science fiction. Yet who would've blamed them for their skepticism? My father grew up in Rhodesia, now called Zimbabwe, in a family where meals were considered sustenance and little more. My mother came of age in London in the aftermath of World War II and had the jaw-dropping stories to prove it. One day, playing with friends in a vacant lot, she discovered the skeletal remains of a German fighter pilot; another time, an unexploded bomb turned up in the yard next door. As a young girl, she drank powdered milk and ate whatever was rationed to her family. Food was sustenance, if sustenance was to be had at all.

All of which is to say that I don't know where my interest in food came from, but I did tend to *experience* it rather intensely, just as I felt certain other pastimes very intensely—none more so than movies. One of my favorite boyhood rituals was spending Sunday afternoons in the cinema with my Dad. My father had, and retains, a commanding presence, but he was never an intimidating figure to me. Quite the opposite, in fact: he was loving and attentive, understood the place of a father in a son's life, and made it a

Rhubarb, Strawberry, and Cucumber Royale

This royale was inspired by fragrance, a paean to the English countryside, specifically springtime at St. Aubyns, when berries are on the bush and verbena and cucumber sweetly perfume the air. Just as I once stood in that garden, eating berries while surrounded by the scent of cucumber, the body of this royale—made of *fraises des bois* and rhubarb, a semifrozen *crème Chiboust* (a pastry cream) with rhubarb and lemon-verbena infusion at its core—is wrapped with a cucumber gelée that is in turn encircled with slivered cucumber. (Young green rhubarb has a whiff of cucumber about it, and this dessert plays on that fact.) To reinforce its botanic origins, the dish is garnished with verbena, *shiso*, and violet petals, and adorned with a hibiscus meringue. All of these themes are underscored by a moat of chilled rhubarb and strawberry consommé with a hibiscus-verbena infusion and a cucumber *granité* to the side.

priority to be that man for me. The first movie I remember him taking me to was *Return of the Jedi* at the Dominion Theatre on Tottenham Court Road, one of London's premier cinemas of the day. To celebrate the release of the third *Star Wars* film, the theater was screening all three of the installments that had been produced to date, back-to-back, in marathon fashion.

"Let's go see all three!" he announced a few days before my seventh birthday, and I could scarcely believe my ears. I had seen the previous movies on television and had amassed an assortment of the action figures and spaceships: Luke Skywalker, Princess Leia, Han Solo . . . I had them all. I was most drawn to Darth Vader, but it wasn't because he was the villain; it was the purity and clean lines of his black-as-night costume.

We saw the movies, one after another, and it was a revelation to me, an all-encompassing sensory experience, utterly overwhelming and transporting. There was even a culinary component to the marathon: Butterkist, a popular caramel popcorn concession item, added to the day, as it did to all my moviegoing excursions. Butterkist has a fascinating, distinctly British history: during World War II, many foodstuffs were strictly rationed, but not the ingredients required to make Butterkist—a state of affairs that enabled the product to rise to prominence and secure a place in the popular culture.

During the breaks between the movies, as my father and I went for a walk or a quick bite, I was so excited that I had a hard time sitting still. I thought it was the greatest thing ever. They call movies escapism and that's what they were for me—a way to forget about the emerging cold war between my parents at home and my growing sense of solitude, and to lose myself in an internal diversion while at the same time taking in the energy of the audience. As I grew older, I often went to the movies on my own, which I know is anathema to many, but which is completely comfortable and natural, even appealing, to me.

As I grew older, there was another, emerging fascination for me. You could often see me, at age ten, tall for my age, standing amidst the commotion of Berwick Street Market—an open-air food bazaar near our London home, complete with vendors announcing specials and prices on the fresh foods of the day, delivering each deal with the full-throated gusto of carnival barkers. Not only was the marketplace a vibrant, bustling hub for farmers and food purveyors who sold fruits and vegetables from their carts, but it was also, incongruously, London's red-light district, with prostitutes

This refined, modern take on the French dish royale of hare (shown on following pages) never fails to remind me of the butcher shop that so obsessed me at Berwick Street Market. But, for all the acclaim in which it's held, I've always found the traditional royale of hare—a labor-intensive, braised mainstay of classic French fine dining—a bit heavy on the palate.

My version of the dish is rendered in five parts. This photograph is the third: with the loin presented as a *ballotine* (deboned, stuffed with a forcemeat, and tied to maintain a shape like a large sausage), with a truffled boudin (sausage) and sweet, vanilla-infused turmeric mousse-line at its center. The *ballotine* is cooked *sous vide* (under pressure, in a vacuum-sealed bag), then sliced and topped with a *jus* that is finished with a drop-by-drop addition of hare's blood, giving it a compelling, metallic flavor.

The meats from the braising liquid are removed and incorporated into a game torte—rather than stuffing the hare with foie gras and truffles, the conventional way to serve it. A pomegranate tuile made with the juice of the fruit adds crucial acidity and crispness that bring balance to the plate. (There's a dialogue that occurs here between the redness of the game and the redness of the pomegranate.)

The composition is completed with grilled baby onions, a strong flavor that fits right in, and some light eucalyptus oil, which adds a pleasing earthiness.

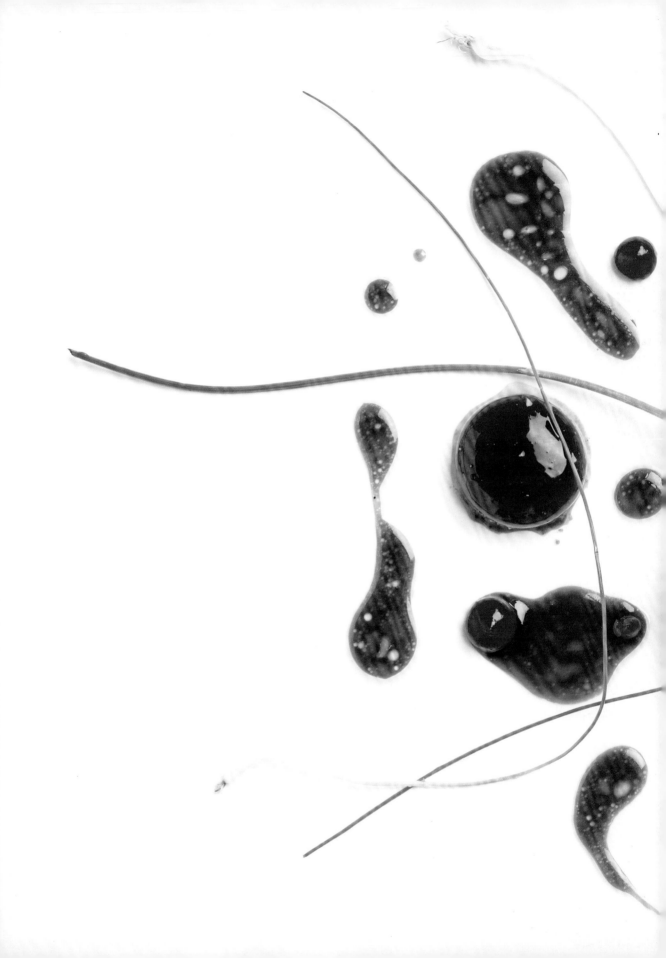

lingering seductively in doorways and flashing neon signs advertising live sex shows.

I'd sometimes find myself at the market on a Saturday afternoon, paralyzed with wonder: fresh fish on ice, vegetable-lined crates, and basket upon basket brimming with my favorite plump strawberries. I was drawn to all of those ingredients and their possibilities. Cementing the moment in my memory is the smell of roasting chestnuts, split open and shaken on a grid over a flaming oil drum, then sold by a vendor in small white paper bags.

My attention always went to the little butcher shops along the perimeter of Berwick Street and the scene in the windows. The shops recalled a Renaissance painting, with hare, partridge, grouse, wood pigeons, and other dead animals hanging in the windows, their full plumage still intact. The butchers made their own sausages, which hung like Christmas lights in the window, and sometimes you could actually see them making it, cranking the red meat into long casings. Most children my age would have recoiled at the bloody spectacle of animals being taken apart, but I would watch with rapt attention as the disparate parts were manipulated and then came together into something as neat and clean as a casing-enclosed sausage. *How do they do that?* I wondered.

If I close my eyes, I can still imagine myself right there, on that street, watching it all unfold, scarcely changed since the turn of the prior century. In my mind's eye, it's always twilight and always Christmastime. The sun is descending behind neighboring buildings, ominous shadows lengthening across the market, the air growing cold, the wind kicking up. And, through it all, my eye remains fixed on that shop, the line of customers, the butchers handing brown paper–wrapped specimens to them. I didn't know anything of cooking yet, and so the entire transaction was a source of mystery. How would those wild animals be converted into something palatable in people's homes?

Of course, I couldn't know it then, but now I realize that in many ways the chef within me began to grow and develop in that market, what with being in the presence of the riot of ingredients and, in the butcher shop, watching the progression from raw to finished product. I still wasn't aware of that chef, but he would make himself known before too long.

When I think back on my childhood discoveries, I must admit that The Food was beckoning to me. It was beckoning in the market—and when my family and I would eat in London's Chinatown. There the conversation and ambient noise would fade away when the food arrived, and I'd find myself lost in a reverie of flavor. It was my first sense that food could be more than sustenance, that it could transport you, teach you about another culture, plunge you right into the bath of human history. My favorite was wonton soup, and not only because of the flavor: a lone woman would often be positioned in the window of the restaurant, patiently filling and sealing the doughy little dumplings, and, as with those Berwick Street butchers, I was endlessly fascinated by her dexterity and by the transformation of raw ingredients into the finished product that was delivered to the restaurant's customers.

Why did I respond to such stimuli while those around me were simply shopping or eating? It's like asking why you're drawn to certain people or places more than others. Chefs come from all walks of life and in all temperaments, and over time I've come to accept that there is no "why." I was simply acting on instinct.

It was this fascination, as well, that led me—at age thirteen, seeking a way to earn some spending money for the annual summer break—to answer an ad in the *Evening Standard* for a kitchen job. A new restaurant was preparing to open, named (prophetically, given where I ply my trade today) New York, New York. I applied for a busing job, but all they had was a dishwasher position. I took it anyway; such was my eagerness for employment in a real restaurant. I fibbed about my age, telling them that I was sixteen and that my national insurance card—the UK equivalent of a social security card—was in the post.

It wasn't long-term planning that led me there, at least not consciously so: my plan at that point had been to follow in my father's footsteps and begin my military training when I turned sixteen. These were peaceful times, and without an ongoing conflict threatening, there was much about the military that appealed to me: its rigor, its routines, and the fact that it was the occupation of my father. I had been on the shooting team at my school, I was drawn to the militaristic ideal of organization and focus, and I was keen to travel the world.

But The Food hooked me first. New York, New York was my first introduction to the kitchen life, and I found myself fully in my element—right at home alongside the harsh lighting, the sizzle and hiss of the hot line, and the cooks themselves. I couldn't put words to any of it at thirteen. All I knew was that, even though I wasn't doing the cooking, I liked being there, *wanted* to be there, didn't particularly care to leave at the end of a shift, and couldn't wait to return the next day. This was in part because life at home had become unbearably sad: my parents had at long last divorced. My mother had moved out of our apartment, and I lived with my father. While he and I remained tight, he had a series of girlfriends, a dynamic I found difficult to navigate and accept. As a consequence, I would often leave the house and roam the streets of Chinatown.

The kitchen environment grew me up fast. Not only did I have responsibilities that I took very seriously (getting plates and pans cleaned and returned quickly to service), but I was suddenly hanging around with people, including girls, in their late teens and early twenties. This added to my addictive desire to be at work, especially as many of the young women changed in the locker room right alongside us, granting me my first look at the opposite sex in various states of undress. On one memorable afternoon, I came bounding into the room to find a coworker standing there in nothing but her knickers, her boobs on full display. There was an awkward locking of the eyes before, red faced, I clumsily excused myself, backing out the door and only managing one word by way of apology: "Whoops."

As food, girls, and adult life infiltrated my days, music became another obsession. I devoured all types of British alternative rock music and most especially The Cure, who, under the leadership of Robert Smith, produced a distinctly British, troubled-youth sound that fit my introverted soul like a glove. I vividly remember listening to their albums on audiocassettes, walking around London with a Walkman strapped to my belt or clutched in my hand, comforted by the feeling that somebody understood this time in my life and in this place.

When I look back at my teenage interests, I realize that in addition to being intensely personal to me, they were also expressions of distinct intimacy. While food may be consumed in the company of others in a restaurant, and music and movies enjoyed in crowded venues, the immediate experience is a profoundly direct one between chef (or artist) and diner (or audience). I might not have had a gift for socializing in those days, but I felt a connection not unlike friendship with the directors and actors, musicians and singers who held my interest.

That said, I did start to come out of my shell a bit at New York, New York. Though I was too young to socialize with them, watching the cooks was a revelation, and I immediately realized that I wanted to be one of them. The food might not have been complicated—salads, sandwiches, burgers, and ribs—but it was all done in-house with fresh ingredients, and I was transfixed by the orchestration of the team. The constant, indelicate clanging and motion could blind you to the fact that there was a sublime collaboration taking place. Orders were called by the expeditor, and each station would get to it, readying any number of dishes that fell to them, then delivering them, plated and ready for the customer, to the pass along with the rest of the order. This particular kitchen was divided into larder (cold preparations), hot preparations, and puddings (pastry), and the organization of each station was fascinating to me; the way they all worked together filled me with awe and admiration. To be able to do what they did, to be able to work like that and keep up, became my first professional ambition, my first sense of what I might like to be when I grew up.

(LIKE A) CULINARY VIRGIN

London 1992

Over the next two years, in my middle teens, I pursued those stirrings that started at New York, New York and began to explore.

In the bookstore, I was drawn to an issue of WHSmith's *Caterer and Hotelkeeper* magazine (colloquially referred to as "The Caterer"). On the cover was a chef, resplendent in his whites, and inside a photograph and recipe for one of his dishes. I didn't know what I was looking at—what comprised that explosion of colors on the plate—but it was my first, vague indication of what a chef, a real chef, did. I was drawn to the bearing of the man in his portrait, the easy confidence he exuded, as well as the visual impact of the food and the beauty of the craft, like a mellifluous foreign language that I wanted to learn and to be able to write in. I saw in the entire package a faint outline of what my own future might look like.

I purchased that and other magazines, and began trying to make the recipes they featured. Never mind that I had never eaten anything of the caliber and sophistication represented. In particular, I was drawn to a terrine, I think because it represented the greatest transformation of raw ingredients into something beautiful and orderly. Looking at that marbled terrine was like gazing at a stained glass window at Westminster Abbey. Before trying my hand at cooking, there was another obstacle to be overcome: I didn't know how to procure the necessary equipment (such as a mold) or ingredients (such as back fat). I strolled Berwick Street Market, only now, instead of merely observing, I had to work up the nerve to participate. Like a juvenile Sherlock Holmes, I went from booth to booth, showing the magazine to the vendors, asking them if they could point me to the sought-after equipment and ingredients. Mostly I was met with quizzical looks or eye rolls that mocked my youth. "I have no idea what you're talking about, boy—I sell carrots for a living," came one memorable reply.

I might have given up, but a North Star emerged in my life, the enfant terrible who had taken hold of the London culinary scene in those days: Marco Pierre White. I first noticed White in a huge spread in the Sunday *Times* magazine, a level of attention usually reserved for prime ministers and other power brokers, and was instantly drawn to the way he mingled everything I was interested in—namely, a rock star attitude and look, and artistry on the plate. I purchased the book White had penned just a few years earlier, *White Heat,* which depicted the chef's life as it had never been captured before on the page. Ten years before Anthony Bourdain's *Kitchen Confidential, White Heat* had a similar effect, pulling back the curtain on what it really took to be a cook and a chef. Before *White Heat,* the chef-penned cookbooks were all about the food, with occasional idealized philosophizing about the life of a chef, most of it conveyed in rapt and precious tones that bore no relation to the grim realities of the cooking trade.

White had turned the British restaurant community upside down when he rose to prominence at his restaurant Harvey's, opened in 1987 when he was in his midtwenties. At an unheard-of young age, White earned one, then two Michelin stars there, but that was only part of what made him an idol to an entire generation of young British cooks. A physically imposing man with a great mane of unkempt hair and an attitude as blunt as a right jab, he was a brash, rebel figure and an unabashed sex symbol. A BBC miniseries about White even featured a shot of the chef strolling a desolate London thoroughfare, a scene reminiscent of Gottfried Helnwein's iconic painting *James Dean: Boulevard of Broken Dreams.* White was more than a genius: he was cool. The world back then had no "celebrity chefs" as we do today, and the only famous toques were French. But White was ours— young, British, and charismatic as hell.

He blew the lid off the food world, revealing as never before the toil, the sheer soul-crushing exertion that the kitchen life demanded. In *White Heat,* much of this was conveyed wordlessly through Bob Carlos Clarke's legendary black-and-white photographs of White and his cooks in all their bedraggled glory, many of the images complemented with Marco-isms (e.g., "We all wear blue aprons in my kitchen because we're all *commis,* we're all still learning") printed on the edges of the picture or in the margins of the page. The contrast between those images—more like combat photos than glamour shots—and the breathtakingly beautiful dishes turned out by White and his team was the perfect summation of why we cooks put ourselves through the inhuman demands of the cooking life: the glory of the end result, The Food.

White's cuisine was classic at heart but made leaps nobody had seen before, such as juxtaposing grapefruit and *rouget* (red mullet). The beauty and integrity of his dishes was staggering. I can still recall a sea bass with precisely diced ratatouille, the feminine elegance of a shellfish *nage,* and the gently brûléed top of a lemon tart. As my appetite for culinary magazines and cookbooks grew, these publications became much more than just reading material; they were the closest I could come to the food of expensive London restaurants, to traveling to other countries, especially France, and to the points of view of the great chefs of Europe. But it would be years before any of them touched me the way *White Heat* had. It showed me the way, sharing an ideal of food and labor that gave me something to aspire to, and—although I hadn't chosen it quite yet—it also prepared me for the rigors of my profession.

Accordingly, I stuck with my interest, and in time, I located the proper shops and specialty markets to begin my kitchen experimentation. But I still had to find my own way. Having read about a dish of pig trotters stuffed with morels and sweetbreads—a legendary Pierre Koffmann composition that had found new life in White's kitchen—I decided to give it a go. I bought sweetbreads from a local butcher, but there was just one thing: rather than a veal sweetbread, he sold me one from an ox, a repulsive, sinewy clump that must have weighed two pounds. I botched the cooking of it and when I tasted it, it was like biting into a bloody heart (or so I imagined).

Clearly I had a lot to learn, but these failures didn't deter me in the least. I plowed ahead with my education and as time wore on, I developed more and more aptitude and finesse, until a crossroads presented itself: when I turned sixteen and met with an army recruitment officer, he handed me a contract. I realized I'd be committing myself to six years of service and wouldn't get out until the seemingly ancient age of twenty-one. I decided instead to go with my gut and devote myself to cooking, seeking a job as a *commis* chef (a prep and line cook) at a more serious restaurant where I could begin my education.

For my first job, I set my sights on L'Escargot, one of the oldest "nice" restaurants in London, first established in 1927. The restaurant had been shuttered for two years and just reopened, in 1993, under the ownership of Jimmy Lahoud, with not one but two chefs—David Cavalier and Garry Hollihead. I had followed all of these developments in the local papers. Both chefs had had their own restaurants and earned Michelin stars in the 1980s. L'Escargot was reborn as two restaurants in one: a brasserie on the ground floor that served pristine, beautiful, grand cuisine such as smoked haddock in a white wine sauce; and a fine-dining restaurant on the second level that offered a more classic French menu with au courant flourishes typical of the White era, such as a ravioli of sweetbread and morels with green asparagus velouté, corn-fed hen with an Albufera sauce (a poultry-based sauce with white truffle and cognac), and a raspberry soufflé with crème fraîche and vanilla ice cream; plus a catering space above that.

What most appealed to me, though, was that the restaurant offered living accommodations to its staff. In light of the unpleasant situation at home, this seemed like the ultimate "two birds with one stone" proposition—get started on the business of learning how to cook, and at the same time get out of the flat and off on my own. L'Escargot, located on Greek Street, was just a few blocks from what had become my father's home on Charing Cross Road, but it would provide the independence, both spatial and financial, that I longed for.

The L'Escargot team let me "stage," working a shift so the chefs could observe and evaluate me before officially hiring me as a *commis* chef. (In the United States, this is known as trailing.) They had me peel tomatoes, pick tarragon and spinach leaves from their stems, and peel garlic. These might seem like unrevealing or unchallenging tasks, but today I understand: so perceptive are the eyes of seasoned chefs that they don't need to see much. Just as they can tell if a piece of fish is done merely by looking at it, they can size up an aspirant cook and his prospects with a quick once-over. Besides, they would be teaching me how to do everything their way; they only wanted to gauge if I was serious and could maintain focus and intensity, not to mention do whatever it took to get the job done.

The two head chefs let me spend some time in the kitchens of both restaurants during lunch service. David Cavalier was very creative and—after the Marco Pierre White fashion—a very boisterous kitchen presence, while Garry Hollihead was a more traditional, archetypal chef's chef, with a mastery of technique and a strong, silent temperament. I didn't help in either kitchen during service; no way they'd let a wet-nosed child get in the way of execution. Instead, they had me stand to one side of the pass and watch the team. The brasserie featured an enormous kitchen and produced about one hundred covers (people served) per meal period. The food was outstanding, such as a beautiful smoked haddock with a poached egg and white wine velouté, and a slow-roasted loin of Welsh lamb with Provençal garnish. But volume wasn't especially appealing to me. I was much more drawn to the intricate food being turned out upstairs, where just three cooks served about twenty-five covers, lunch and dinner, five days a week.

The difference between an everyday eatery like New York, New York and L'Escargot was stark, especially upstairs. There was a hush over the line during service, a reverence for the work at hand and a sense that something important was being undertaken. Amusingly, despite the venerable setting and attitude, the cooks didn't wear the classic uniform of checkered pants and white jackets. So ubiquitous was the influence of Marco Pierre White that every kitchen in London was populated by Marco wannabes dressed in sweatpants, T-shirts, and blue aprons with white stripes—a sartorial statement that extended to the chefs themselves. By the same token, White's use of a Villeroy & Boch charger plate with a basket weave–patterned rim made it de rigueur in most fine-dining restaurants of the time, including L'Escargot.

After service, Cavalier asked me if I wanted a job as a prep and line cook. I didn't mess about, responding with an emphatic yes. I was keen to get into that kitchen and begin cooking, even though I had no idea where all of this might lead me.

He hired me on the spot, and we agreed on a weekly wage of 100 pounds, roughly equivalent to US$150—a pittance even in those days, but that's normal. Restaurants of a certain caliber are forever engaged in a glorified barter with young cooks: the cooks provide labor for nothing or next to nothing, and the restaurants dispense knowledge and experience that can only be earned on the job. This might sound like a racket, but it's a long and proud tradition and also, in many cases, the only thing that keeps the price of a fine-dining meal from skyrocketing into the stratosphere. In any event, I didn't care about the money or lack thereof; I was eager to get in a real kitchen and cook, so that was all that mattered.

It wasn't until after the handshake that I got to see the living accommodations that had drawn me to L'Escargot. I was unabasedly excited as one of the cooks led me there for the first time. It was something to have just turned sixteen and be living on my own, but I was about to learn that "on my own" was a relative term. The first thing that hit me was the stench: when my guide flung open the door, the sour smell of sweat hit me so powerfully that I instinctively drew my head back and my eyes started to tear up, the same way they did when I was chopping an onion. Just a year or two older than I, the cook chuckled the chuckle of a world-weary veteran, and I felt the chasm between his experience and mine expand even wider. My stomach sunk. I hadn't known what to expect, but I certainly didn't expect *this*: a dimly lit two-room flat with mattresses arranged around the floor, about six per room. (In time, I would discover that behind the bedroom was a back bedroom where the pastry chef, Bernard, lived. He had declared it his own and padlocked the door, and that was that.) At the foot of each mattress was a suitcase or duffel bag, secured with a padlock, and, taken together, the two items constituted the personal living space and possessions of each tenant.

If I had any illusions about what it took to become a cook, they were dispelled right then and there. I also quickly realized that I had merely forgone one type of military existence for another: the whole experience had a *You're in the Army Now* feel about it, from the discipline of the kitchen brigade to this barracks-like setup. Things only became more militant from there. I asked to be assigned to the upstairs restaurant, and the chefs granted my wish, dispatching me to the hot appetizer and vegetables station. It was everything I wanted, but it was also sink-or-swim and was something of a nightmare. In a kitchen like that, there were no prep cooks—you readied your own food, from peeling vegetables to butchering fish and meats, prepared the dishes in advance, then finished and fired them at the lunch or dinner hour. It was a lot to take in, and the environment intensified it. There was no extraction (ventilation) in the kitchen, so it would get up to a hundred degrees during service, prompting me to periodically step back from my station and pour an entire bottle of water over my head.

The food upstairs at L'Escargot wasn't inherently complicated. A main course might be as simple as a nicely cooked piece of corn-fed chicken, accompanied by potatoes or mushrooms, and orbited by bits of celery. The menu was small—five appetizers and five main courses—so there wasn't really that much to master on any given day; readying ten prepared portions of each dish would put you in good stead for the next service. But it was all new to me, the standards were high, and the precision alone was daunting, as everything required deft knife work. For example, one of the first things I did was a *brunoise* (very fine dice) of ratatouille. It might not sound like much, but for me it was a crash course in knife skills, as I cut half a case of red pepper, eggplant, zucchini, onion, and garlic down to infinitesimal, uniform dice. Because they cooked at different rates, during service, I had to sauté each one to order, then bring them together in a tomato reduction.

My first few weeks at L'Escargot served as a seminar. Among the other things I made then was *pommes dauphine* (a Parisian-style gnocchi) made by mixing *pâte à choux* with riced potatoes, grated orange zest, and nutmeg—which I would shape, to order, into quenelles (three per order) in the palm of my hand, then deep-fry them, whereupon they would balloon up into perfect golden arrowheads. I learned how to braise a pork neck, which was the first time I ever cooked anything *sous vide,* or under pressure. (It's a sign of how much this technique has matured over the past two decades that I now realize we did it all wrong back then: we braised it old-school in a pan, then reheated it in bags, whereas today we cook it in the bag from the get-go.) There was a classic veal *jus,* which we'd simmer for three days in a huge cauldron, never letting it boil, then add an entire bag of shredded torpedo shallots and cook them down until they infused the liquid with a honeyed sweetness. The flavor of that *jus*—its perfect complexity and primal intensity—was revelatory to me, though I never got to taste more than the small spoonful required to okay it for general use.

Add up all the little lessons, and I was privy to a first-rate culinary education. I did not attend a cooking school nor did most of the young men and women I came up with in the kitchens of London. Most American cooks consider matriculating at an institution a rite of passage, but where I come from, you learned by doing on the job. The system works, if you become a careful curator of your own education, staying in jobs that continue to develop and expand your knowledge, and choosing well when the time comes to move on to the next one. The strength of the European system is apparent by the repertoire of potato preparations I learned at L'Escargot: in that one restaurant, in just one year, with one vegetable, I learned to make *pommes puree* (in the Joël Robuchon style, with butter), *pommes fondant, pommes dauphine, pommes Anna, pommes soufflé, Turban de pommes, pommes dauphinoise, pommes frites,* and *pomme rosti,* to name just a few. It's as complete an education in the craft of potato cookery as you could ever hope to attain, even at the best modern cooking schools.

Never a terribly social person, I found that I rather enjoyed communing with my ingredients, considering them, contemplating them, even coming to understand them the way I felt I understood myself. This may sound a bit eccentric, but it's something that, over the years, I've found I share with other chefs. For example, I'd be turning potatoes, slicing them, blanching them, and frying them, and pondering everything about them. For such a humble ingredient, it has an enormous place in Western cuisine and in Western history. It has nourished man for centuries and been at the forefront of important milestones: Ireland's potato famine, for example, or the way it nourished immigrants to America when they first arrived on its shores. It's built civilizations up and torn them down.

It's also one of the more versatile ingredients available to chefs, part of why each chef has his own take on the potato. Under the learned leadership of Cavalier and Hollihead, I became expert in the potato's many nuances and how to get the most out of it. Most cooks don't think of potatoes as seasonal, but they most certainly are. Different potatoes are at their prime at different times of year, mostly due to how dry matter solids (which give the tuber its defining flavor) behave. For example, Yukon gold potatoes are perfect for *pommes fondant* in December and furthest from it in June. This kind of information is crucial to properly respecting your raw ingredients and just one of the countless lessons I gleaned in those early days at L'Escargot.

Ironically, cooking for service—when all of your prep work coalesced in *à la minute* fashion—came pretty quickly to me. But prep was my challenge and, in my early days, my downfall. I was a quick study with certain jobs, like those ratatouille vegetables, but other ingredients were just too foreign to me, and I was doomed to fail. We made langoustine tempura, and I'd never seen either langoustine or tempura before. The shellfish came in alive and snapping, which in itself was a revelation, and I tore my hands

Composition Pommes de Terre

This dish is my tribute to the potato and to my time at L'Escargot, combining three preparations I learned there in one composition. The base is a *pommes fondant,* which I prefer to make with Yukon gold potatoes at their peak. The center of this butter-cooked preparation is punched out and filled with *pommes aligot,* a preparation similar to *pommes puree* that I give an airiness by applying an *espuma* technique, piping it from a N_2O (nitrous oxide) canister.

This composition is an ideal accompaniment to any fish, poultry, or meat, and is also delicious on its own. The recipes for these preparations can be found on pages 231–232.

up taking them apart out of their hard shells. Perhaps my worst offense was the first time I deveined foie gras, one of the most luxurious and costly of ingredients. I'd never tasted or even heard of it, and nobody told me to keep the lobes together as I deveined it, to keep it from falling into pieces. I botched it terribly, butchering it in the very worst sense of the word: when I was done removing the veins, it looked as though a fox had attacked it.

These moments, in turn, provided my introduction to yet another military aspect of kitchen life: the drill sergeant–worthy onslaught by the chefs who lorded over us. Whenever I made a mistake, it seemed, the chef who ran the upstairs kitchen for Cavalier and Hollihead was right there to witness it and would unleash a deafening attack: "What did you do? You fucked it up!" To a boy of sixteen, this was intimidating and terrifying, both verbally and physically, as the chef would impose himself, standing so close, screaming so loudly, that I would have to lean away just to absorb the blow. Once the punishment had been administered, he would stalk away, grousing about "the fucking guys they give me up here."

"I'm sorry I don't know everything," I'd plead, following after him like a stray animal. "Teach me." But he was clearly too frustrated to invest the time, and I'd give up asking, pick myself up, and return to my work.

(I was also once scolded by my kitchen hero. Marco Pierre White was friends with the owner of L'Escargot and would sometimes eat there. When he was scheduled to come in, word would spread among the cooks instantaneously and anticipation would permeate the afternoon, a pulsating awareness that "Marco's coming." One day, he sauntered through the kitchen and caught me out of the corner of his eye. He turned and looked right at me: "Cut your hair," he admonished me. I did, the very next morning.)

More supportive was a seasoned cook in the upstairs kitchen, Simon Davis, who had just come back from Guy Savoy in Paris. Simon had also worked with Michel Guérard and with Marco Pierre White at Harvey's; there's a photo of him in *White Heat,* which impressed me endlessly. He

---

WHITE ASPARAGUS Another ingredient that I first discovered at L'Escargot is beautiful white asparagus, from the South of France, presented here as I sometimes prepare it today, with a ramp *croquant* and a paste of onion and hazelnut praline, a song to spring. The recipe for the asparagus can be found on page 233.

Scottish Wild Wood Pigeon, Oyster Leaf, and Caviar

This woodsy dish—in which a *farce* is fashioned from the liver of a wood pigeon and set between the two breasts, with a chestnut in the center, then slow poached to create a warm *ballotine*—evokes my first days at L'Escargot with its classic technique. The oyster leaf is from Scotland, and its salinity, along with the creaminess of the caviar, offers a perfect foil to the *ballotine*. The vinaigrette on the side is made from wood pigeon carcass, slow roasted with red grapes and Banyuls vinegar, and reduced to a delicious syrup.

was the very picture of the rock-star chef. In his late twenties, Simon possessed chiseled good looks, a leather jacket, an easy confidence around the stoves, and a ridiculously gorgeous French girlfriend, who'd be waiting for him after work like a dutiful wife at the prison gates. More to the point, he had a mastery of seemingly anything that might be asked of him in the kitchen. Mercifully, after witnessing my early floundering, he chose to share his hard-won knowledge with me; once the chefs had conveyed the menu each morning, he'd make a few minutes to school me in my tasks, setting me up for success. (Simon would occasionally tell me that the technique he was showing me was the one they used at Savoy or in White's kitchen, which gave it the stamp of approval for me.) He was also the guy who told me to begin keeping a notebook in which I could record kitchen notes and recipes as I went from kitchen to kitchen and in time would use as a sketchpad for my own ideas. That seemed light-years away to me, and it was, but the vote of confidence was empowering.

But his most urgent and lifesaving guidance was technical. If, for example, I was assigned the *farce,* or filling, for the mushroom ravioli, he'd see me standing there, lost, and demonstrate. He'd show me how to salt raw chicken to help it break down in a blender, then add egg whites and half the cream, process it, and gently fold in the remaining cream. He taught me that holding that final cream portion until the end kept me from overworking the mixture, allowing it to achieve an impossibly silky texture. Then he showed me how to pass it through a *tamis* (a fine-mesh sieve sometimes called a drum sieve for its shape) and how to do a test cook of the filling, to assess the flavor and texture and determine if any corrections were required. He showed me how to make the endive tarte tatin we served alongside our pigeon dish—halving and coring the vegetable, slowly caramelizing the halves in an olive oil–slicked pan, then separating the leaves and layering them in a mold, with chopped truffle in between, topping it with puff pastry, and baking to order. He showed me how to cook a sweetbread properly and how to fillet a red mullet. And he was the guy who straightened out my tragicomic foie gras deveining technique, or lack thereof.

In a harsh and unforgiving environment, Simon showed me some human kindness. I'm not sure why he singled me out for such lifesaving attention, but I like to think it's because he saw something in me—that chef within, that I went beyond *"Oui, Chef"* and asked how and why certain things were done—that indicated ambition or at least seriousness to him. In time, he became something of a big brother to me. He'd invite me to join him for the short break between lunch and dinner, and we'd grab a coffee together downstairs. When there weren't pressing technical issues at hand, he'd recount his own professional history, telling me about his three years in France. (This was before the rise of Spain, when France was still considered the only place to go for "finishing school" as a cook.)

Occasionally, my insouciance would betray me, as when he mentioned that friends of his had worked for Joël Robuchon and I replied, "Who's that?"

Simon looked at me with unmistakable horror but quickly masked it with a supportive tone.

"He's the best chef in the world," he said.

"Right," I said, looking away sheepishly. We both laughed.

Simon's coolness was only magnified by his ongoing battle with the chefs, who would berate him for insisting on salting everything—from pasta water to stocks—with *fleur de sel* (sea salt), which they believed should only be used as a finishing agent. Though he'd been admonished many times not to do it, he would surreptitiously continue the practice when nobody was looking. "In France," he'd tell me, "they season *everything* with sea salt." Today, as a chef-owner in my own right, I see that he and his higher-ups were both correct: the gentle salinity of sea salt is almost always a better choice, but the expense requires that one pick the times when it really matters to use it. In hindsight it was my first lesson in the decisions foisted on us by the intersection of cooking and commerce.

Another constant reminder of that delicate balance was the restaurant's nonexistent family meal—industry-speak for the nightly staff meal. While respectable employee meals are de rigueur in most upscale restaurants today, at L'Escargot, they were an afterthought. Often, a cook would be sent to a market around the corner, then return with Snickers bars that he dispensed to the rest of us, to fuel us for the long service ahead. (I'd often supplement these after work with a carbo-load of Walkers potato chips.) Here, too, Simon taught me a trick: we'd help ourselves to pieces of bread that nobody would miss from the waiters' station and dip them in the pot of tempered chocolate at the pastry chef's station. It wasn't much, but it was better than a Snickers bar, warm and sophisticated, and it had the extra benefit of annoying Bernard, the pastry chef, who'd often return to his station to find bread crumbs in the chocolate.

As a cook, a working student of the plate, Simon was an inspiration to me, somebody who I wanted to emulate and impress. And the example he set went beyond the culinary: understanding the path he'd taken, from L'Escargot to other restaurants and back again with new knowledge, was crucial to me understanding the path I'd need to take. There's no one way to become a chef. Yes, there are cooking schools, but the real things are learned on the job, in restaurants, cooking under pressure. And there's no set amount of time to be at any one job—some guys work for years under one chef, while others move along to the next adventure every twelve months like clockwork. Both approaches can work. The thing is to know what you're after and when and where you want to go to achieve it.

But such decisions were a ways off for me. For the time being, I was at L'Escargot and, as time marched by, I got into the rhythm of the working day and week, arriving at a point where I could hold my own and start to learn things about who I was as a cook. I realize now that my predilection for visual, graphic food was already present. The chefs' little foie gras and duck terrine glazed with a gelée made from Sauternes lodged in my memory (today I serve a foie gras that's coated with a hibiscus-beet gelée). The beautiful pastries that Bernard turned out, such as a raspberry soufflé and lemon tart, spoke to me with their brilliant colors and precise shapes (you could set a level atop his soufflé and have it register as perfectly straight). From afar, I admired much that went on at the hot station as well—especially the skilled, precise butchery and cooking of fish, such as *rouget,* watching as the cooks took the fillets off the bone, gently trimmed the fish, removed the pinbones, then very delicately cooked the fillets, skin side down, to achieve an almost glass-like finish on the skin.

As my culinary aptitude swelled, I began to develop predilections, not for things I liked to eat (because, ironically, I still scarcely got to eat anything) but for things I liked to cook. One of the first things I came to love making, almost from the first time I did it, was pasta. The tactile pleasure, the downright sensuousness of making the dough, kneading it, then rolling and cutting it—I loved the entire process and was able to lose myself in it entirely. (No wonder I'd been so taken with the woman preparing wontons years earlier during family trips to Chinatown.)

One of the first pastas I made was a sweetbread and morel ravioli. The satisfaction of starting with a handful of ingredients—flour, egg, sweetbreads, morels, butter, herbs—during the groggy, early-morning hours, and dispatching the finished dish during dinner service never got old. Decades removed from that kitchen, I could prepare it for you perfectly today because the steps are emblazoned in my mind and muscles. First, you sauté diced morels with minced shallots, garlic, and picked thyme leaves, then set the pan aside, off the heat. Quickly, you take pinky-size bits of sweetbread, dust them in flour with a pinch of curry powder, and sauté them in foaming butter just until bronzed. You add the sweetbreads to the morels, along with some chicken mousse, and fold them together to bind them; then spoon the mixture onto a ravioli circle, set the top on it, and crimp the two together. Amazingly, we made the ravioli to order, and the dish was rounded out with a quick glaze of truffle butter, some sautéed morels, and spears of turned asparagus, and finished tableside by a spoon-over of asparagus "cappuccino."

It was also about this time that I began to realize a curious thing about myself: I was a bit clumsy with the cooking basics but had a natural aptitude for more complicated technical work. Ask me to fry an egg, and the results would be inelegant. But ask me to make some tortellini, and I'd pick up on it in a snap—filling, folding, and twisting the little parcels with the efficiency and consistency of a machine. The chefs suspected I must have been trained to do it in Italy, but I had never made them before in my life. The same went with pastry, which figured in to some of my hot-appetizer preparations: where most young cooks take time to develop the tactile memory to make perfect dough, my fingers picked it up all at once.

I came to believe that, while I wasn't sure I had a special gift for cooking, I was born with a certain *feeling* for food, a unique way of perceiving it and a natural affinity for working with it in certain ways. It's not an intellectual or thought-related skill set, but rather a simple animal attraction to the tasks that appealed to my senses, that pleased and calmed me, that gave me the same feeling of being close to a loved one, of being at home.

I was an anonymous worker bee, but I was developing the pride of a chef in certain dishes every time I put one up on the pass. It's worth mentioning, however, that becoming a true chef, while it was my inspiration, was the furthest thing from my mind. Here again, I come to the military analogy: a fine-dining environment like L'Escargot teaches you to cook, and that's it. You are not there to think for or about yourself. You are a cell in an organism, a member of a team, and it's the kitchen and the food—the mission—that counts, and nothing else. Seeds for future dishes may have

been planted in those days, but I wasn't thinking about what my own style might look and taste like, or anything of the sort. I was interested in only two things—survival and learning my craft.

Not only did an attitude like this teach me well, but it trains the overwhelming majority of cooks for their careers. I'm fortunate to have ultimately become a chef, but simple mathematics dictates that most people who cook for a living will spend much of their lives as just that—cooks, not chefs—and that's fine.

One of the aspects of life at L'Escargot that I came to be most fond of was the one that so horrified me initially: the barracks, which I came to appreciate for a number of reasons. When you choose the cooking life, you remove yourself from many of the rites of passage that most people take for granted, and the barracks helped make up for that loss with an alternate-universe variation. Having decided against college, I deprived myself of the social conventions that would have helped me develop as an individual, such as the dorm-room rap sessions, impromptu parties, and the like. These cooks had carefully defined identities, which helped immunize them to the rigors of the scene, evident in the proliferation of tattoos, piercings, facial hair, and other aggressive declarations of confidence. (When I took the job at L'Escargot, I had taken to wearing mostly black clothing and pulling my shoulder-length hair back in a ponytail; I fit right in.)

In the barracks, I also came to learn that each cook was partially defined by his taste in music. Bernard blasted French death metal (yes, there is such a thing) from his room; another cook listened to country western, usually and mercifully through a set of headphones. As I began to mature, my tastes expanded to include contemporary and alternative bands such as The Sisters of Mercy, Fields of the Nephilim, Ned's Atomic Dustbin, and The Jesus and Mary Chain. In time, I even came to listen to American rap pioneers such as Public Enemy and N.W.A, groups that none of my friends, or anybody else I knew in London, were even aware of, but that, despite the seeming incongruity, spoke to me with their own distinct brand of alienation.

Each cook also had his own favorite cookbooks, and we'd sometimes share them with each other. The awe that aspiring chefs heap on a top toque's cookbook is something to behold. I remember gathering with my coworkers, looking over a beloved classic or a just-published recipe tome, ogling and talking about food photographs with the hushed reverence most teenagers reserve for centerfolds, our eyes caressing the images, our minds overflowing with possibilities. In addition to the perennial *White Heat*, Ferran Adrià's book about the food of the Mediterranean (*El Bulli: el sabor del Mediterráneo*), published in 1993, had caught my eye and admiration. He wasn't known in London yet, and was just beginning to find the style that would make him a legend, but his food was already very interesting and compelling.

Less healthy, but no less a part of the atmosphere, were the crew's after-hours drinking binges, of which I was a sometimes participant. One of the unfortunate by-products of the celebrity-chef phenomenon is the glamorization of the social lives of cooks. The exploits of toques have become known to even the most casual observer of my industry, and chefs have developed a reputation as rowdy party boys.

The general public finds this entertaining, and young cooks find it appealing, a convention that they feel gives them license to indulge. But there are profound reasons for this aspect of the chef's life that ought to be considered. For most cooks, the day begins early in the morning and doesn't end until well past midnight—bruising hours that normal working people endure only at the height of major projects or deadlines. Most of those hours are passed in the physical company of others but in reality are relentlessly isolating. The business of prep demands unfailing attention to detail and almost absurd repetition. A young cook might perform the same mundane tasks—peeling and turning a particular vegetable, or shelling and cleaning langoustines—up to fifty times a day for months on end.

Service ups the stakes. One has to maintain a rhythm from the first order to the last, turning out a handful of dishes with robotic consistency. The ultimate paradox of the cooking life is that for all of the labor and concentration that goes into the production of each dish, the finished product should look elegant, effortless, almost as though it sprang to life, fully formed, on the plate, without the aid of human thought or hands.

To produce that effect never ceases to be stressful. Just as a Broadway diva will confess to nausea in the moments before a performance, any honest chef will tell you that he still feels the flutter of butterflies when the first orders of the night roll into the kitchen. Stress isn't unique to chefs, but cooks are deprived of the social conventions of most workplaces: the water-cooler chitchat, lunch breaks, and so on that help a great many people get

Agnolotti of Cauliflower, Coffee, and Caviar

Since working at L'Escargot, I've loved making pasta, which to this day I find to be a meditative, almost cathartic, morning exercise into which I can utterly lose myself. Making pasta transcends mere recipe-following, requiring one to develop a sixth sense for the unique rhythms of the task. When a new cook begins working with me, I spend a week making pasta side by side with him or her, to walk them through all the steps and help them develop an intuition for the look and feel of proper pasta.

The *agnolotti* pictured here is ultimately a very simple dish, in which the caviar serves more as a seasoning than an embellishment, bringing an umami-like quality to the cauliflower.

through their days. Moreover, in the time when I came up, if you made a decision to become a cook, to pursue The Food, you essentially committed to shutting off your life for a few years, subordinating the development of your personality to the gathering of knowledge and the honing of technique. As a result, we essentially end up stuffing a full day's worth of socializing into those few, precious hours between when we've wiped down our stations and when we turn in for the night, which is also the only time you are able to uncork your true personality, to stop being a soldier and be a person again, to reconnect with yourself. Another less-positive side to the need for release: occasionally, if two colleagues had had a contentious night in the kitchen, we staged our own version of *Fight Club,* standing around in a circle as they worked out their differences.

Put another way, the discipline that we exhibit in the kitchen is the untold story behind the excesses that are often displayed outside of it. Much as I love the life, I have to admit that cooking can strip one emotionally bare. You have to prove yourself not just every day, but in every task and in every dish put up on the pass. There is nowhere to hide as a cook, no opportunity to phone it in, not even for an instant. If you let up, lower your standards, or just plain get lazy, you will be found out, if not by the chef, then by the customer who sends your work back. As a young cook, you are constantly reminded of this—either getting savaged by the chef yourself or witnessing one of your comrades in arms getting ripped by the boss—and you are only as good as the last dish you put out.

For all of these reasons, the nightly decompression that takes place after service is an essential part of a cook's life, a necessary release of tension and a chance to share the feeling that, after surviving a night together, you're on R&R, savoring a well-earned break. That said, it must be acknowledged that some chefs have difficulty calibrating their celebration. The stories of drinking, drugs, and philandering in my industry are all true, and not nearly as glamorous or funny as they're often made out to be. Mostly they are tragic, ending or interrupting careers, or branding a cook with a hard-to-shake reputation.

Still, the moments of toil and release create a bond between chefs. Indeed, many of my most cherished professional memories are of the silent moments after service, looking up from scrubbing my station or from a just-cracked-open beer, and catching the eye of a kitchen mate in an infinitesimal, wordless glance that says, "We did it. We pulled it off . . . again." Those nights weren't the norm. Oftentimes after service, all any of us wanted to do was to get into the barracks and crash, banking as much sleep as possible between the end of dinner service and the commencement of prep in the morning.

But the upstairs kitchen was closed on Sunday and Monday, and so Saturday nights were special, a weekly party such as only professional cooks could throw. Throughout the day, a member of each station would make or stash a few extra portions of whatever he wanted to share with the others. Bernard might produce a few extra chocolate tarts; the meat cook would reserve some foie gras trim or duck breast. As for me, I'd gather up some *pommes dauphinoise* or another garnish that we wouldn't keep after the weekend because it wouldn't survive the two days of cold storage.

Around one thirty or two o'clock in the morning, once the last of us had finished scrubbing down his station and the unit had reconstituted at the barracks, we'd bust out all those things and have a feast. The meat guy would sauté the duck, I'd cook the potatoes or risotto, Bernard would bring the tarts or some such, and one guy would go out and buy an ungodly amount of beer. Then we'd lay it all out on the one table we had for ourselves, sit around, fire up the telly, and unwind almost until sunup.

Sundays were precious and cruelly short. We'd sleep as late as possible, then lounge around, savoring the fact that we didn't need to be anywhere and didn't need to be on our feet. Our youth was irrelevant; we were physically and emotionally depleted, and it required idling most of the day to recharge our weary bodies. In time, when we were all up and about, we'd go for a bite at a local pub, then come home and nod off. (As a sign of my relative youth, I'd also do my laundry at my father's house at some point in the day, which offered a perfect, two-hour opportunity for me to catch him up on my progress.) Just about anybody who grew up cooking when I did had a similar experience with Sundays.

For my first year at L'Escargot, I was confined to very specific culinary tasks and education, not even thinking about the chef I might one day become, but my budding creative instincts did find an outlet, albeit an unexpected one. On New Year's Eve, after one of the most brutal services of my life to that point, some fellow cooks dragged me to a rave. We piled into a taxi and drove to an abandoned post office on the outskirts of London. There were about two thousand people there, lights crisscrossing the darkened space, a snake pit of arms waving rhythmically above a dark sea of bodies. And it was all set to music spun by a DJ.

I was transfixed by the scene and the energy, and by the next morning had decided that I wanted to be a part of it. I began socializing in the scene, returning to that rave and to many, many others, and met members of Spiral Tribe, a sort of DJ collective that spun all over England. One of the guys affiliated with Spiral Tribe owned a record shop in central London and became my unofficial tutor in all things DJ, showing me how to use turntables and a mixer and selling me all the necessary equipment which, for budgetary reasons, I purchased secondhand. I loved DJing; in many respects, it was my first true chef-like experience: I took disparate influences, blended them into my own creation, and projected them out to a public for them to experience and enjoy.

My big break came when I was mixing records in a store and a popular DJ heard me. To my surprise, he was impressed and asked me to do a set with him. Next thing I knew, I was a regular presence at raves from London to Holland, working them into my schedule whenever I could, often leaving town after service in the wee hours of a Sunday morning to get to my next precious gig. For my name, I took Kraken, after the sea monster in the movie *Clash of the Titans,* the perfect union of my two nonculinary obsessions: music and movies. When I finally became a chef, there were times, many of them, when I'd look out over the dining room from the kitchen and for a moment feel the same sensation I did at age seventeen—in my T-shirt and jeans, my head down, a single earphone held to my cranium, pulsating to the music I was spinning, the only one in the place who knew what was coming next.

I worked at L'Escargot for just under two years, from ages sixteen to eighteen.

Toward the end of my first year, a delicious rite of passage occurred when a new kid came into the kitchen. Only a year younger than I, he seemed a generation my junior in attitude and body language. I had stepped onto that great conveyor belt that mints cooks and chefs, and here was the next one being placed on the assembly line behind me. The new cook was put under my charge, and I was delighted to have somebody to hand off my grunt work to, somebody who I could have scrub the stoves and chisel the grease off the equipment at the end of the night—not that I was exempt from my own tasks, such as climbing inside the refrigerator and detailing every square inch of it, every nook and cranny, every night.

I also began to save what money I could to start dining at restaurants around London and expand my culinary horizons. For my adventures, I bought myself a shiny, green, double-breasted suit. I thought it was quite distinguished, but in hindsight I realize it looked ridiculous on me, especially with my string-bean physique. Usually, I'd go for lunch, when most restaurants offered a prix fixe menu, a relatively economical option at the time. Often, the staff at the restaurant had no problem identifying me as a young cook, and once in a while my status as a solo diner caused others to take pity on me, as when a tableful of bankers at Joël Antunès's Les Saveurs invited me to join them for dessert and beckoned the chef out to meet me.

About that same time, I moved out of the barracks. Much as I loved the camaraderie I found there, I had reached a point where I needed to get out on my own, so in my second year at L'Escargot, I secured a 25-square-foot room for myself in North London. It had a bed, a television, and not much else, but in addition to some necessary privacy, the domicile gave me a place to store my ever-growing collection of records, that I organized in wine boxes from the restaurant and that soon dominated the flat.

For my second year at the restaurant, I was assigned to the pastry station and fell in love with cooking all over again. In most professional restaurant kitchens, the savory and pastry worlds are completely segregated, and the cooks who specialize in one discipline have little or no interest in the other. But I enjoyed working pastry. In addition to tasting great desserts for the first time, I loved the precision and the satisfaction of baking something as delicate as, say, a soufflé and having it come out perfectly.

The unique demands of pastry taught me a mind-set and discipline that benefit me to this day, and I'd encourage any young cook to be exposed to a great pastry chef at some point in their development. The greatest value of pastry was the precision required. In those days, cooking savory food wasn't necessarily rigid. Even in a restaurant of L'Escargot's caliber, you were taught to add a splash of this and a pinch of that, and then to taste and correct for seasoning. Not that desserts were terribly complicated at L'Escargot—in the style of the day, they might be as simple as strawberry sorbet with a spun sugar antenna plunged into it. But even the most elemental desserts require exactitude, right down to the prep work. Tempering chocolate was especially challenging in the roiling heat of that kitchen, as was rolling out a *pâte sucrée* because of its high butter content.

Similarly, baking desserts was much less forgiving than, say, roasting a lamb saddle. A minute or two beyond what was required could dry out a custard or blacken a crust. So for preparing desserts, we were taught to cook gently, to put a lemon tart in the hot oven and turn it off, allowing the residual heat to set the custard ever so slowly. Our method for making a chocolate tart, like that of other kitchens in London, was a version of Joël Robuchon's much-celebrated dessert. Where his was essentially a crème brûlée base (milk, chocolate, cream, and egg), ours was made with a sabayon (sugar and eggs whisked to a frothy thickness over gentle heat), to which we folded in melted chocolate and butter, poured into molds, and gently baked.

My pastry work also gave me a foundation for some of the visual flourishes and flights of fancy that, years later, would become a hallmark of my own personal style. Many of the signature contributions of the most important contemporary restaurants have their origins in pastry, as well. Ferran Adrià drew heavily on the pastry arts in his work at El Bulli with savory *croquants* and other flourishes. A pastry-driven approach such as his, rooted in exacting standards and precision, veers away from the standard protein-starch-sauce formula that has defined savory cuisine in the Western world for generations. I myself have followed in that vein, with savory meringues and other pastry-inspired elements. Moreover, I've tried to incorporate the discipline of pastry into all of my cooking with recipes that require cooks to weigh out all ingredients, carefully monitor exact cooking times and temperatures, and portion each serving identically. It helps them learn to do things the right way and helps me achieve one of the most elusive and important goals of any chef: consistency.

INTO THE FIRE

London 1995

By their nature, young cooks move from restaurant to restaurant, country to country, continent to continent. This was one of the things I loved about the early years of my career—the mercenary aspect of it, the awareness that you were actually expected to move on at some point, to roll up your knife kit and set sail for the next kitchen, the next adventure. This was especially true then, as it is now, for young cooks who don't attend cooking school. The way I came up, a cook created his own curriculum, learning on the job and determining what the best next step was in his development.

Unlike in many careers, the right steps for cooks vary from person to person. A native of Lyon, France, might be an expert in the ways of puff pastry and charcuterie by his early teens, while for somebody from London, those might be the last tumblers to fall into place. And decisions are not always made for the sake of knowledge alone. Cooks might take a job just to work in a country that attracts their curiosity or to work under a chef they respect or from whom they believe they might take inspiration. It's a process that, depending on your temperament and tolerance of uncertainty, is either extraordinarily exciting or perpetually terrifying.

There was only one next step I wanted to make in those L'Escargot days, and it was the same one that many of my peers would have wished for as well: to work in the kitchen of Marco Pierre White, who had just moved from Harvey's to his eponymous restaurant at the Hyde Park Hotel (today a Mandarin Oriental hotel). We all referred to it simply as "The Restaurant," as though there were no other place to dine or to work. Among London cooks, White's kitchen was known for being famously tough on the chefs, and customers there were the most demanding in town. White himself had earned a singular reputation for his erratic behavior in the kitchen— newspaper profiles proliferated, each with what seemed a mandatory story that illustrated the chef's volatile temperament.

Simon once said about working for White back at Harvey's, "Before you're even in the restaurant, you're running, already having heart palpitations." Working for White would be a test of my fortitude for sure, but my attraction had deeper significance. During the Reagan era of the 1980s, Americanism had all but dwarfed my native culture on all fronts, leaving us in the shadow of our cousin across the Atlantic. But things were changing with the resurgence and redefining of British culture. Pop bands like Oasis and film directors such as Danny Boyle of *Trainspotting* fame were garnering worldwide acclaim, and the emergence of a new British cuisine followed in their wake. Where our food had long been a punch line for international writers and travelers—as if all we had to offer was roast beef and Yorkshire pudding—all of a sudden we were demanding respect, and White had been the catalyst for that, starting back in the decade prior. Against a backdrop of French-accented conformity, this punk wunderkind was more than a breath of fresh air: he was exciting, dangerous, and unpredictable, and it's almost impossible to explain the spell in which he held young British cooks. We didn't want to be like him; we wanted to *be* him.

For me, White's kitchen would be the ultimate early test of my still nascent talent and the best possible place to rise to the next level. It would also, simply put, be cool. The upstairs maitre d' of L'Escargot, Patrice, who had once worked for White, had heard about my interest in The Restaurant and arranged a "stage" for me. (In a chef's world, doors open at random: next opportunities are often discovered at after-hours pubs or thanks to a casual exchange.)

Everything in the kitchen at Marco Pierre White seemed bigger and grander. The space itself was physically larger than L'Escargot, with row after row of gleaming copper pots and silver trays, all the trappings of a beautiful three-star Michelin restaurant. At each station, chefs and cooks—about twenty in all—worked with an intensity I'd never witnessed. Their heads were focused downward, and their movements were economical, precise, and lightning quick. It seemed almost to defy the possible, as though I were watching filmed footage that was being fast-forwarded. The noise also seemed heightened, especially the admonishments of the chefs—"C'mon, c'mon, c'mon. Move your ass!"—that were almost nonstop and mingled with the other ambient noises of the kitchen to create a bizarre industrial house music that served as a soundtrack to the hive of activity.

Despite my two years of experience cooking in a top London kitchen, I instantly felt queasy at the realization that I suddenly knew nothing. As I continued to scan the space, taking it all in, I discovered that even the most mundane tasks were being performed slightly differently than they had been at L'Escargot. The butchering of chicken and fish, the shaping of vegetables, and so on, were all done to White's specifications, and I grasped for the first time that every kitchen lives by its own rules, each restaurant a universe shaped by its own god. Some gods were more demanding than others, and the specificity in White's kitchen was breathtaking. For example, where that shallot-infused veal *jus* had many applications at L'Escargot, in White's kitchen all the stocks were tailored to the dish in which they'd be used. And our purveyors moved heaven and earth to supply fish and meats of the size and quality we demanded, to fulfill White's vision and standards for each plate. If, say, we had four-pound sea bass on order and the ones that arrived weighed six pounds, well, you could be sure that those would be returned before the morning was out.

One area in which there was no difference between L'Escargot and Marco Pierre White was the screening process: a shift spent trailing, which here basically amounted to being shoved into a corner and told to pick spinach and stay the hell out of the way. Once they saw I could handle the environment, or at least was up for the challenge, there was the job offer, the handshake, and then the trial by fire began.

I was stationed on *garde manger,* where my first tasks were elementary: picking chervil, slicing new potatoes and cooking them for a lobster and truffle dish, and—before too long—preparing a terrine of foie gras with

Colston Bassett Stilton with Frozen Quince "Crème"

My homage to the resurgent British pride of the 1990s, this dramatic composition presents traditional British flavors in an unconventional package, the powerful Stilton blue cheese taking a rock-star turn against a glam backdrop of sweet fruit. The quince "crème" is actually a simple sorbet fashioned from quince and lemon juice that captures the crispness and fragrance of the fruit without the toothsome texture. I like to serve Stilton a little cooler than most chefs, as you might chocolate from the refrigerator, slightly tempered so that it melts on the palate but isn't too soft. That's how it's presented in this dish, for the best interplay between the cheese and the crème.

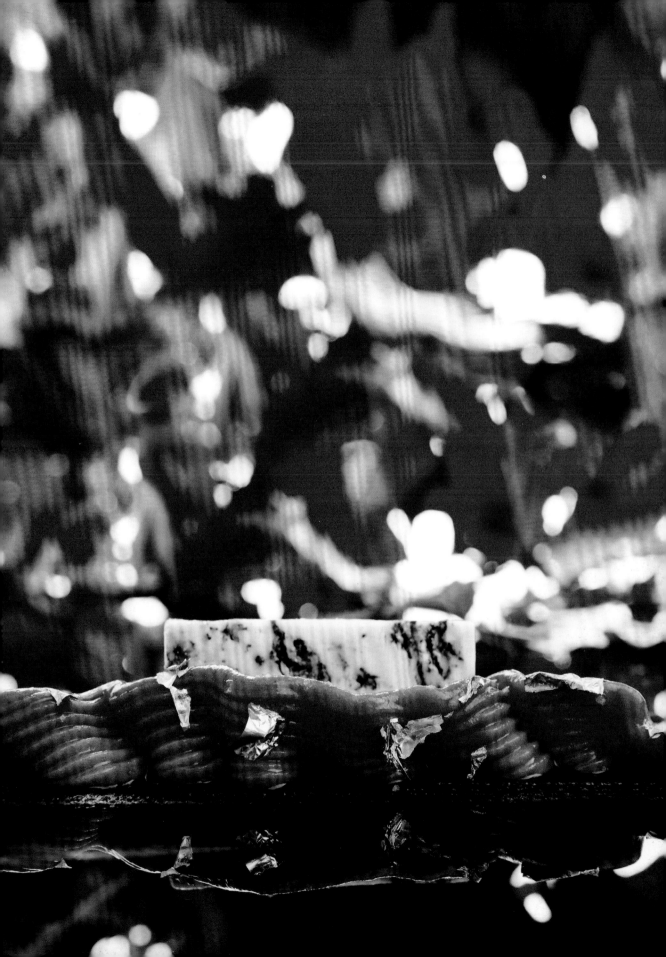

a gelée made from Sauternes. All of the dishes were featured in *White Heat,* and I could scarcely believe that I was there in that kitchen preparing them—or parts of them—myself.

The menu at The Restaurant was much more ambitious than what I was used to at L'Escargot. Instead of five first courses and five mains, here there were about a dozen of each course, and they were all more labor-intensive, requiring intricate techniques. Even though there were twenty cooks, there was more to do and more was expected of each of us. As a temporary means of survival, I cribbed from those around me, surreptitiously picking up ways of organizing myself and my station to work as quickly and efficiently as possible.

In such a large kitchen, with more complicated food, synchronicity became a huge part of my development. So much of becoming a professional chef depends on the innate ability to sense where the cooks next to you are with each dish and to adjust your own timing to synch with theirs and with the overall kitchen unit. I'd liken it to what members of a band must do with every performance, almost intuiting what has to happen from one moment to the next for an hours-long show every night.

Going into White's kitchen was, as White himself described it, like going into the SAS, part of the British special forces. His team was elite, the best of the best in London at the time, and it was expected that you could pull your own weight. Even for a young cadet like myself, once you were shown something, you were expected to have the hands and the know-how to replicate it immediately. If, for whatever reason, the person next to you didn't show up on the day, it was expected that—based solely on having observed that person—you would be able to jump in and do his work. To survive, one had to be cross-trained, ready for anything, and calm under fire.

I was impressed by the lengths to which White's kitchen went: the devotion to flavor would have been absurd were the results not so spectacular. In many respects, the kitchen was as parsimonious as any in London, but it was also almost comically extravagant. For example, we roasted a few racks' worth of whole chickens every morning, then wrapped them in cellophane to allow the juices to collect. Then we'd puncture the plastic, drain the juice, and *discard the chickens.* The juices were used to flavor our *jus*—a sensational, decadent, and spectacularly wasteful commitment to producing the most delicious possible product. Would I do that myself today? Probably not. If nothing else, the societal pressure to use the chickens themselves in another preparation would be hard to resist. But I have to be honest: I respected White for that uncompromising approach, and if I close my eyes, I can still taste that *jus* today.

To me, all of this was exhilarating. It was a shock at first, to be sure, but there was never any doubt that it was what I wanted—I knew I was in the right profession. It was what every person in that kitchen wanted. If you didn't want it, you wouldn't have ever set foot in there in the first place. The common purpose was absolute.

By this time, I had moved to Deacon Road in Fulham, another district of London, with a waiter from L'Escargot who now worked at White's other restaurant, The Canteen. Our inexpensive living quarters were not remotely close to either restaurant. Because the Underground stopped running at 11:30 p.m., and I didn't finish in the kitchen until about one in the morning, I had to take a night bus home. I'd stand out on the street for about forty minutes waiting for the bus at Trafalgar Square, a mass-transit hub, where I entertained myself watching the inebriated get into late-night brawls, then travel another forty minutes to get home. If I was lucky, I could be in bed by 2:30 a.m. and get four and a half hours of sleep before waking up and starting the cycle over again. This was nothing out of the ordinary; it's what young cooks do all over the world in the name of education and advancement.

Much more than at L'Escargot, probably more than in any other kitchen I'd ever worked in, there was a rigidly defined hierarchy at Marco Pierre White. New guys like me were on the bottom rung of the ladder. Above me were the more seasoned cooks and *chefs de partie* (station chiefs), who exhibited the hardened air of those who had been to war. These were the guys who had Marco's ear and spent social time with him outside of the kitchen. Because of the spotlight trained on that restaurant and on the star chef at its helm, their access to the inner sanctum infused them with a sense of power and prestige.

As for White himself, I never interacted with him directly. But I watched him at the pass, hunched over plates, working quickly to finish them before they were whisked to the dining room. His movements were a mass of seeming contradictions: astonishingly quick but very precise; aggressive but balletic; fluid yet forceful. White was a big man, hulking almost, and hailed

Guinea Hen and Langoustine

This is a dish that positively screams of spring. Guinea hen and langoustine is a pairing that recalls Marco Pierre White's dish of rabbit and langoustine, and is my play on the classic marriage of poularde (young hen) and crayfish. The guinea hen is taken off the bone, rolled in its own skin, and caramelized to crisp the skin. The langoustines, featured in a boudin (sausage), positively explode with flavor, and these and other elements are bound together by a potent crème made from Stilton, garlic, and ramp—a dish made for the spring when the ramps are still wild. I've included the recipe for the Stilton-Green Garlic Crème on pages 233-234, which made on its own is lovely with scallops or other shellfish. You can use it to dress chilled green vegetables for a Caesar salad-like effect.

from Leeds, a northern working-class town, and his kitchen demeanor put proof to that lineage: he was in every way very direct, with no faffing around, not even with guests, with whom he spoke in a very elegant but concise manner.

The pace in that kitchen was relentless from the moment you arrived in the morning until you left well past midnight. There was never any letup. During the winter months, I only saw the sun one day a week, Sundays. Nevertheless, I stuck it out and, before too long, began to prove myself. Verbal abuse ricocheted off my hardened exterior; I was able to hold my own during the heat of a service. For all of the unbridled machismo of the kitchen, there was also a deep and unspoken camaraderie—the after-work beers were all the more well earned. As it had been at L'Escargot, staff meals in Marco's kitchen were all but nonexistent. We didn't sit at a long table and eat and sip wine before service; if we were lucky, we'd have a bowl of cornflakes or the end of a baguette with some jam. The European kitchen mentality is that you put your head down and work, to the exclusion of everything else. Cooking at the level of what we did at White's restaurant required 1,000 percent attention, and when it was all over, there was nothing left. You were shattered, a shell, comatose.

Eventually, I got accustomed to the life and developed the emotional calluses necessary for survival. But I can't lie: in those formative years, there were times I thought about throwing in the towel. On weekends, when I would see friends of mine in the DJ community in Holland and Germany, it would never fail to hit me at some point that the twenty-four-hour party they lived wasn't just a weekend phenomenon, but a way of life. And there was an emerging frustration: having gone straight from the all-male crucible of a boarding school to the equally male-centric world of professional kitchens, I was deficient in my interactions with women. I cringe remembering my awkward chat-up lines at bars—a pale, disheveled string bean clumsily bragging that I worked for Marco, to little or no effect. Then I'd slog home on the bus and try to fall asleep to the thudding of my flatmate's lovemaking.

Does that sound like a lonely life? It was. I wanted friends and the companionship of a woman, but life in that kitchen didn't allow for anything more than passing acquaintances in both the kitchen and the bedroom. This affected me most profoundly when I was privy to a glimpse of "normal" life. Once in a while, the chefs would dispatch me to borrow an ingredient from a friendly kitchen in the neighborhood. It was an intense and foreign experience to leave the kitchen, beginning with the sunlight, something I saw so infrequently. I'd linger in the street for a little while, watching people going about their day. It stopped me dead in my tracks to realize how foreign the whole scene seemed to me, almost like watching an alien race. I was especially fascinated by people chatting spontaneously and nonchalantly, as if they had all the time in the world and nowhere to be. I didn't have friends like those people did. I kept remembering something Simon had said to me back at L'Escargot, about how at some point he had "stopped bothering to learn most young cooks' names" because the vast majority of them would be moving on before he knew it.

White's kitchen was much like the special forces in that it created a culture of self-screening. The demands were so trying that if you didn't want it bad enough, you'd resign in short order and move on to something else. And I'm not going to lie to you: there were times, many of them, when I questioned whether being a chef was worth it. When you're standing out in the snow at one in the morning after a crap service, waiting more than thirty minutes for a bus, wondering why you paid rent for a flat you spent less than five hours a day in—all five of those hours unconscious from exhaustion—and knowing you'd be getting off the return bus just six hours later to do it all over again. . . . Well, why wouldn't you question your profession at moments such as those?

Though he'd never worked in a restaurant, my father proved to be a great source of strength to me during this time. We'd connect about once a month, usually for dinner on my night off. When I told him that I was struggling with the work I'd chosen to take on, he propped me up with the rigid love of a military man: "This is your *life*," he said to me. "You have to make it happen. This is what you want. *Make it happen*." Thanks in part to such stern encouragement, I stuck it out.

There were still moments of longing, however, especially for that elusive first serious girlfriend. I would pass an occasional summer Sunday, the entire day, sitting outside a pub, drinking cold pints of beer and staring longingly at all the girls who went by in their summer dresses. Decompressing and dreaming of a normal life, I wondered if such a thing were even compatible with a life centered on The Food.

SUMMER CRAB COMPOSITION Those lazy Sundays I spent girl-watching at British pubs are captured in this dish of peekytoe crab, lemon balm, anise hyssop, and nasturtium petals. The focal point for me, though, is the gelée, shaped like a summer dress and fashioned, appropriately enough, from Asian white beer.

One day, I realized with a shock that I had been at Marco Pierre White for a year. I couldn't believe that that much of my life was gone. To say that the time had flown by would be an understatement—and yet, a few of the more seasoned chefs had moved on, there were new kids younger than I, and I was an emerging veteran—not a *chef de partie* by any means, but a solid working cook, somebody who functioned well and helped keep the organism on track.

The chefs moved me to the fish station, and a new chapter opened up for me. I fell in love with fish at that restaurant—not just the dishes themselves, but every part of the process. White had access to the best product money could buy, and the fish were something to behold. The most impactful to me were the ten-pound turbots: I'd stand there at the table and stroke the clean lines as though the beast were a new pet. Just as I'd had that feeling of communing with the ingredients at L'Escargot, I felt a personal bond with the variety of fish that we worked with at The Restaurant, and began to believe that each one had its own innate personality. The muscular turbot suggests a prizefighter to me, and today I treat it accordingly, pairing it with assertive flavors. Sea bass is fast, so I came to think of it as a sprinter. Salmon and trout lack the nuance of the bass, so they require straightforward accompaniments.

A typical day at the fish station went something like this: My station mate and I would be in the kitchen by seven in the morning, which was about the time the fish arrived. I would survey it all to be sure it was of the quality we expected, checking for signs of freshness, such as clear eyes; the sweet, clean smell of the ocean; and rigor mortis. If there were any concerns, I'd update the sous-chef immediately so he could have it out with our purveyor, request or (if need be) demand replacement fish, and adjust the menu if necessary.

Next up was the butchering, which I found intensely satisfying. For me, there's an almost ceremonial rhythm to the craft of butchery, a ritual that begins with the sharpening of the knife and the cleaning of the board. Then there's the scaling and gutting of the fish, removing its head, clipping off the dorsal fin, cutting down the length of the backbone with the knife, and teasing the fillet off the bone—working precisely and leaving no flesh behind. Then, laying the fillets down, inspecting them with a surgeon's eye, and taking tweezers in hand to remove the delicate pinbones, periodically dipping the tweezers in a bowl of water to clean them. Then, trimming the

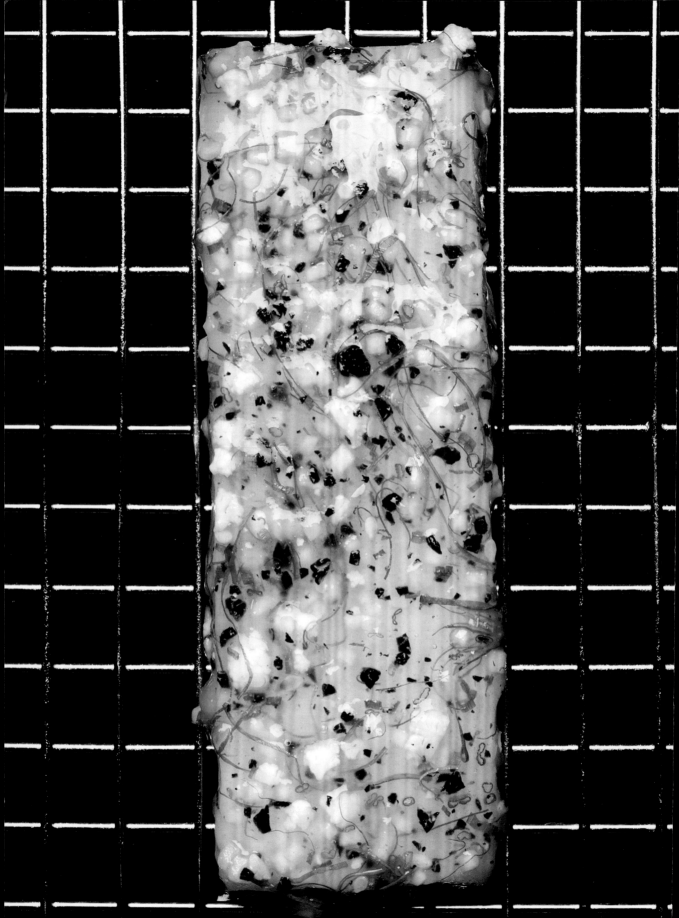

JOHN DORY WITH GREEN MANGO, CELERY, BLACK TRUFFLE, AND BUDDHA'S HAND Depicted above in a progression that reveals its assembly, the dish pictured on the left reminds me of my days at The Restaurant, because the combination of fish and Savoy cabbage was central to one of White's signature compositions. John Dory is a unique fish that yields three fillets and inspires my imagination; it also has enough texture and flavor to hold its own amid the other assertive elements here. The Tapioca Celery Jus (see page 234 for the recipe) is also a fine sauce for shellfish, especially lobster.

One of the most iconic images of chefs, especially European ones, is that of the temperamental taskmaster, hurling sauté pans at young cooks and cursing everybody from the front-of-the-house staff to the customers. It's become a cartoon image, but in reality these figures are as terrifying as an abusive parent. In my early days, it hit me that some chefs thought nothing of screaming the most insulting, personal, and hurtful comments at their minions. The most awful thing I ever witnessed was the morning a young cook walked into work, his face a mush of pain, and told the chef that his father had died during the night and he'd need to miss a day of work.

"What are you going to do about it?" asked the chef. "He's gone. Work your shift and take care of your affairs afterwards."

There's not much I can add to the canon of well-publicized incidents in this genre, except to say that everything you might have heard is true. I can also confess that I myself have been known to raise my voice an octave or ten in the kitchen. You know what they say: those who are abused as children are the most likely to abuse as adults. While I've moderated my tone over the years, I'd be lying if I said that I completely regret my outbursts, because it produces the desired result, and that's worth a lot in a kitchen, more than almost any other consideration.

What rarely gets remarked upon, however, is the culture of sabotage that goes on among young cooks. This is less of a factor in the United States, but the air of competition in European kitchens is so cutthroat that it leads nascent chefs to engage in behavior more appropriate to a penal colony than to a bastion of fine cuisine.

For example, in my first week on the job in one kitchen, I was tasked with making langoustine consommé, a time-consuming process resulting in a clear, nuanced liquid that was like gold. One day, while vacuum-packing it, I noticed that a colleague had dropped a roasted chicken leg in the bottom of the cauldron to cause the consommé to cloud, ruining it beyond repair and requiring me to start over from scratch.

Then there was the *chef de partie* of the meat station in one kitchen who made a habit of stealing my tomato *concassé*, a laborious chopped tomato preparation that required an investment of time and concentration. He would just smile at me when I'd return to my station and find it had gone missing, and because I lacked his seniority, there wasn't a damn thing I could do about it. I couldn't even tell the *chef de cuisine*. Just like in prison, there's nothing worse than a rat.

I learned, though. In time, I learned. Just as my knife and plating acumen developed, so too did my instincts for self-preservation. The next time that prick stole my *concassé,* I gave him some payback: During service, when *his* back was turned, I scurried over and shut off his oven so that when he went to pull his food out, it was cold. There were few moments more satisfying than when he gazed around the kitchen looking for evidence of his saboteur and found me, waving back, doing my best impression of the smile he'd sent my way the day prior.

This is all part of the education of a cook, just one of the many tests that probe whether or not you have the stuff for survival.

fillets into perfectly chiseled portions, wrapping them individually in plastic wrap, and standing back to survey the work.

For me, the most important thing at that time in my development was to try to be better the next day. Fish is one of the ultimate tests of a cook's skill and mettle: there's no place to hide if you screw it up. Make a hash of a ten-kilo turbot and you take your knives and go home. It's as simple as that. Hence, the discipline.

Turning something wild into a beautiful plate of food, the journey of it from one state of being to another, was transporting. Even today, when the dinner service arrives and I put the finishing touches on a dish, every part of me is gratified. Just like some of those dishes from L'Escargot, there are Marco dishes that I could prepare right now, so indelible is the memory: the turbot with grilled new potatoes and a tomato-and-cockle butter; a sea bass dish from Harvey's with crisped skin, cream-enriched *nage* spooned over the top, and a spoonful of caviar for good measure; Scottish lobsters that we would split, cook under the salamander (broiler), and finish with béarnaise sauce; a scallop and oyster *nage;* and *rouget* with ratatouille. These weren't, on paper, terribly complicated dishes, but they were the epitome of proper cooking. These were the days before xanthan gum, hydrocolloids, and other additives that chefs such as myself use today (which help make cooking fail-safe). We plied our trade with a knife, a whisk, a bowl, a spoon, some tweezers, heat, and a pan. It was good, solid, well-prepared French food.

Having rhapsodized this way about Marco Pierre White, I must also admit that one of the more profound epiphanies of my career has been that no matter how privileged you may be to work in certain settings, even a summit such as The Restaurant, there is always a time to move on. It's a moment when you must recognize that, despite the trust that's been invested in you and what you were able to learn, the only way to truly honor that investment is to push off and continue your development elsewhere. After two years at The Restaurant, I sensed that it was time to seek out the next evolution and to expand my repertoire beyond classic French cuisine.

DISCOVERING THE NEW WORLD

About two years into my time in White's kitchen, I heard that Jean-Georges Vongerichten, a New York City chef of French descent, was going to be opening an outpost of his pan-Asian/French hybrid restaurant Vong at the Berkeley Hotel in London. Having enjoyed Chinese food since childhood, I felt the pull of other Asian flavors. It seemed like the perfect next step for my own idiosyncratic journey, combining French technique with a new world of ingredients. It would also be an adventure in learning to cook for volume: Vong would have more than one hundred seats, and we'd be cooking food that wasn't Michelin bait per se.

I answered an ad in the *Evening Standard* and, after a brief meeting with Jean-Georges's on-site executive chef, was hired. It was actually pretty easy to secure the job, not only because of my growing résumé, but also because the global export of American dining concepts was just beginning to take hold, and Jean-Georges—though one of the kings of New York City, if not America, at the time—was more or less an unknown quantity in London.

I got off on the wrong foot with the chef when I confused my start date, showing up one Monday later than he wanted. It's the kind of thing I'd sack somebody for, but fortunately they were more forgiving and didn't give the job away. There were just seven of us in that kitchen, and I was to man the fish station, which meant that I was responsible for all the butchering, cookery, sauce work, and garnish. A typical day would require me to crack eighty lobsters, dice up all the vegetables required for garnish, and make eight different sauce bases; one of my favorites was a stock made with whiting, lemons, oranges, limes, sumac, and hazelnuts that we served over monkfish. It was hard, manual work, and mentally very demanding.

I didn't care much for the volume at the time, but in hindsight I realize that from a business standpoint, there was much to learn from Vong, which was designed and engineered to produce both good food and an enormous profit. The kitchen wasn't much bigger than others I had cooked in. Because the food was built for speed, we could produce enough of it to serve a full house, with labor costs comparable to those of the other places I'd worked. In a world in which many of the top restaurants are, at the end of the day, money losers, this place was unapologetically built for success. The food was distinct and delicious, but the real genius was in the overall conception and execution, in dishes such as lobster with Thai herbs, and a langoustine satay with oyster *vin blanc* and fresh kaffir lime leaf.

Vongerichten himself arrived on the scene a few weeks prior to the opening and made quite an impression on me: a slender man dressed from head to toe in black Prada, he exuded the calm aura of a spiritual guru. The first day he showed up, gliding through the kitchen with his beautiful girlfriend on his arm, I was awestruck. He was such a contrast to the beaten-down chefs I'd seen throughout London that I couldn't help but stare at him. "That's a chef?" I remember thinking to myself. Jean-Georges was the first chef of his level that I really got to interact with, and I took an instant liking to him. He may not have been in whites for that first visit, but he was a chef's chef through and through, and he knew the nuts and bolts of the kitchen and the cuisine.

He also had a mastery of all the ancillary requirements of the modern chef. He greeted visiting journalists gregariously, offering them personal tours of the kitchen and dining room, and was utterly at ease during all of the photo shoots leading up to the opening of Vong London. Vongerichten was also a celebrity on the same level as our bold-name guests. When we opened, Mariah Carey was a frequent diner, and when he visited her table, it was all hugs and kisses, as though he were one of her gang rather than a kitchen slave. Another frequent guest was one of my favorite directors, Luc Besson, whom Vongerichten had gotten to know when the filmmaker was in New York making *The Professional* and became a regular at the original Vong in Midtown Manhattan. When the London restaurant opened, an early lunch visitor was soccer superstar Pelé, who ordered the salmon wrapped in *feuille de bric,* sliced and served with a citrus vinaigrette. I made it for him and was thrilled when he came back the next day and ordered the same thing.

All of that had nothing to do with cooking but everything to do with success. Where even a titan like Marco pretty much chained himself to the stoves, Jean-Georges showed me a different aspect of being a chef—a stylish, high-living ideal that was undeniably appealing.

Beyond Jean-Georges, his imported team of cooks was less antagonistic than what I was used to. They were free of the tensions that coursed through the London cooking scene, like the Marco-inspired abrasiveness of many chefs or the generations-long tensions between French and British guys. Jean-Georges's cooks were serious and specific—they knew what the chef wanted and how to guide us there, but they weren't aggressive about it. Their attitude was industrious and collaborative, and this, too, was refreshing. The kinder, gentler environment also fostered a new and rare kitchen friendship: an Aussie named Jason, whom I'd met during a "stage" at La Tante Claire between working at The Restaurant and Vong, had also taken a job at Vong. He and I began dining around town on days off and when we could afford it, trying the better restaurants in hopes of edifying our palates.

I didn't love everything about Vong. The restaurant, after the fashion of its New York City mother ship, had a window into the kitchen that let the guests see us cooking, which was a first to me. Because we were on display, we were part of the décor, and so all the cooks had to wear colored skullcaps, with a different color for each section. They were polyester, hot, and itchy, and drove me crazy. But my meager issues were nothing compared to the disdain exhibited by the cooks who ran the other food service for the hotel, especially the head chef, an old-school British guy who would make a point of leaving his classic, haute, Savoy-esque food up on the pass for hours, so that as we walked by, we'd have to see it, as if to say, "See what we do."

It was a perfect illustration of what was going on in London cuisine at the time. The old guard were being left behind, both stylistically and in the

Thai-Spiced Blowfish

This Thai-spiced blowfish has a crust of red curry paste and burning laurel leaf, and I sometimes augment it with fresh coconut juice poured over it at the table. We didn't serve this dish at Vong, or even a version of it, but I probably wouldn't have come up with this abstract and sensuous connection of French and Thai food had I never cooked there. The recipe on page 236 produces a streamlined version of the dish. I suggest serving it like a tandoori with no additional sauce—let the natural juiciness of the fish speak for itself.

media, by forward-thinking chefs, both homegrown and imported, and they didn't like it one bit.

As the kitchen came together and I got to see more and more of the repertoire, I was impressed by the food. The base recipes were rock solid, the flavors were fresh and clear, and the dishes I worked on made an impact that is still with me today. There was a lovely lobster dish of curry paste that I'd make by combining shrimp paste and red, yellow, and green curry pastes, and sweating it down; then I'd add apples and carrot, then turmeric, chiles, and lemongrass. We didn't really cook out the apple and carrot flavor, so they remained in the foreground. For service, we'd warm it up and finish it with a spoonful of whipped cream—it would soufflé up, right over the top of the lobster—and a chiffonade of cilantro. It was simple but very tasty. We also made a langoustine saté that was served over a piped-out shrimp and langoustine mousse. But the main thing was the sauce: we added a puree of fresh oyster and a pinch of lime leaf to a sauce based on a *vin blanc,* a traditional sauce of white wine and cream.

There was real freedom in Jean-Georges's food, not just in the rule breaking, but in the unabashedly big flavors, the spice, and the acidity that I'd never encountered in such a sophisticated setting. Asian ingredients are part of just about every chef's larder these days, but it was borderline revolutionary at Vong and very exciting: new flavors unleashed by French technique. During an era in which the food in Michelin-worthy restaurants was rigidly classical, having food of this caliber produced with the same methods and at such incredible volume was template-shattering.

Southeast Asian food—with its lime leaf, lemongrass, chiles, palm sugar, and fish sauce—was a whole new world: fragrant, alive, intoxicating. The use of a variety of citrus at Vong was a revelation to me, the first time I'd seen certain distinct acidities in cooking. I'd used lemon in classical French cuisine, but Vongerichten called on quite a bit of other citrus, such as mandarin and especially kaffir lime. It began a love affair between me and this family of fruits, which has only grown and developed over time. I think of lime as the femme fatale of the citrus world, a seductive, perfumed experience unto itself that can overtake you if you're not careful. It's a fruit that brings out the explorer in me. I'm endlessly fascinated by its possibilities, not just of the juice itself but also of the oily skin and even of the intensely fragrant leaves. There's a distinctly female sexiness to lime that compels me. Today a number of limes find their way into my cuisine, such as Persian limes, limequats, and mandarinquats. But it all began at Vong, with what at the time seemed an audacious yet perfectly natural mingling of French technique and Asian flavors.

As a chef who sometimes thinks in terms of colors, lime also epitomizes green. The 2.0 version of my signature Green Apple–Wasabi Sorbet on page 251 is served atop a frozen lime half, the apple, wasabi, and lime united by their common color. Also new to me at Vong was the opportunity to plate my own food. In other kitchens I'd worked in, we'd deliver our work to the pass, and the chef would plate and fuss over it until it was just right.

Through it all, Jean-Georges continued to impress. First, he was just a good guy. I didn't get to cook side by side with him because he was too busy running around, keeping tabs on all the moving parts of his growing restaurant group. But I still remember the day he took the time to ask me to make him the langoustine saté, and his complimentary and enthusiastic appraisal upon tasting it. Early on in Vong's business days, he took a bunch of us chefs on a tour of an Asian supermarket, curious about what ingredients were available locally. Spotting some sesame bars that he knew from overseas, he bought a handful and handed them out to us. As we stood outside the market, tasting and hanging out with the boss in a way I never had before, he talked to us about his time in Bangkok and how they cooked there, contextualizing the snacks we were eating by describing how he'd discovered them at open-air street markets in the Far East.

My entire experience of Jean-Georges planted a seed in my head, a curiosity about New York City: Vongerichten was born and trained in Europe, but had found his great success in Manhattan. Everything about him was refreshing to me, from his open, approachable attitude to the freedom in his food. Proud Brit though I am, I can't help but admit that this was all incredibly refreshing to me. To a kid who never felt quite at home amid the stifling scene in London, Jean-Georges made me want to see where he came from.

His fame, and pursuit of fame, also flew in the face of what I have to admit is a stifling aspect of British culture: the idea that you cannot get too big for your britches, that only certain people are preordained to make it, to achieve a certain level of success. The uniqueness of his food—the unapologetic trumpeting of Asian flavors in a refined context—was also something that I didn't think a Brit would have been capable of in those days. Marco, god among men that he was, still operated within the template of classic French cuisine and came up in a time when one had to be validated by the imprimatur of the greats. Vongerichten, on the other hand, created something altogether different, which he somehow made seem utterly natural.

It wasn't that I had outlandish ideas of my own yet, but the oppressive structure of British kitchen life, reflective of the country's class system, silently bothered me, almost to the point of depression. And so, here was Jean-Georges, a jet-setting, Prada-wearing original, commanding attention on the world stage as though it were the most natural thing in the world. The fact that he found all of this success in New York City, I reckoned, was all I needed to know.

The restaurant opened strong, was packed every lunch and dinner, and earned Best Newcomer of the Year from the *Evening Standard*. It was an exhilarating, dizzying month and a half. But when Jean-Georges himself got on a jet plane to his next adventure, the air went out of the enterprise for me. He said he'd see us all in six months, and the time stretched before me like an eternity. My infatuation with the flavors had settled down in Jean-Georges's absence, and all I was left with was the volume of customers waiting to be satisfied. I fell into a semidepression, and whether I knew it right away or not, began to search for something new.

Around this time, my lunchtime dining tour took me to Pied à Terre, where a chef named Richard Neat had earned all kinds of attention and buzz by going against the Marco grain and creating something distinctly his own. Where White's food was grand and perfect, but elemental—a beautiful piece of meat, flawless sauce work, and garnish—Neat's was intricate, with more ingredients per plate, harmonized as though he were drawing on the canon of classic cuisine, when in fact, some of the ideas were unique to him. And so with my pal Jason, I made plans to drop in one day and enjoy the astonishingly inexpensive lunch prix fixe, available for a little more than twenty pounds.

What I encountered at Pied à Terre blew my mind. I still remember the *dourade,* gently cooked, with a lovely ratatouille and white bean quenelle and a sardine and onion puree. (Where had he thought of that puree?) Neat had cooked under Robuchon, and from the books and magazines I had read, I recognized the influence. The same went for my meat course of pork, prepared several ways including a crispy pig ear, braised cheek, and stuffed trotter. It was elegant food, but groundbreaking in its identity, a personalized rendering of state-of-the-art French cuisine.

My wandering professional eye couldn't help itself—I wanted out of Vong and into Pied à Terre. One night, just a few days before Christmas, I prepared all my *mise en place* and quit, telling the chef I was leaving and not coming back. It was an irresponsible thing to do, a violation of the code between cooks. To give no notice was bad enough, but to leave on the spur of the moment was unforgivable. I wasn't proud of it then or now, and I regret it to this day. But when I look back, I realize that I was simply young and in love, smitten with Richard Neat's food and powerless to stop myself from impulsively pursuing it.

A TASTE OF FRANCE

London 1996

I didn't realize the kind of chef I myself might become one day until I went to work for Richard Neat at Pied à Terre at the age of twenty-one. Part of the reason was timing. I had chosen cooking as my vocation years earlier and sacrificed the last of my teenage years to pursue it, but had necessarily maintained the image of myself as a foot soldier rather than a commander, not indulging in fantasies of My Future. What would have been the point? When you spend more than a dozen hours a day engaged in the repetition of a handful of tasks, imagining a grander position is a sure recipe for discontent. And besides, I hadn't *earned* the right to think of myself as a chef.

But now I had grown from a boy to a man, and the chef within was feasting on a rich diet of influences—the techniques and compositions offered not only in the kitchens of L'Escargot, The Restaurant, and Vong, but also in those I'd dined in around town. Physically, I had grown to my current height of six feet four inches and had the kitchen confidence, the swagger, of a mature and confident cook.

I had also developed what you might call food fluency. Having spent the better part of the past few years developing the vocabulary and grammar of cuisine, I was ready to think and speak in complete sentences, if not paragraphs. I had a mastery of basic ingredients and technique, and even a bit of a knack for the exotic complements of Vongerichten, but lacked any instinct or inclination for how to put it all together in a way that would distinguish and represent me. Neat would change all that by causing a sea change in my perception of food as a means of self-expression.

When I started at Pied à Terre in January, the chef had just received his second Michelin star and was cooking the most of-the-minute modern French food I had seen in all of London. Neat's food was hypercreative and—most important—superpersonal, to an extent I'd not seen before. He wasn't just cooking; he was actually saying something with the food, expressing *himself* on the plate, as compared to most of his contemporaries, for whom quality and consistency were expression enough. As for what he was creating, each composition was nothing less than a graphic work of art that inspired a reaction in the customer. He had a modernized nouveau sensibility that was more Parisian and feminine in its level of detail and elegance than Marco's robust style, with lots of little, dainty elements on the plate. When the dish arrived at the table, it wasn't just food that was being delivered; it was something that demanded at least a moment's attention and contemplation before the conversation was resumed and the meal consumed.

Where flavors were concerned, Neat's were classical, but the ways in which he deployed them were unheard of. Rather than the requisite foie gras and Sauternes, or *rouget* and bouillabaisse-inspired dishes—combinations that it seemed everybody in town was drawing on—Neat served dishes that could only have been dreamed up by him, such as *rouget* tartare, date paste, and cauliflower puree. The earthiness of the *rouget* and cauliflower played against the sweetness of the fruit, conjuring a sort of classic umami flavor but in a distinctly French way.

Moreover, the precision and elegance of the plating, and the intricate techniques employed to attain them, left everybody else in the dust. For example, there was a croquette that required the cook to fold chicken mousse and crabmeat together, pipe that into a leek, roll it in plastic wrap, then unmold it, bread it, and fry it *à la minute*. I'd never seen a leek used in that manner, nor would I ever have thought to use it that way, and such flourishes were the rule rather than the exception in Neat's food. Another of his signature dishes involved a snail encased with chicken mousse, poached and rolled in dried morel mushrooms so it maintained its natural coiled shape. This was served atop potato fondant with garlic confit below and baby girolles (chanterelle mushrooms) all around. As if that weren't enough, we'd shave tagliatelle-like ribbons of asparagus, blanch them, use a fork to wind them into a perfect bobbin, and set that in the center of the plate, with a garnish of chervil and a spoon-over of chicken *jus* and the snail's braising liquid.

Sometimes the preparations were simpler, but it was all fresh and exciting—even some revelatory decisions about otherwise familiar dishes, such as a crab and skate terrine that we served cold rather than hot. Some dishes were distinguished simply by the precision they required, such as langoustine tortellini cooked as they were at Robuchon to a degree of doneness (*cuisson*) specified by the customer, and the petit fours made from little opera cakes that we'd cut into 1×1-centimeter cubes.

Neat's food upped the game, operated on a level above what I'd experienced before, in terms of both sheer technical wizardry and that incredible, visceral reaction it inspired. *Audacious* didn't even begin to describe the summary effect; it was nothing less than a man sharing everything of himself with the guest—his talent, craft, vision, and palate. I wasn't in the dining room to witness it, but I loved the connection Neat's food made with diners, and I only had to see my own reaction to glean this. I also loved the feeling of ambition his food rebooted in me. Having developed the full complement of basics, I was ready for new challenges as a cook, and the intricacies of Neat's cuisine asked that of me, while providing constant inspiration.

The kitchen at Pied à Terre was minuscule, much too small for the fourteen of us who worked there, and Neat was a big man—not Marco big, but imposing to be sure. For all of his uniqueness, he wasn't above trying to be a little like Marco himself, growing his hair long and wearing sweatpants in the kitchen. Moreover, his menacing air was underscored by an eye that wandered at times; he scared the cooks a little bit.

But I was able to pull my own weight and had developed the thick skin of a working cook, so I didn't really have anything to worry about. Besides, the tight quarters afforded me a front-row seat to the machinations of my new culinary role model. I was keen to know where inspirations such as his came from. In time, from observing him, I realized one of the main lessons of my professional life: that true chefs are completely absorbed by The Food. Neat was the first chef I'd met who was engaged in what I'd describe as a symbiotic relationship with his cuisine. It was no wonder I'd felt such an inexplicable, love-at-first-sight type of attraction to what he was doing at Pied à Terre because I soon discovered that Neat himself was locked in a permanent, operatic relationship with food. It consumed him.

I'm sure there are those who found Neat's relationship with The Food bizarre, frightening, or just unnecessary, but it resonated with me. I'd been obsessed with other things in my young life, namely music and movies, but not having had the talent for a career in those fields, beyond my DJ skills, the interest was essentially recreational. That began to change under Neat, who operated on another plane altogether. Having long ago mastered the technical aspects of cooking, he was now essentially dancing with it, improvising with it, acting as the conduit through which their shared muse expressed itself. It didn't take long to realize that everything about his food—the flavor combinations, the stylistic flights of fancy, the intuitive leaps that tied it all together—could only come from somebody who spent every waking hour, and then some, either thinking about food or actually cooking it.

This made perfect sense to me. I thought of the way I related to food, assigning or imagining personalities and dispositions for ingredients as I'd done since L'Escargot, and began to understand that those observations weren't mere quirks, but actual ideas that might become the beginnings of my own distinct style. I never had a chance to discuss this perceived kinship with Neat—he was far too impenetrable and unapproachable for that—but I felt certain that he must have had his own similar version of interacting with The Food.

Of course, that level of immersion comes at a cost: Neat spent so much time alone with his thoughts that human interaction seemed an intrusion for him, and so his personality could be as unpredictable as the weather. Today I understand where he was coming from. It's tough to switch gears and interact with others, even cooks, when you live in such a private mental space most of the time. There's an almost unfathomable gap between what goes on in the mind of a chef and executing it in the physical world of the kitchen. Bridging that gap can sometimes feel like a Himalayan haul.

In part, I think Neat relished the isolated vibe he exuded, and he would play mind games with the staff, most of them designed to create a sense of urgency in the kitchen. On occasion we would arrive to begin work in

Lamb

Richard Neat was the first chef I saw use multiple cuts of the same animal in one dish, and not primal cuts—for example, one of his compositions featured the trotter, ear, and cheek of a pig. As a cook, it gave me more of a feeling for the animal and a sense of how to tell a story on the plate. These three lamb preparations (shown opposite, and on pages 76-77), based on elements of a *navarin* (stew), are part of a progression of dishes I'm apt to serve in the late winter or early spring months, using the tastiest parts of the animal—its neck, cheek, and tongue. The sheer ambition of the progression, and the variety of plating techniques it calls on, owes a debt to my formative days in Neat's kitchen. (I must point out that the lamb I use today is from Keith Martin's Elysian Fields Sheep Farm in Pennsylvania, which is remarkable for its consistent excellent quality.)

Lamb neck with pumpkin, coffee, and hibiscus. The recipe for the Braised Lamb Neck can be found on page 237.

Lamb cheek, braised very gently, then served with white beans and pickled red onions that cut the richness of the other ingredients.

Small cubes of pickled lamb tongue, paired with pickled cucumber, and dots of cardamom crème around the perimeter of the bowl.

RABBIT AND CUTTLEFISH This is from a progression of rabbit dishes that recalls the audacity and ambition of Richard Neat, as well as his penchant for using lesser items in a sophisticated way—in this case, a cuttlefish preparation that's almost Sicilian in its effect. To the left is tortellini of rabbit and cuttlefish wrapped in squid ink pasta. (The recipe for lemongrass velouté, which is poured over the pasta, can be found on page 242.) Above is the progression's main plate, an array of rabbit preparations, including Rabbit-Cuttlefish Rillettes, my play on rillettes (potted cooked meats, bound with fat), which wraps rabbit confit in cuttlefish, shaping the combination into little balls that are adorned with a green bread crumb mixture. The recipe for the rillettes can be found on page 240.

CRAB/ASPARAGUS/ALMOND MILK This is another Neat-like composition, with many of the springtime ingredients elevated by intricate knife work and plating techniques. I've cooked crab just about every place I've ever worked, but it was working for Neat when I truly came to love it.

OUR OPERA This is my contemporary play on a classical opera cake, which takes banana and coffee as its main flavors. Although the layers look very traditional, the cream piped over the top is infused with Madras curry powder. I love the simple symmetry of this dish and the elegant integration of the yellow and chocolate tones.

the morning, only to learn that he had locked the fridges. We'd do what we could, prepping newly arrived ingredients, all of us exchanging nervous glances. Finally, with mere minutes to spare, the chef would unlock the food vault, and we'd almost trample each other to get at what we needed and finish preparing for lunch service.

Another similar bit occurred during service, when Neat wouldn't tell one of the *chefs de partie* that he needed a particular dish for a table until the last possible second. When the captain emerged in the doorway, he'd nod surreptitiously at the chef, who would then say *"envoyez,"* whereupon the cook running that station would go into a frenzy, preparing the dish in record time.

Neat also had a temper and an absolute devotion to perfection, which can be a lethal combination. During one service, upon discovering that a squab was overdone, he punched a hole in the white drywall, stuffed another squab into it with its head protruding, and drew a dialogue balloon on the wall next to it, writing "I am one well-fucked squab" inside the balloon.

For all its apparent dysfunction, I related to this part of Neat's mental makeup. With the notable exception of Vongerichten, I'd worked for stern taskmasters my entire career to that point, and the same was true of every young cook in London. It was part of the social contract of any kitchen worth its salt. What I appreciated about Neat was that he was just as unique in his tantrums as he was on the plate. That squab's head sticking out of the wall was just another work of art as far as I was concerned. I mean, how many other people would even *think* to do that?

Nevertheless, some guys just couldn't withstand the tension and would either quit or be sacked. One morning, a bunch of us cooks were eating a breakfast of cold chicken pies from the previous day's service. Neat was at his station, in a foul mood, hacking chicken wings that we used to make *jus*. He was enraged about something and held the cleaver in both hands, assaulting the wings with a special vengeance. With each clobber of the cleaver, the entire kitchen seemed to shake. Those of us who'd been there awhile were accustomed to such displays, so we went about our business, doing our best impressions of people who didn't notice the thudding. But down the line from the chef was a new cook, on his very first day in the kitchen, picking parsley and trying to take our lead and ignore the display; still, he couldn't help but shudder with each blow of the cleaver. The man eventually put down his parsley and simply walked out of the kitchen, never to return. As the newcomer passed by him, Neat brought the cleaver down again and gave him a look that said, "What the fuck is that guy's problem?"

But Neat could also be the supportive and protective boss every cook desires, and he'd sometimes get our backs in a surprising and touching way. There was a Northerner (a casual way of referring to those from Northern England) high up on the totem pole at Pied à Terre who had worked for Marco as well. Like so many guys in London at the time, this guy thought that he *was* Marco. One day, apropos of nothing, the Northern guy was all over a young cook who was *brunoising* (very finely dicing) a carrot. "How old are you?" he demanded. "You're just a southern shite, aren't you? Won't amount to anything, will you?"

As a subordinate, the young cook just stood there and absorbed the abuse, but when Neat showed up for service that night, somebody relayed all of this to him—whereupon he emptied the Northerner's locker, gathering his clothes and knives, and hurled it all into the street. "Don't you ever fuck with my boys again!" he bellowed.

As bizarre as all of this side action could be, it was white noise to me. Neat was the first chef who inspired me creatively, and just to be in his presence was worth it all. L'Escargot was about a block away, and I'd walk by every day and look at the tradition-steeped menu and think how far I'd come in just a few years. This was nowhere more apparent than in that notebook I'd begun keeping back at L'Escargot. It was no longer merely full of other people's basic recipes; instead I had begun to track my own new ideas, such as a tempura of *rouget*.

And so it was especially disheartening to me when, after I'd been at Pied à Terre just six months, we learned that Neat would be pushing off and that Tom Aikens would be replacing him. Aikens was a respectable talent, to be sure, but I had come to Pied à Terre to work for Neat, and with him gone, there was nothing there for me. I decided that it was time for the next adventure and that it would be a good thing to shake up my world a bit, to leave familiar London for something new, to act on the sense of wanderlust that had been planted at Vong and set my sights on my next destination.

CITY BOY

1997–1998

The logical next step for me would have been to go to France, which at the time had long been considered a finishing school for young cooks. (It still is, of course, although in many ways Spain has nosed ahead as the mandatory stop on one's culinary CV.) You could become a perfectly skilled cook in London, but going to France was a rite of passage that many dreamed of, but few attempted or pulled off. It was the center of the gastronomic universe at the time, with a culinary culture that couldn't be replicated anywhere else. In addition to my own professional older brother Simon, many of the best London chefs of the day had spent time in France, such as Gordon Ramsay, Richard Neat, and Tom Aikens. So I had it as a goal to cook in France myself. In addition to stamping my CV with a French credential, I also wanted to learn proper French, not just the paltry kitchen French I knew at that time. I took my stab at a long and proud tradition among young cooks, penning letters to an ungodly number of Michelin two- and three-star restaurants, offering my services for little or no money, in exchange for the technical wisdom and palate-sharpening cuisine available there.

I wrote to no fewer than twenty-two restaurants. Despite what would be considered a short but formidable work history in London, not a single chef or restaurant responded to my overture, not even to turn me down. It was an exquisitely humbling experience, a reminder that in the fine-dining universe, for all of the toil and sacrifice I'd logged to that point, I was just another anonymous worker bee, with miles to go before I made a dent. (It probably didn't help my cause that rather than enlist the help of a bilingual friend, I translated the letters myself with nothing but a French-English dictionary to guide me; I can only imagine how unintelligible they must have been.)

The question, then, was what to do next. I knew that I was in need of stimulation, of something new, but for all the great restaurants in London, I felt sure that there was nothing there for me. Having worked for White, Neat, Vongerichten, Hollihead, and Cavalier, I reckoned, where my hometown was concerned, there was nowhere to go but down.

All right, I thought, *if I can't go to France, at least let me expand my horizons and get out of the city*. A chef friend of mine suggested that I go to a fine-dining institution, and I decided that I should go to Raymond Blanc's Le Manoir aux Quat'Saisons, a luxury hotel in Great Milton, Oxford, in the countryside. So much about Le Manoir made sense for me, not the least of which was the fact that its culinary lineage was mind-blowing: a number of the best young chefs in England had cut their teeth there, including White and Neat. Moreover, working for a big operation rather than an intimate dining temple, and for a Frenchman rather than an Englishman, would all be new experiences for me.

I phoned up Le Manoir's chef, was invited to "stage," and made the trip to the countryside by train, the gray cityscape of London giving way to a blur of green. After a night in a bed and breakfast, I took a taxi to Le Manoir the next morning.

The application process alone was a window into the differences between the often improvised hiring practices of a smaller, stand-alone restaurant and one that was affiliated with a stately hotel. Instead of a few hours in the kitchen followed by an offer and a handshake, I was directed to a human resources department, where I filled out an "official" application for the first time in my life. The next step was to "stage" for two days, after which it would be determined whether a job offer would be forthcoming.

The first thing that struck me about the kitchen at Le Manoir was its size: it was massive. It was a Sunday, and there were thirty-four people cooking for one hundred guests plus a private party. The room exuded a sense of history and importance appropriate to its place in professional British cookery, and that is what had drawn me there. I had worked for the best of the new, but other than as a *stagiaire*, I hadn't spent time in a legendary restaurant such as La Tante Claire (but for a few days) or Le Gavroche—and now here I was at the Oxford of kitchens. The detail that stands out most vividly in my memory is the bronze bust of Blanc himself that lived opposite the stove, with all of his medals and accolades hanging off it like Christmas tree decorations. I was endlessly fascinated by the display—a physical representation of what one might achieve in this industry if you were talented and hardworking enough.

On my second day as a *stagiaire*, the chef asked me to cook a dish of my own. Although I had a growing repertoire of ideas in that notebook of mine, this was the first time I'd been asked to actualize one of them in a professional setting. I slow-roasted some sea bass and served it over a langoustine and fennel blossom risotto.

The chef seemed impressed. "Have you done this before?" he asked.

"No, Chef."

"You just made this up?"

"Yes."

He poked at it with a fork, flipping the bass off the risotto, silently evaluating it. As he cut himself a piece of the fish, he asked me what I thought. I wasn't sure how to answer. "You tell me," I said.

He took a bite of the bass, and I detected the first hint of his estimation. "The fish is cooked beautifully," he said. He took a bite of the risotto and frowned a little.

"The risotto's too al dente." He looked at the dish again. "And I'd have much preferred if you'd set the langoustine on top or around the risotto. To show them off." I didn't agree, but I could see he was impressed, at the very least with my technical ability.

I was hired and assigned to the meat station. The first order of business, as it often was, was to find living accommodations. I entered into an arrangement with a junior sous-chef and a pastry chef, in a house about two miles from Le Manoir. I had never lived in a house before—since leaving home at the age of fifteen, it had been nothing but crap flats in sketchy neighborhoods. Though luxurious by comparison, this new home was a bit disorienting. I didn't know what to do with all that space. There was a proper kitchen, and when I made my morning cup of coffee and opened the back door, I found myself staring at miles of rolling hills and green pastures that flowed right on out to the horizon. It never ceased to feel like something out of a dream. I also traded in my bus fare for a bicycle, on which I rode the bumpy country roads two miles to and from work every day. The morning ride was idyllic, a lovely, meditative way to begin the day. The reverse commute at night was harrowing, as motorists, many of them drunken guests from Le Manoir, nearly ran me off the unlit road.

That nightly ritual became a metaphor for my feelings about the countryside. As lush and lovely as it was, I have to admit that the country never felt like home to me. Open fields and an unobstructed view of the sky are probably very healthful settings for the vast majority of the human race, but the truth is that I found the expansiveness overwhelming in only the wrong ways, like a giant abyss coming at me from all directions, amplifying my essential loneliness. I wouldn't have been able to put these words to it at that time, but the truth was that I was a creature of the city, meant for the concrete canyons of a modern metropolis, where the tight spaces and skyscrapers whittle the universe down to a manageable scale and keep your more troubling thoughts at bay.

Where I found solace was in the culinary benefits of the setting: Le Manoir was the first restaurant I worked at that grew much of its own produce. Rather than receiving vegetables in crates or from outdoor markets, I got to pull turnips, leeks, and other vegetables right from the earth. There was also a dedicated grounds crew who could be seen out the kitchen windows pushing wheelbarrows to and fro. These details put one in a pleasant state of mind, constant reminders of the connection to the raw ingredients and where they came from; this also fostered a sense of calm in the kitchen.

Decidedly less mellowing was a daily ritual. Le Manoir employed a full-time staff member whose only role was to work the fish market at Billingsgate in London, procuring the absolute best fish possible. However, the fish team had to have its orders in by midday the day prior. So, on a busy day, while working our way through one hundred lunch covers, the on-site go-between might turn up at the nearby fish station screaming with great urgency, "On order! On order! What do you need? What do you need?"

And then there was Raymond Blanc himself. Though he was more concerned with the business of the restaurant and the expansion of the physical property at that time, he was often around and he was unlike any other chef

I'd encountered. This trim, sprightly Frenchman disproved many of the more prominent clichés that attached to his countrymen. He wasn't a screamer. He didn't loathe Brits, whom many Gallic whisks delighted in calling, with condescension and arrogance, "Roast Beef" (the implication being that that's all we could cook). Moreover, this largely self-taught man had an inexhaustible love of cooking and a passion for sharing it with others. I appreciated this, even though I couldn't necessarily relate to it. The emerging truth, between my inability to embrace the country and my regard for Blanc as a lovable curiosity rather than necessarily a soul mate, is that I saw myself more like the misanthropic Marco—brash, urban, and unapologetically antisocial. Fittingly, a few years prior, the two men had appeared together in a BBC special, where the differences between them came into high relief: Blanc waxing poetic on the gift a chef gives his guests, White expressing his belief that the guests had little or no appreciation for the toil that went into it.

Unsurprisingly, given his reputation, Blanc romped around the kitchen like a jackrabbit, a living, breathing illustration of this different, sunnier point of view and another way of life from what I had seen in other kitchens. Where others thrived on seriousness, Blanc was too irrepressible to let that define his roost. I remember one day, while he was walking down a corridor to the prep room, he spanked a line cook with two big squeegee sponges, leaving his ass soaking wet before zooming away like the roadrunner. Executed by another chef, the move would have been seen as abusive; with Blanc, it was utterly playful and amusing, even to the victim.

There were times when he could seem as absentminded as Inspector Clouseau, like when he was flambéing veal kidneys, poured green Chartreuse into the pan, and a mushroom cloud of flame shot up, singeing his eyebrows. *"Merde!"* he exclaimed, as though he had no idea that flame plus liqueur might equal fire. But lest we read anything into such moments, they were balanced by evidence of his laser-like eye for detail. One day, a cook, a woman of Scottish descent, was walking through the kitchen, a tray of *navarin* of lamb neck in tow. From among the chaos of the kitchen, his eye trained on the contents of the tray, the one thing amiss, like an intelligence drone. He leapt over the pass, intercepted her, and eviscerated her.

"You stupid girl," he bellowed. "Do you not care? Do you not care?!"

As for the food itself, Blanc was unencumbered by the slavish devotion to convention that defined most of the cooking in fine-dining establishments. There was no rigidity in his personality, his kitchen, or his food. In

This winter dish never fails to remind me of my Le Tarion days because of its mingling of French classicism with a contemporary sensibility. I think of it rather like dressing up a rugby player in a Savile Row bespoke suit.

To prepare this *tête de cochon* (head of the pig) dish, we debone a pig's head, but rather than adhere to the traditional method of rolling it, we take strips of the face, cheek, jowl, and back of the head and make a garlicky mixture, almost like a *salchicón*. This is rolled up into strips of the pig's face to achieve a balance of meat to fat in every portion. (The magic of any *tête de cochon* is the interplay between the fat of the head and the immense flavor in the cheek.) It's vacuum-packed and cooked *sous vide,* which breaks down the gelatin, and the result boasts what I think of as a refined viscosity; in the eating, it's not unlike foie gras. It's complemented by a tapioca cracker, fresh violet leaves, and anchovy, which helps pull all of the disparate flavors together, much as it does in, say, a Caesar salad.

Fond as I am of this dish, I serve this as an accompaniment to other dishes; a larger portion would simply be overpowering. The recipe can be found on page 243.

this way, although his cuisine rang more classic than that of, say, The Fat Duck's Heston Blumenthal or El Bulli's Ferran Adrià, I recognized a kinship of nonconformity between him and those rising stars. For example, there were lovely pressed duck confit, shredded, seasoned with Xeres vinegar and chopped black truffle, pressed into a ring mold with foie gras in the center and frisée alongside, and a mosaic of cured Scottish salmon, caviar, and pickled carrot set within a salmon consommé.

There was also a Cochon de Lait for two, a choice of rack or saddle of pig that was cooked on the bone, then crisped under the broiler to burnish the crackling, before being served with baby Savoy cabbage sautéed in pig fat. (One day, I had the pork under the broiler and felt a poke in my ribs. I turned to see who it was, ready for a row, but there was nobody there. I looked down and saw Raymond Blanc, giddy at his little joke. "It's good to be tall, yes?" he asked. I found it so delightfully quirky that it took me a moment to offer up the only appropriate reply: "Yes, Chef!" "Ah, yes!" he exclaimed, and off he went.)

Blanc's attitude fostered a sense of fun in the kitchen that sometimes led to harmless lapses in discipline. There was a dish of frisée lettuce with foie gras and *pata negra,* an Iberian ham that's similar to prosciutto de Parma, but more intensely salty and flavorful. It was so delicious, and we were so perpetually underfed and hungry, that we snuck slices from the leg that hung in the fridge, hiding them in our bib aprons. It was like crack cocaine to us: at first you'd nip off a minuscule slice, but in time you'd take more and more. The leg got so whittled down that I can still hear the *chef de cuisine* upon discovering it, screaming out: "Who the fuck keeps eating the *pata negra?*"

PHEASANT EGG AND RAZOR CLAM   This dish belongs to Le Manoir for me, reminding me of spring, when pheasant eggs begin to appear. The bubble is a spherification of olive oil and razor clam, which I think of as the veal of shellfish for its big flavor. When the spherification is popped and the clam is released, there's an intense umami effect. Though photographed in extreme close-up, this is in reality a small dish that leaves you wanting more.

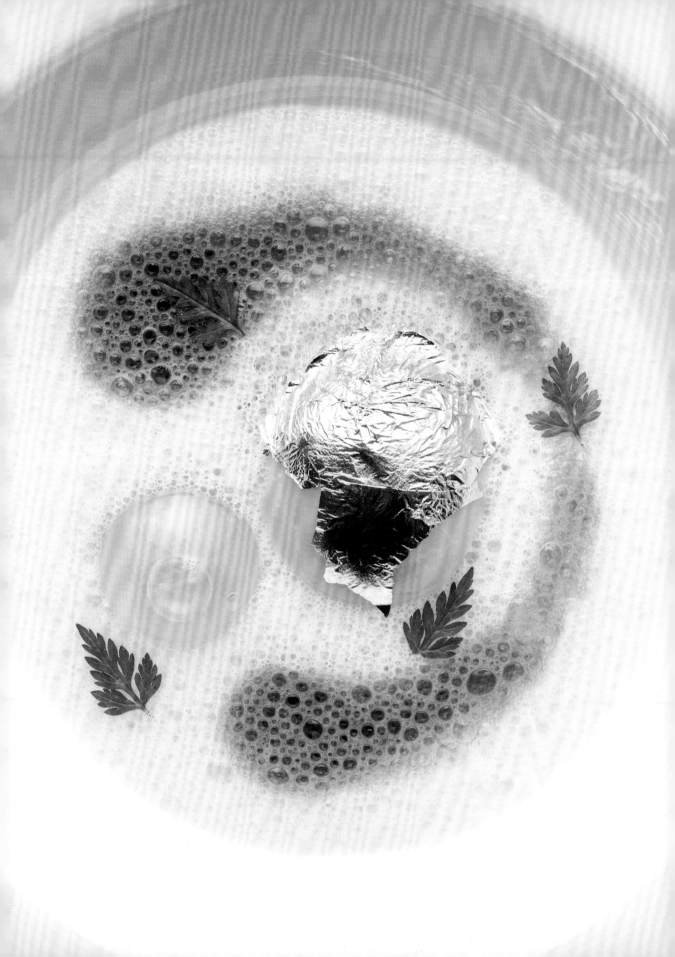

Oyster/Almond Crème/Beet/ Tropical Red Spinach

This dish, featuring kusshi oysters, harkens back to my classical days of preparing oysters en gelée. The shucked oysters are set in a light gelée of their own juice with a delicate infusion of green cardamom. Paired classically with caviar to accentuate the salinity and metallic quality of the oyster, it's supported here with a delicate almond milk crème (a dairy-free blend of almonds and water) and lightly smoked Chioggia beets. On the face of it, the combination skews slightly odd—a mixture of land (beetroot), tree (almond), and sea (oyster)—but the experience of eating it is unmistakably oceanic.

I got off to a great start at Le Manoir. Though assigned to the meat station, I was also one of the rotating cooks who periodically did a breakfast shift for the hotel, which I enjoyed because it was a chance to cook a whole category of food that most chefs never get to, and it led to a pleasant tradition in that kitchen: competitions to determine who could make the best scrambled eggs.

To cook breakfast required arriving at half past five in the morning, but in return you got to cook such dishes as smoked salmon omelet with caviar, fried egg with brioche, scrambled eggs with smoked salmon, and, if requested, coddled eggs. It was just you and a member of the pastry team, one on each side of the oven, standing by to serve the guests of the hotel's twenty rooms.

As for lunch and dinner, having cooked for White and Neat, I knew a lot of techniques that the other kids didn't. For example, one night the sous-chef came over to me and asked if I knew how to make tortellini.

"Yes," I told him matter-of-factly.

"No, seriously."

"Yes."

"I need one hundred fifty goat cheese and lemon tortellini."

"No problem."

I set about making the tortellini, and it was sheer bliss. Was I already old enough to have fond memories? I guess I was, because it brought back thoughts of L'Escargot. I was lost in a reverie, a cook's high if you will, and when I came out of it, there were one hundred fifty beautiful tortellini on the work station before me. The sous-chef came over, picked one up, examined it, looking for a flaw, didn't find it. Picked up another one, turned it over like a jewelry appraiser, put it down.

"You've done this before," he said.

"Once or twice."

"Okay then," he said, walking away.

And that, dear reader, is how rapturous praise was conveyed in a British kitchen circa 1997.

Of course, there were also the usual bits of kitchen sabotage and subterfuge. Like the cook who had worked for Alain Ducasse in Monaco and thought he was the shit. He and his *commis* delighted in taking all the pans and trays from the meat station and hiding them in their fridge so that, during service, I couldn't find one to save my life. But I was older and wiser now, and I knew how to get revenge. My favorite trick was to grind a handful of peppercorns and toss them on the flat top, where they'd crackle and explode like a sort-of mace. Of course, the key move here was to drop the peppers, then casually turn back around as though nothing had happened, and ignore the screams of your victims. (As is also the case in many kitchens, there were some transgressions that were beyond the pale, like the time a head chef passed off the effort of a sous-chef—a pigeon dish with a balsamic and endive tarte tatin alongside—as his own in a magazine article. Word of the intellectual pilfering spread through the kitchen like wildfire and quietly enraged the other young cooks.)

All of this probably sounds like a swell existence for an up-and-comer such as myself, and professionally it was. But I remained bored and increasingly depressed in the country. I would spend my Sundays counting the cars that went past my window and came to loathe the treacherous bike ride home each night. The rhythm of every day, every night, every week was utterly the same, and the monotony was unbearable. After a year, I resigned. The *chef de cuisine* told me that he took my departure as evidence that I had no stamina.

It was a compliment, I supposed. They'd have no trouble replacing me, so he must've been disappointed that I was leaving, taking my hard-earned knowledge elsewhere.

Around this time, *Caterer and Hotelkeeper* magazine published a series of profiles of the most influential, avant-garde French chefs. The food that caught my eye was Pierre Gagnaire's. It was arresting, in some cases not even instantly recognizable as food, but suggestive of nautical creatures, magnified microscopic organisms, or perhaps something extraterrestrial. There was a beauty in his compositions, and they filled me with a sense of wonder. Neat's food had showed me that personal expression was possible on the plate; Gagnaire's showed the extremes to which that notion could be taken. I literally could not believe my eyes.

Fuck me! I thought, instantly recognizing that my next move had to be to Paris. I couldn't get there quickly enough but had no idea how to do it.

LIGHTNING
STRIKES

Next thing I knew, I was in a nomadic mode, back in London, sleeping on a friend's couch, and trying to figure out my next move. Faced with the need for income and to remain in circulation, and with the fear of growing rusty, I worked, helping an old kitchen colleague get a new upscale modern bistro off the ground in Fulham. But my heart wasn't in it: to tell the truth, I was a bit rudderless. It was something to have worked for Marco Pierre White, Richard Neat, Raymond Blanc, and Jean-Georges Vongerichten all by the age of twenty-two. The Big Question in my life was as enticing as it was daunting: What next?

The obvious answer was the same as it was before I had pushed off for Le Manoir: Paris. I thought about the cooks I'd admired in the kitchens I'd worked in—guys like Simon Davis back at L'Escargot—and the one thing they all had in common was a turn in the City of Light. Nothing else made sense for me just then.

The last thing I expected when I walked into work one morning was for my life to change, but that's what happened when a cook named Gregory casually mentioned to me that he had worked for Pierre Gagnaire in Paris.

I thought instantly of that article I'd seen just before leaving Le Manoir, in which I'd been so knocked out by Gagnaire's food. I had studied his compositions for hours on end and come to realize that one of the things I loved about them was that you couldn't detect the lineage in them. With most chefs, it is possible to look at their repertoire and make educated guesses as to where they had lived and for whom they had worked. Even with somebody as brazenly original as Richard Neat, you could see traces of Robuchon and Le Manoir. But that wasn't true of Gagnaire. He was an utterly unique culinary artist. A true original. And this above all else made him compelling to me.

When Gregory revealed this detail from his professional past, I was more direct than I probably had ever been about anything: "Gagnaire? You worked for *him*? Can you help me get a job there?"

The old adage that "You don't ask, you don't get" never proved more true. Later that day, Gregory handed me a scrap of paper with a phone number on it, the kitchen line at Pierre Gagnaire, the chef's eponymous restaurant, in Paris. "Speak to Michel, the chef," he said. "He's expecting your call." I phoned up and, employing what little broken French I had picked up in kitchens, managed to get him on the line.

"How is your French?" he asked me.

"*Un peu,*" I said. A little bit.

"Okay," he said. "Come over and say hi."

And that was that. Next thing I knew, I was packed up and on the Eurostar en route to Paris.

Making the decision to relocate to a foreign land was no small thing. But it didn't matter that I didn't know the language or how the currency worked, or that I didn't have any friends there. The next thing for me to do was to go to Paris and work for Pierre Gagnaire. It was as simple and absolute as that.

Disembarking at Gare du Nord, I didn't even have to leave the train station to realize that Paris was a world unto itself. The magnificent soaring space, with sculpted support posts that seemed to extend up to the heavens and natural light pouring in from all sides, was a marvel of both engineering and artistry, a far cry from the stark, utilitarian train stations of London. Even the acoustics—a pleasing blend of voices, footfalls, and train squeals—were exquisite, like something remembered rather than being lived in the present.

All of this only added to an immediate and growing feeling—by no means unique to me—that Paris was a dream, and the sensation was reinforced by my first foray into the streets, the endless, rambling boulevards of the city, with its relentless architectural beauty. The deep culinary culture also seduced me: the smell of fresh baked bread emanating from *boulangerie* after *boulangerie;* the dainty, impossibly beautiful detail on pastries lined up in shop cases; the food on view through restaurant windows. Above all, there were the Parisian women. Walking the streets, I was almost drunk with the realization that "I'm in Paris." If I closed my eyes, I could imagine La Belle Époque all around me. I wasn't just in the land of all that glorious food, but also on the home turf of Robuchon, of Ducasse, of Gagnaire.

I met with Michel, a straightforward, calm *chef de cuisine,* whom I'd put in his midforties at the time. He was happy to have me work as a *stagiaire* for him but made it clear that there was no money to be made. I happily accepted the offer. Having led a Spartan existence for the last several years, I had some money squirreled away, as well as two credit cards that I was prepared to max out in the name of my own professional development.

Initially I put myself up in a flophouse, but once I knew I'd be staying, I phoned my father and for the first time in my life asked him to wire me some money so I could put down a deposit on a month-to-month rental. As I remember it, the room I secured was roughly one meter by one meter on rue de Lourmel in the 15th Arrondissement, which was essentially an outer borough. In a life filled with unremarkable living quarters, this was probably the worst and for sure the smallest: upon entering, the door hit the bed, which in turn was set into a cutout section of the wall. There was a sink (the toilet was down the hall) and a dresser, and for the entire time I lived there, my suitcase was parked alongside, a constant reminder that I was just a visitor and that, at some point, I'd be leaving Paris and returning to "normal" life.

I was once again living in the tunnel, my life reduced to little more than my puny flat, the kitchen where I worked, and the commute between the two. Sometime before leaving Paris, I learned the expression *tête don guidon,* or "head on the bike," which means that you are very focused on the task at hand and nothing else, and that's what it felt like at the time.

At first, before I worked my way into the kitchen and greater responsibility, I was assigned the most fundamental tasks, such as standing in the corner and peeling girolles, helping out in pastry, or shuttling ingredients

This winter dish of meaty turbot and shellfish (shown on pages 104–105), such as razor clams, grilled mussels, and Nantucket scallops (the scallops are topped with salted butter), is a warm, elevant answer to a *plateau de fruits de mer,* which I came to love on the rare occasion that I dined out during my time in Paris. The turbot is brushed with a reduction made from the juices of the shellfish.

and preparations to and fro, upstairs and down. But I had a front-row seat for the Gagnaire Show, and the food did not disappoint. The sheer volume of ingredients and techniques that were new to me would have been overwhelming were they not so exhilarating, including Japanese ingredients such as fresh wasabi and herbs such as mustard flowers that I'd not touched, smelled, or cooked with before.

And the French ingredients, while not as exotic, were something to behold: wild hares, plump pigeons, *poulet de Bresse*, wild ducks with regal plumage that looked like something out of a fantasy movie, and pristine seafood such as baby soles from Normandy, huge brown torto crabs, and delicate little squid called *la piste*. To all of this, Gagnaire would apply classical French technique to unite seemingly incongruous ingredients on the same plate: like the baby Japanese eggplant caviar that was seasoned with cumin and powdered yuzu and served with apple mostarda.

Gagnaire used certain techniques repeatedly, to bring a vibrancy, life force, and emotion to his plates that I'd not seen from any other chef, much along the lines of what I'd witnessed in the article that had piqued my interest. But the effect in person, and in three dimensions, was breathtaking. For instance, he made *croquants* with orange, lemon, spinach, eggplant, pumpkin, and onion, just to name a few, and deployed them in a variety of contexts—such as crab with smoked tomato jelly and a variety of *croquants*; and a papillote of white fish, whole except for the head, cooked on the bone in a *vadouvan* spice dough, and served with foaming butter and a spinach *croquant*.

More generally, there was the small white fish called whiting, cooked with white wine and shallots, which was nothing unusual until he paired it with pigeon. There was squid ink gnocchi, which was also not especially revolutionary until it was plated alongside green mango and snails. And ribbons of squid, slowly cooked, then chilled, with an *écume de mer* (beer made with salt water) foam over the top and a piece of confited foie gras. And a side dish of rabbit kidneys and liver, prepared as a *fidueà*, with the rabbit loin served alongside with white asparagus.

Dessert was no less eye-popping. For example, a *baba au rhum* was perched atop a bed of mango confit, a bitter almond cream spooned over the top, blackberries alongside, and a tuile of cumin and cashew nut paste on top for texture. (Having maintained my love of berries and of surreptitiously enjoying them, I often nibbled on them when nobody was looking.)

Tart Rouge

The first chef I'd ever seen create a dish based on a color was Pierre Gagnaire, who served a tart rouge. To me, it was poetry on a plate, a fresh new way of looking at food, just one of many ways in which this modern master opened my mind. It doesn't seem that revolutionary today, but at the time, the very idea of it was revelatory. Food in London wasn't as cerebral as what was going on in Paris in general or at Gagnaire in particular.

Over the years, I've served a number of color-themed offerings. At Gilt, for example, I served a variety of compositions under the label "Vert" (green). My tribute to the color red features parsnips cooked with Campari, *pâté de fruit* of pepper, red *shiso*, trevise, and red onion, all in a little boat fashioned from a savory tart dough.

This play of earth and sea was inspired by Gagnaire's ability to seamlessly unite disparate, seemingly incompatible ingredients; were the man a politician, he no doubt could achieve world peace. Here, a paste is fashioned from the scallops, then rolled and shaped into a ravioli that melts in the mouth, giving way to a lemon-verbena cloud inside. The black rice is squid ink risotto that is dehydrated and fried into a chip, and the porcini bring an earthy, meaty gravitas to the plate. It's all set atop a light lemon-verbena gelée with a black olive paste beneath. The recipe for the Scallop "Pasta" can be found on page 244.

Monkfish with Vadouvan Spice

I introduced this dish at Atlas, my first prominent chef position in New York City, and it quite literally wouldn't have become a part of my repertoire had I not cooked under Pierre Gagnaire. He introduced me to *vadouvan* spice, which in many ways ignited my lifelong love affair with a variety of spices. Here monkfish is cooked in a quasi-tandoori method, lightly caramelized in a dry heat under the broiler, with no fat whatsoever, and allowed to finish cooking by its own carryover heat. The result is astonishingly tender and moist, and is paired with a royale of foie gras with cucumber, dried kaffir lime, and the citrus fruit combava, another ingredient Gagnaire introduced me to. Japanese in its simple beauty and Indian in flavor, the two influences seamlessly enmeshed. That's one of the many things Gagnaire made possible for me.

In addition to the sheer, template-shattering originality of the food, there were Gagnaire's idiosyncratic plating techniques. He had a penchant for side dishes or flotillas of plates sent out to a table en masse. For an *amuse-bouche,* he might dispatch six plates per person, so for a table of five, we'd send out thirty individual dishes. By the same token, a first course might comprise a number of thematically related dishes. One composition featured various preparations of langoustine. At that point in my career, I'd had plenty of experience with langoustine, but nothing prepared me for the meditation on langoustine that was on display in a series of plates featuring a langoustine tartare, consommé, and royale.

All of this blew my mind. My exhilaration at being there and witnessing it was tempered only by a curious and sometimes painful aspect of my life in Paris and at Gagnaire. For the first three months, I scarcely spoke to anybody, save for the excruciating briefing session each morning, when a *chef de partie* would have the thankless task of explaining to the lone Brit in the kitchen how to do what needed doing that day. My technical skills at this point were formidable, but Gagnaire's methods were so different from anybody else's that the more seasoned guys would have to spoon-feed me. For example, one dish required me to slowly cook a piece of lamb over very low heat, turning it constantly, so as not to extract its water content or cause the fibers to tense up. It was the kind of thing that had to be demonstrated to me at length, never mind what happened to it after I cooked it. It was served with a bitter Seville marmalade and a reduction of lamb juices enriched with a touch of cream, and adorned with a huge brown butter and orange tuile. (In hindsight, it feels like Gagnaire put tuiles and *croquants* on everything. I came to think of them as little hats, as though the dishes weren't fully dressed and ready to leave the pass until they had their hats on.)

There was also the age-old bias against Brits to be overcome, which I'd not had to bear in any of my previous kitchen stints. But in time, I proved myself in the kitchen and came to be included in the camaraderie, despite

---

BRIOCHE NOIR I share this as an homage to Pierre Gagnaire, the man who opened my eyes to food. This is his creation. I think it's beautiful and timeless as a Prada handbag.

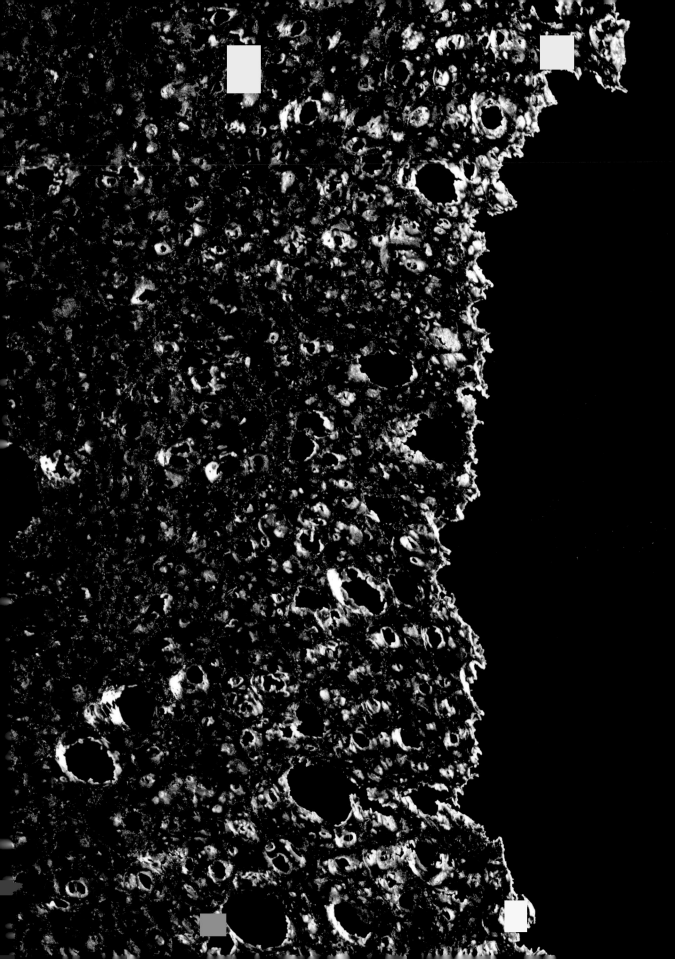

Flatiron of Wagyu Beef

with Black Eggplant Meringue

The direct inspiration for this dish was the char on a piece of steakhouse beef. The challenge for me was to conjure the flavor of steakhouse meat, while cooking the beef in a method elegant enough for the restaurants I've led. I decided to employ the method I was taught for preparing that lamb at Gagnaire, slowly and tenderly bringing it to doneness in a sauté pan over low heat.

The char flavor comes from blackening eggplant, then using it both in a meringue that accompanies the meat and in an eggplant oil that's employed as the cooking medium, taking on a deep, caramelized flavor and some actual caramelization, but with no aggressive heat applied directly to the meat. The technique is the very antithesis of steakhouse cooking, demanding gentleness and patience on the part of the cook; if you're attentive and the kitchen is quiet enough, you can literally hear how much fat and water remain inside the meat. I think of this as *sous vide* without the bag: the effects are quietly stunning and the impact of the first bite never fails to pleasantly surprise.

Japanese Mackerel, Black Olive, Bergamot

Japan meets the Mediterranean. Chef David Kinch of Manresa first introduced me to beautiful Japanese *goma* mackerel, served here with a black olive crumble and black olive fat with bergamot confit and edible sweet potato leaves. The fish's aromatic smokiness and umami have a natural affinity with the black olive, and the confit provides a counterbalancing note of gentle bitterness.

the language barrier. I picked up a little French, and the guys would invite me out with them after service—not every night, but a few times a week, and always at the end of Saturday night, which ushered in our one-day weekend. It was rather touching how some of the cooks took me under their wing. Knowing full well that I hadn't any money, they would pick up my drinks and pay for my food if we went out to dinner at brasseries such as Au Pied de Cochon. It was nothing fancy, just oysters, pig trotters, and sliced foie gras terrines, but it was a moving show of generosity and my only real exposure to French cuisine outside of Gagnaire's four walls—where, incidentally, I never had the chance to enjoy a meal during my period of employ.

Gagnaire himself lived up to his reputation as a bit of a madman. Though the sous-chefs and *chefs de partie* conferred with him on the pass, *stagiaires* like me had precious little direct contact with him. *"Bonjour mesdames et messieurs,"* he would say upon striding into the kitchen, and that was the only time we "interacted with him"—instead receiving his brilliance via the chefs for whom we worked or by stealing sideways glances at him during service. But it must be said that his love of spontaneity affected all of us. New ideas presented themselves to him constantly, as though the dishes were not finished entities but rather sentences in an ongoing dialogue between himself and The Food.

As a result, he was constantly changing things during service, crumbling an eggplant *croquant* over a dish because it suddenly didn't look right to him. We *stagiaires* cringed a little every time he crumbled a *croquant* because of the work that went into them. The method, developed by chef Michel Trama, involved dipping thin slices of an ingredient, usually a vegetable, into a liquid and blanching it, then putting it on an oil-slicked tray and slow drying it in a low oven. It doesn't sound that complicated, but doing it right demanded exactitude and patience. At other times, he'd create a new dish out of thin air by pulling together bits of *mise en place* from different stations. This would cause a ripple of confusion and chaos down the

---

FOIE GRAS/KAMPACHI/CAVIAR Spontaneity: A dish created on the spot from components, perhaps for a special guest.

line, and it happened every single night. It wasn't easy to cook in that context, but it was worth every moment of drama to be that close to his genius.

There was little practical about this, but I felt that I'd encountered a culinary soul mate, somebody who moved me even more than Richard Neat. On an intuitive level, everything about Gagnaire made perfect sense to me, from his plating techniques to his love of improvisation. After years of learning the *craft* of cooking, here I was face-to-face with the *art* of cooking. For the first time, I felt that I was experiencing the ultimate in the possibility of food, not just of the flavors but of the graphic aspect of it as well as of the emotion it could provoke. Above all, the feats he performed with food left me with one overriding impression: anything is possible.

And there was something else, something that I'd been slow to recognize but that had to be admitted: my natural, national identity had been working against me. That British impulse toward modesty, the ingrained inclination to always be the gray man, to not stand out or call attention to oneself, was in reality something that was holding me back. Watching Gagnaire, both the man and his food, I realized that I wanted to be as outspoken on the plate as he was, to express myself as freely and audaciously as he did. It was a life-changing lesson. The chef within was just about ready to hatch.

EMPIRE STATE OF MIND

Despite my belief that every job has a natural life span, I would've gladly stayed at Gagnaire for considerably more time than the ten-plus months I was able to, but the simple truth was that I couldn't afford it. Having racked up about 7,000 pounds in debt, I informed the chef of my need to leave, and the moment I did so, I was overcome with sadness. I remember standing on rue Balzac just outside the restaurant and wondering if I'd ever come back to that place again, ever get to lay my hand on my touchstone.

The thought of returning to London was anathema to me. I felt that I had taken what the city had to offer me as a cook, but that I wasn't quite ready to be a chef. Or was I? I didn't know. My thinking was too clouded to make any real decisions. To clear my head, I took a short side trip to the Alps along with a friend I'd met at Gagnaire. Never a terribly athletic sort, I decided to try my hand at snowboarding. Sitting on the top of Black Run, I thought it looked remarkably easy, but as soon as I pushed off, I was tumbling head over tit for 100 meters, dislocating my shoulder on the way down. It was the perfect metaphor for where I was in life just then, headed from the summit to the depths in one fell swoop. (On the other hand, the food in that region was to die for, especially the Reblochon cheese and local ham. And of course the scenery: all those snowcapped vistas and expanses of sky were just what the doctor ordered.)

I returned to London in 1999 feeling a bit like a man out of time at twenty-three years old and after just a year away. Marco still ruled the roost, and Gordon Ramsay was fast on his heels, but there was nothing new for me there. I still pined a little for Richard Neat, who had retired, and I didn't have a toehold in newer restaurants like The Fat Duck, which under chef Heston Blumenthal had been open for four years and was fast climbing the ranks.

Full of doubt, I did what any young man might do at that time and met my father for one of our dinners. As usual, he had the answer. I mentioned that I was thinking about traveling but that it seemed irresponsible given my financial status. He encouraged me to follow my instinct.

"You've worked here," he said. "What do you want to do *now*?"

The truth, which I hadn't even really uttered to myself, was that I wanted to go to New York City, to follow up on that seed of an idea that had been planted in my mind all the way back at Vong. My British friends thought I was mad when I told them I was going to visit New York City. "Be sure to bring a gun" was the most common tongue-in-cheek advice they offered. To uninitiated Brits, New York still suffered from the blood-soaked reputation it had earned during the financially strained, crime-infested 1970s and 1980s. To visit New York City was to invite some form of violation, from mugging to murder. One acquaintance told me this horrific tale: "I had a friend who was walking down to 42nd Street and some guy offered him a ride and he got into this cab and . . . *it wasn't a cab*. They locked the doors and drove him to the Bronx and shot him in both legs." Based on this and other hearsay, in my mind's eye, there were gang members camped out on every street corner in Manhattan, waiting to shoot tourists like me, rummage through my pockets, and leave me in their wake like a discarded cigarette butt.

And yet none of that mattered. I had arrived at that time in my life again, that periodic moment of clarity when the chef within sensed what the correct next move was. I had learned to crawl in London, to walk in the countryside of Oxford, to run under the tutelage of Gagnaire in Paris, and now it was time to fly—to get across an ocean and consummate the attraction I'd had for New York City since cooking under Jean-Georges Vongerichten.

And so, with my friend Vaughn, a fellow cook from London just a few years older than I—despite all the warnings and protestations of friends and loved ones—I made a fact-finding visit to Manhattan in the late 1990s.

The flight to the city still shimmers in my memory. I felt an explorer's sense of pride, like I was discovering the city for myself when, out of the vast expanse of sea and sky between England and the States, suddenly there appeared the island of Manhattan, its signature buildings coming into high relief as we approached: the Empire State Building, the Chrysler Building, and at the foot of the island, like a double exclamation mark, the Twin Towers.

The skidding, screeching touchdown. The shove-fest of claiming my luggage and clearing customs. The queue for the taxi and the lurching ride into Manhattan. These were all things that, I suppose, would have been off-putting to many of my friends back home, but felt curiously familiar and correct to me. This was New York City as I had imagined it, and for all of its harsh indifference, I felt right at home. I instantly chucked my paranoia, my plans to avoid eye contact and check over my shoulder, and decided to embrace the city with open arms.

Vaughn and I checked ourselves in to an economy hotel in Chelsea and began exploring the city, walking for miles with no particular aim or destination. We roamed the length of the West Side Highway, along the Hudson River, oblivious to the fact that the landmass on the other side was New Jersey; we scurried like mice through the crooked maze of Greenwich Village, ducking in and out of clothing shops and record stores, bars and cafes; and we luxuriated in the majesty of Central Park, that great, democratic oasis of rolling green and sequestered, wooded pathways, in the heart of New York City—the perfect rejoinder to anybody, like my friends back home, who find Manhattan harsh and unbeautiful.

And, of course, we ate. Our first stop was the Gotham Bar and Grill because back in London, at my favorite bookshop, Books for Cooks, I'd seen a book about cooking with port that featured a dish by Gotham's chef, Alfred Portale, that was finished with a port reduction. The chef, known for his artful presentations, stayed in my mind, and at Gotham I had my first taste of succulent Maine lobster, in a salad with avocado and caviar. As with Vong in London, I was amazed by the quality of food Portale was able to put out in a restaurant that looked to be serving about two hundred lunches.

"The Gold Bar"

Glitz and glamour. Timeless elegance. The little black dress of chocolate desserts, with gold foil as the perfect accessory. Techniques learned in Europe finding expression on the other side of the Atlantic. Though I didn't work pastry at Le Manoir, Blanc's kitchen was the first place I ever tasted a proper chocolate ganache, which was poured into a terrine and allowed to set. My ganache, like that one, is fashioned with salted butter and pure black cocoa. To me, this skyscraper-shaped dessert, which I make today with the superlative Mast Brothers chocolate from Brooklyn, captures the essence of New York City. The gold foil represents . . . take your pick: opulence, wealth, ambition, the river of light that illuminates Manhattan at night. For me, this dessert is emblematic of the never-ending ambition that New York inspires, each bite a taste of liquid gold, as satisfying as it is addictive, leaving you forever wanting more, more, more. "The Gold Bar" recipe can be found on page 245.

"Red"

This is my tribute to another aspect of life in New York, especially to a newly arrived visitor: the sensation that life is moving at a million miles a minute, that you've been dropped into a pinball machine . . . and you're the ball. The ephemeral nature of Manhattan, the constant forward motion and blink-and-you'll-miss-it opportunities, is captured in this almost textureless dish, whose solids all but evaporate on the palate. It's full of bold, round flavors—red cabbage puree, huckleberry meringue, lime radish—but the absence of proteins means that they are gone before you know it, like the flash of a strobe light, a kiss from a stranger, or any of the other fleeting lures, both real and imagined, that come at you always in this unrelenting city.

The recipe for the Red Cabbage Gelée can be found on page 247.

At Daniel Boulud's eponymous restaurant, I was struck by how much fresh life he was able to breathe into his unmistakably French menu with dishes like sweet corn soup with watermelon and peekytoe crab. At Gray Kunz's Lespinasse, I enjoyed a roasted turbot with citrus confit, and there too was impressed by the vibrancy and flavors, as well as the ambitious menus relative to the number of seats. Executing that level of artistry across so many meals was still unimaginable back in London or Paris. At Bouley and Bouley Bakery, I discovered that food in the classic French mode was alive and well in New York, even in the hands of an American chef.

After ten days, as it had after my time in Paris, the very thought of returning to London was something I almost couldn't bear. I was like a bluefin marlin that had been hooked. I printed my CV and gave it to a number of chefs around town, including Alex Lee at Daniel and the sous-chef at Lespinasse, but on hearing that I didn't yet have a working visa, both of them gave it right back to me. And so, even though I didn't have a job waiting for me in Manhattan, I flew back to London, paid my rent with a few consulting gigs, secured a visa, closed my bank account, and set a date to return to New York City. For good.

With the decision to remain in New York City came the need to find work. And so, when I returned to Manhattan a few months later in summer 1999, I was a cook in need of employment. Too embarrassed to return to Daniel or Lespinasse after they turned me away for lack of a visa, I walked in off the street and handed my CV to Brian Bistrong, a soft-spoken, gentle soul who was David Bouley's *chef de cuisine* and chief lieutenant.

Bistrong scanned the document—his eyes widening as he worked his way down past the legendary establishments, one after the other—then looked up at me and said, "You want *my* job?"

I was both flattered and taken aback. "No, I'm new to the city. I just want to cook."

Brian hired me on the spot. I later learned that after I left, he pinned my CV to the employee bulletin board and showed everybody the hit parade of European chefs I'd worked with. There was already a serious crew at Bouley. In addition to Brian, there was Galen Zamarra on meat, Doug Psaltis on garnish, and Eric Greenspan on fish, and all have gone on to successful

Halibut Jamón

My tribute to the cultures of both smoked fish and cold cuts in New York City. *Jamón,* Spanish for "ham," is the name I apply to my cured local halibut. I apply a *vadouvan* spice mixture to the fish and cure it for eighteen to thirty-six hours, depending on the fattiness of the fish, then thinly slice it as one might a sturgeon or smoked salmon. (In this recipe, I call for twenty-four hours of curing, which should be adequate regardless of fattiness.)

The Halibut Jamón is pictured with a yuzu sponge, mandarinquat (a tart cross between a mandarin and a kumquat), goat cheese Chantilly, and green mango chutney—each contributing a distinct sweetness or acidity that complements the natural sweetness of the fish and the spice in the cure. You can also serve the cured fish on its own or even on a bagel as you would smoked salmon. The recipe for the Halibut Jamón can be found on page 248.

This wintertime canapé was inspired by my first formative days in New York City. Having been raised, since my teenage years at least, on morning croissants—the baked good of choice among Michelin-level cooks in the UK and Europe—I was caught by surprise at the popularity of bagels among New Yorkers. As emblematic as they are of the city, I've never quite warmed up to them. They're just too dense and leaden for me, especially first thing in the morning, which is a painful time of day for most cooks. But I appreciate it as a part of the landscape, a local institution. And so, in the "when in Rome" spirit of an adopted son, I created this tribute to New York's favorite morning tradition. It's roughly the size of a quarter and flavored with orange zest. Another dimension is achieved by smoking the yeast. In short, if I were ever going to begin my day with a bagel, this is the one I'd do it with. The recipe can be found on page 249.

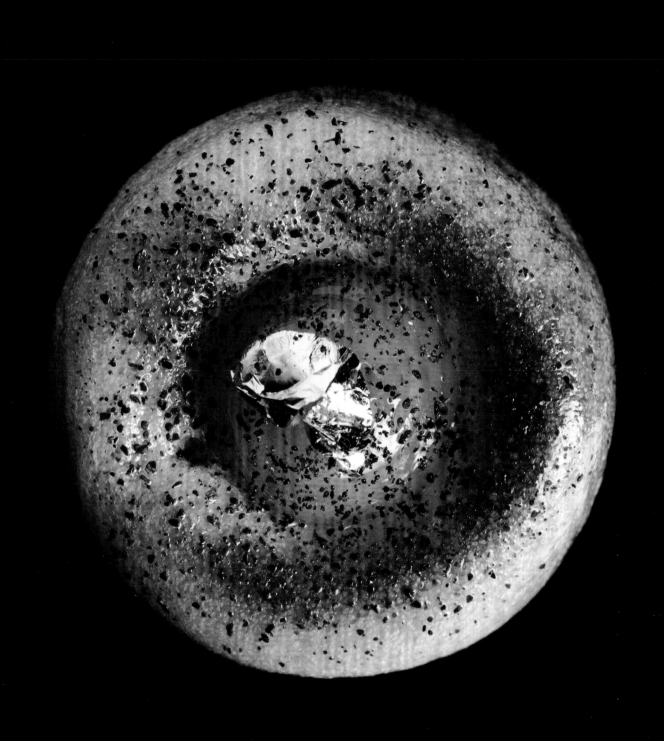

careers in their own rights. It was an all-American crew, and the introduction of a foreign kid was conspicuous, to say the least. My accent was more pronounced than it is now, creating a bit of a barrier and prompting people to ask if I was from Scotland or Ireland.

I was *chef de partie* on the fish station. Josh DeChellis, who had helped open Union Pacific, was the a.m. fish guy, so we ran it together for a few weeks, before I was promoted to sous-chef and more kitchen-wide responsibility. Josh and I got to be buds. I enjoyed his joie de vivre and some of his hilarious kitchen colloquialisms, especially his use of the word *guy*. Josh is from New Jersey but worked in California for a while, and that laid-back vibe shows up in his language. "Hey, can I take my guy and ride it in your guy?" he'd ask. Eventually, I decoded his shorthand and discovered that he was asking to braise his lamb in the *jus* I was using for another preparation. To a cook of my background, it was like another language altogether.

In addition to the upscale dining experiences on offer in New York City, I quickly began to explore the international cuisines of the city, taking the lead of my kitchen colleagues. One of the things that struck me straight away about American kitchens was that the less taxing days left the cooks with energy to burn at the end of the night. Befitting the hour (when most upscale establishments were closed) and their budgets (one thing that was the same on this side of the Atlantic), each cook had a regular itinerary of so-called ethnic joints, casual eateries where the foods of other cultures were served. Just as I'd gravitated to London's Chinatown as a child, I was drawn to many of these restaurants and fascinated by what I found and tasted there.

Josh also introduced me to high-end sushi at Sushi Yasuda and Japanese cuisine in general, filling in blanks I'd been left with after my introduction

---

ANAGO/FOIE GRAS/PISTACHIO CRÈME This dish of foie gras wrapped in warm sea eel, then seaweed, and paired with lightly toasted, unsweetened green pistachio ice cream was inspired in part by my first taste of sublime Japanese seafood in the sushi restaurants of New York, as well as by a dish of eel and foie gras that I admired at Martín Berasategui's restaurant in the Basque region of Spain—both filtered through French cuisine. To me, this dish oozes sex appeal, like gazing at Monica Bellucci.

to some key ingredients at Gagnaire. I had never tasted products such as Santa Barbara uni or Japanese *kinmedai,* and the simplicity and cleanliness of the cuisine, not to mention the utter perfection of the fish itself, was a revelation to me—one of those moments when I saw ingredients a little clearer, opening a new chapter of food and cuisine in my life.

I also made time, when I could afford it, for some high-end dining. The talk of the town at this time was a kitchen wunderkind named Rocco DiSpirito, a former *chef de partie* from Gray Kunz's kitchen at Lespinasse who had exploded into national prominence at Union Pacific in the Flatiron District in 1997.

DiSpirito used a lot of Asian techniques and ingredients, but with a fundamentally French sensibility. Some of his dishes were simply rendered but noteworthy for the combinations. One early signature was a bay scallop and uni served on the half shell and enlivened with tomato water and mustard oil. Another dish audaciously combined watermelon, calamari, and cilantro. I, along with much of the New York City dining cognoscenti, was knocked out and saved up my money to eat there every three or four weeks.

One day, while savoring some fresh air outside Bouley after the dinner service, Josh, who'd worked at Union Pacific, was on the phone with DiSpirito. He abruptly handed his phone to me.

"I'm looking for a sous-chef," DiSpirito said.

"I was just offered a sous position here," I said.

"Great," he said. "Good for you."

Things were looking up for me quickly in New York City. For the first time in my life, I was a sous-chef, at Bouley, and I took advantage of the autonomy it brought to begin feeling my oats in the kitchen, running my own stuff on the menu. With visions of Gagnaire and his gift for spontaneity

BLACK OLIVE GNOCCHI, OCTOPUS, GOAT MILK CHANTILLY   Another tribute to my sushi-love, this one centered on octopus. Believe it or not, I didn't realize it looked like a Japanese flag until I saw this photograph. (The recipe for the Black Olive Gnocchi can be found on page 250.)

Santa Barbara Uni/Black Kombu Gelée/ Spring Pea Puree

It wasn't until I came to New York City that I had proper sushi, which to me is about as close to perfection as food can get: pristine natural product expertly shaped and minimally manipulated. One of my favorite delicacies quickly became Santa Barbara uni, so naturally compelling, with a complex mouthfeel, that you needn't do anything to it. This dish pairs uni with black kombu gelée (made with a lemongrass-infused dashi base) and a vegetable puree that I change with the seasons and my mood: sometimes I make it with peas, sometimes with carrots, sometimes parsnips. I also sometimes shave raw black truffles over this dish for an earth and sea effect.

The first time I visited a New York City Korean restaurant, where little grills are embedded into the tables and customers barbecue their own food, I almost set myself aflame. Rather than cooking my beef piece by piece, as you are supposed to, I put all of it over the grill at once, causing a terrible flare-up. Despite this traumatic beginning, I quickly came to love Korean food, and this dish of squab and plum, which looks French, tastes distinctly Korean and honors that discovery in my early New York days. It combines squab with plum and a kimchee consommé. Other touches have nothing to do with Korean food but round out these flavors nicely, such as a liquid yogurt gnocchi, which brings a lactic element to the plate, balancing the barbecue flavors.

still fresh in my mind, I began improvising dishes: combining apple and lime puree with almond cream; lobster-poached butter with chanterelles cooked with sansho pepper; and other compositions.

After just seven months on the job, Bouley had his *chef de cuisine*, Galen Zamarra, terminate me. I was never quite clear on the reasons, but the truth was that I was happy to be cut loose because I was emboldened by how my personal creations were working out in the kitchen, looking to make the leap to my own chefdom, and perfectly happy to be pushed out of the nest.

And so, with spring in the air and the sense of optimism and possibility all around, I answered an ad in the *New York Times:* the owners of a restaurant were looking for a new head chef. The time to leap was now.

TOE IN THE WATER

In the spring of 2000, I took a meeting with the owners of Le Gans, a sixty-seat restaurant in the meatpacking district, on the fringe of the West Village—one of those industrial, cobblestone regions of the city that time seemed to have left behind. The neighborhood has since become trendy and restaurant-laden, but at the time was barely colonized, save for a bistro Keith McNally had just opened called Pastis, and Le Gans, named for Gansevoort Street. The owners, two Moroccan gentlemen, were wary of hiring me. They had a good thing going, having earned two stars from the *Times* and wanted to be clear with me that they were running a *French* bistro.

I assured them I could do bistro food, and I did: *Paul* bistro food. There was a salad topped with goat cheese croquettes and dressed with a fig vinaigrette; *dourade* tartare with black olive jelly and microgreens; and rabbit leg stuffed with squid and chorizo, cooked with a shellfish and squid ink *jus*. Simple stuff that I was able to execute with the meager staff—just myself and two other cooks. It was such a modest space, with such a skeleton crew, that there was no sense of truly arriving as a chef in my own right, though it was gratifying to set my own menu.

Looking back, I have to admit that it wasn't really the right food for the place or the neighborhood. But I was a young chef, full of ideas, and looking to stick my toe in the water. Some friction soon developed between me and the owners, highlighted by a somewhat absurd exchange we had every morning: I would tell one of them that we put milk in our tea in England, and he would snap back, "No you don't!" as if he had greater insight into my homeland than I did. The ritual was a reflection of our larger differences.

Nevertheless, I had a good time at Le Gans. I was living in a rented room in another cook's apartment on MacDougal Street in Manhattan's fabled SoHo (never mind that the name was borrowed from London), and Le Gans's neighborhood was colorful in its own right. Often I'd do some of my prep work outside and would look up to see James Gandolfini, at the height of his *Sopranos* fame, hanging out outside his apartment and smoking a cigar. "How you doin'," he'd say with vintage New York delivery. When I left the restaurant at two in the morning, I found myself in the company of groups, *packs*, of transsexual prostitutes, who I saw so frequently that I began to know some of them by name. (Hi, Shaniqua! Hi, Kiwi! Strawberry!) It was also an exciting time for me to be in New York because the great French chef Alain Ducasse was opening his restaurant in the Essex House and there I was, at the very same time. Not that I put myself on the same plane as that living legend, but it was still thrilling to be a chef in his company.

Because so many up-and-coming cooks knew me from Bouley, word began to get around that something interesting was going on at Le Gans. A lot of cooks came in after service, including Josh and a talented whisk named Tom Rice, a friend of Josh's from his Jean-Georges days whom I'd met one night hanging out at a downtown watering hole called Liquor Store Bar. One day, Josh called me and said, "Rocco's coming in," and that evening I did a tasting menu for him and a date, featuring, among other dishes, a carpaccio of *dourade* with green olive oil, black olive gelée, and fresh tomato paste; and a yogurt *panna cotta* with delicate candied tomato gelée.

At the end of the meal, I came out to the table to say hello to DiSpirito, and his appraisal was enigmatic: "Everything exceeded my expectations." As I walked away from the table, I couldn't help but think to myself, *What the fuck did* that *mean?*

I also had my first experience with the chef-owner dynamic. One of the owners had a hair-trigger temper and would lose it constantly. If a customer bothered him, he would kick him out, and he'd threaten to fire front- and back-of-the-house staff for any transgression on a daily basis.

That summer, after just two and a half months in the job, I took my girlfriend of the time to Paris for a week. I returned to a kitchen that I scarcely recognized. I could feel it the moment I walked in—the same sensation, I imagine, you get when you realize your home has been broken into. It just felt different, and upon closer inspection, I learned that things *were* different. Everything had been moved around, and much of it had been changed. I rummaged through the refrigerator and all of the *mise en place* was altered: instead of chorizo, black olive jelly, and squid ink *jus*, there was mustard vinaigrette, canned artichokes, and jarred asparagus.

I slammed the door closed, ran into the dining room, and pulled a menu from the stack in the compartment built into the maître d's podium: it was the exact menu they had before I came to work there. Frisée salads, *croque monsieur*, steak frites, profiteroles. Bistro 101.

It didn't take a genius to figure out what was going on: they were going to push me out. I didn't really care, because I didn't want to be there, but I'd be goddamned if I would give them the satisfaction of firing me. When they showed up later that morning, I asked if we could sit for a moment.

"Listen," I told them, "I did some thinking while I was away, and I don't think this is going to work out. I'm giving you my notice."

They looked at each other and could barely contain their relief.

"It's probably for the best," one of them said.

For once, we were in total agreement.

SHADES OF GREEN

A friend tipped me off that a relatively new Midtown restaurant named Atlas, not yet a year old, had lost its chef. Freshly in the hunt for a new position after the coup of Le Gans, I phoned them up and inquired about an interview.

Atlas was way up on Central Park South, the three-block stretch of 59th Street that frames the southern edge of the park. I knew next to nothing about this region of Midtown. My life had been downtown, living in SoHo, working for Bouley and then at Le Gans. But I liked the location. It didn't have the grittiness of downtown or the elegance of the Upper East Side, but I appreciated the international vibe on the street—lined with posh hotels that drew a moneyed, global clientele—and the majesty of one of the world's great urban parks across the way.

Truth be told, despite my short-lived stint at Le Gans, I wasn't truly ready to make the quantum leap to chef at a restaurant like Atlas, a proper establishment in a prominent location and staffed with a full complement of cooks. Nobody is. Until you actually do it, there are simply too many responsibilities you haven't had, too many decisions you haven't made, too much pressure you haven't had the privilege of bearing. I was only twenty-four. Relatively young to be handed the keys to the kitchen of a place like Atlas. But something told me that I could handle it.

Still, I didn't have any illusions. I didn't think that one minute I'd become a chef and the next minute my name would be written on the plates or lit up in four-star glory. I had more to learn than I already knew. But I knew that until I took the chance of becoming a chef, of devising my own menu and managing my own crew, I would never grow into that position. And I felt that I had amassed enough knowledge and technique, and had enough ideas scribbled and sketched in those notebooks I'd been keeping, that I was ready to take the first steps down that path—and that any owner or owners who took me on would be in good and capable hands. My entire adult life had been about becoming a chef, and I knew that the transformation would continue for years to come. But I had to actually be enlisted *as a chef* in order to take those precious next steps.

The general manager, an affable but somewhat disheveled man named Jimmy, greeted me when I arrived for my interview. I'm not one of those cooks who shows up in a T-shirt and denim. Jean-Georges Vongerichten taught me that, not directly, but by example. You show up in a suit. It makes a difference. People see all of that and they figure you for a man, not a boy. I was dismayed to learn that Jimmy wasn't just the GM; he was also acting as the chef. What was *that* about? True, he had once cooked in some top kitchens, even Gray Kunz's at Lespinasse, but you can't just tap the GM—a guy who no longer cooked on a daily basis—to be the chef. Cooking doesn't work that way, like a switch you can just turn on and off. If they thought that it was, I figured the place was in bad shape. I had no idea how right I was.

Formerly a dentist's office, the restaurant had undergone an expensive build out. The dining room was amoeba-shaped with irregular sight lines, but well-apportioned, with generous space between the tables and a pleasing view onto the park. The horse-drawn carriages gliding to and fro outside were a regal touch. The menu, though, was odd: buffalo steak with Hoppin' John sauce? Really? And what was with the cottage cheese and fruit available on the dessert menu, priced at $22, no less? (I'd later learn it was to accommodate friends of the house who dependably followed the latest dieting fad; at the moment, it was Atkins.)

A meeting was scheduled with the owners, a husband-wife team. Atlas didn't serve lunch, so we met midday in the dining room, with the summer sun pouring in through the windows that faced the park. After all the usual pleasantries, they asked if I could do a tasting for them at lunch the next day. I agreed and didn't ask them any more questions, because frankly I didn't have any. I needed a restaurant, a proper restaurant, and they had one.

"Do you want to give us a list of what you'll want?" the husband asked.

My response, driven by my successful improvisations at Bouley, caught their attention. "I'll just have a poke around the fridges and see what you have, and I'll make something from that." I paused, then added, "But if you could have some artichokes and caviar on hand, that'd be lovely."

Eyebrows were raised. I guess they thought me brash, and I guess they were right. As I saw it, I was about to burst out of the cook's cocoon and reveal the butterfly within. There was a feeling of anticipation and confidence welling up in me, and the plain truth was that I couldn't wait to get into that kitchen and show what I could do. My plan was to improvise a meal like my hero Gagnaire: working like an octopus at the pass, taking this and that from here and there until before any of us knew it, he had fashioned new and unheard-of dishes from out of thin air. That was the way I aspired to cook, and I planned to put it all on the line and cook that way for my audition lunch. If I couldn't deliver, I figured, then I wasn't ready for the job.

"All right," I said. "See you tomorrow."

I informed Jimmy that I'd come back around nine thirty the next morning, and left. I played it cool for my date with destiny and strolled into Atlas the next day at ten o'clock, to find Jimmy panicked by my thirty-minute tardiness. "They're coming at one o'clock," he said.

"Don't worry," I said. "It's only four people." As it turned out, it would be six—including pastry chef Della Gossett, Jimmy, the sommelier, and a friend—but none of that concerned me.

In hindsight it was a foolish way to go about an audition menu, but what can I tell you: I was a confident twenty-four-year-old. I meant what I'd said to the owners. I was going to go into the walk-in and spin six courses out of whatever I found there. And what I found was promising: lovely Granny Smith apples, pristine diver scallops, striped bass, lamb, and the artichokes and caviar I'd requested.

I'd never done an audition menu before, and I quickly discovered that this is one of the more pleasurable bits of cooking a young chef can engage in. It's just you, and you get to perform all parts of the process, from basic prep to cooking, plating, and finishing dishes—there aren't any cooks to manage or waiters to contend with. The entire enterprise rises or falls on the strength of your performance. Oh, if only cooking were like that every day!

The first thing I did was take a moment to commune with all those ingredients, to engage in the kind of dialogue I knew that Neat and Gagnaire did with The Food. Your mind—knowing what the possibilities are and what your hands are capable of—leaps ahead several steps, presenting you with a menu of possible outcomes. Where most people see an array of fruits and vegetables, fish and meats, you see a meal. And so, with very little actual thought, I knew that I would serve the scallops raw, as a tartare, enrobed with a green apple gelée, and finished with a regal coat of caviar. The artichokes called out to me next: I decided to pair them with sour oranges, green apple tapenade, and a warm vinaigrette enlivened with chorizo (after the style of that *rouget* dish I'd seen Gagnaire make), and serve all of that with the striped bass. For the meat course, it would be roasted lamb loin with a pickled ginger and black trumpet crust with sautéed chanterelle mushrooms and baby marble potatoes alongside.

I procured a sheet of paper and made myself a work list, then had at it, silently converting ingredients into food, calling on some of my favorite tricks of the trade. To make the apple gelée, I juiced the green apples, clarified the juice to separate out the starch, put it into a quart container, then waited for it to separate. Then came my favorite trick. Most cooks would skim the foam off the top, but somewhere along the way, I'd learned to punch a hole in the bottom and let the clarified portion drain out; then I poured that through a coffee filter to further refine it. For dessert, I sliced pineapples, made a vanilla and chile syrup with a touch of orange juice, and set some raspberries to macerating. While they did that, I butchered the lamb, cleaned and cooked artichokes, made a compound butter of garlic, thyme, shallot, and minced pickled ginger (come service time, I'd cook the mushrooms in that, along with the *jus* from the lamb). I saved a few easy tasks that didn't involve cooking for last, such as shucking the scallops.

There were other cooks in the house, readying their *mise en place* for dinner service, but I didn't call on them for anything, except to ask for a bucket of ice or another stack of mixing bowls. Otherwise, it was head down

Green Apple–Wasabi Sorbet
with Extra-Virgin Olive Oil and Maldon Sea Salt

One of the dishes I added right off at Atlas was a palate cleanser: Green Apple–Wasabi Sorbet with Extra-Virgin Olive Oil and Maldon Sea Salt. It was a telling exercise in developing a dish instinctually that began with a combination that intrigued me: crisp, tart green apples and icy, hot wasabi. It was a satisfying sorbet, but I wanted it to have more of a presence in the meal, to linger on the palate. So I turned to an olive oil from Provence, which actually has a slight hint of banana, what I think of as a greenness. I finished it off with a grain of Maldon sea salt, perched atop the sorbet like an ice flake. By the time the dish debuted on the menu, I had the idea of waiters finishing it at the table with a drizzle of the oil. The sorbet became my signature palate cleanser at Atlas, though I retired it for years, only revisiting it in 2011 at Corton. The recipe can be found on page 251.

and all business. As far as I was concerned, for those three hours, there wasn't another soul in the universe.

The time flew by, and when Jimmy informed me that my "guests" had arrived, I was ready.

To give a full sense of the way a meal at Atlas might unfold with me at the helm, I started them with an *amuse,* a gazpacho of cucumber with lemon crème. While they sipped on that, I prepped the scallop tartare on chilled plates, applying slivers of the gelée ever so gingerly, then topping with the caviar. Before the runners took the plates out to the dining room, I studied my handiwork and nodded. It was as I'd pictured it a few hours earlier.

Next, I turned my attention to the fish course. I was flowing by this point, just riding a wave of instinct and muscle memory. And within minutes, there was a wind at my back—the knowledge that I was doing well, evident by the fact that the plates from the first course came back clean (every chef's measure of success or failure). After the fish, out went the lamb, followed by dessert. I bound the raspberries and topped them with thin sheets of pineapple, like a ravioli, serving it with a quenelle of vanilla ice cream and tonka beans over the top. For good measure, I followed this with classic vanilla *sablés* (French butter cookies), to give a sense of the full breadth of my training.

At the end of the meal, I was summoned to the dining room where I was promptly offered the job, at $61,000 a year.

"Fine, great, I'll take it," I said. It was a typically green and unseasoned decision for me. I didn't ask about health benefits or bonuses, or equity, or any of the things a more seasoned chef or businessperson might have asked. But what can I tell you? All I wanted was a kitchen to call my own and a chance to begin the process of self-expression and self-discovery essential to developing as a chef. I took the weekend off to collect my thoughts and planned to hit the ground running the following Monday.

It turned out that, for the worst of reasons, Atlas as I inherited it was a great place for a fledgling chef to develop a feeling of confidence because it was in such disarray that you couldn't help but feel like the long-awaited savoir. On my first day, I was staggered to discover that the cooks, used to preparing dinner for just a few customers each evening, were turning up in the middle of the afternoon. It was about as cushy a job as you could get, or as they could make it, and as antithetical to my way of work-ing. I was also shocked to see one of the guys start butchering meat—a task performed first thing in the morning in every kitchen I'd ever worked in—at five o'clock in the afternoon, half an hour before we opened.

On a technical level, most of the staff was plainly out of their league. I remember the first day I got there, they had tried making foie gras terrines. One was overcooked, a second wasn't seasoned properly, and neither was the third. One after another went into the bin until finally I put an end to it.

"Guys, you know what that stuff costs, right?" I asked them. My first day on the job, and I was already going after my crew for being oblivious to food costs—just like a real chef. I didn't hurl any terrines or langoustines, as I'd had hurled at me back in those London days, but it was those lessons that prepared me to toe the line when I saw this abuse. And it was the hard work I'd done back in the day that allowed me to stop everything and hold an impromptu tutorial in the finer points of terrine making.

Before too long, a terrible dichotomy was at work: my confidence in my own ability was swelling, but I had very little faith in the cooks. Neverthe-less, I felt great urgency to overhaul the menu and replace the existing items with my own. My goal was to replace at least two dishes each week so that by the time we (hopefully) drew the attention of critics and diners, a cohe-sive menu would be in place.

It wasn't long before having the freedom to do my own thing opened the floodgates of creativity. I was combining ingredients in new ways, and my style was quickly beginning to take shape, with what I would eventually come to think of as "graphic" presentations. A parsley and lico-rice soup encircled by bite-size salt cod beignets verged on kaleidoscopic. Clearly inspired by Gagnaire, I stuffed pig trotters with braised pork, then topped them with an attention-grabbing foie gras foam and paired them with a little salad of pickled anchovy and cucumber relish to cut the rich-ness of the dish. (It sounds outlandish, but the combination of salty pork and tart pickles will be familiar to anybody who's ever sampled from a char-cuterie plate.)

Having newly fallen in love with sushi, I was eager to incorporate sushi-inspired influences on the menu. So there was a freshwater eel with a red wine glacé served on a bed of watermelon. Another tribute to my sushi-love was rosettes of raw bigeye tuna topped with Granny Smith apple ravioli and sauced with lime puree and soy vinaigrette.

I also recast the restaurant's standard roasted chicken as a poached chicken topped with a chicken liver and artichoke foam. I served it atop another flavor combination borrowed from Gagnaire, basmati rice tossed with tarragon, mushroom, and chestnuts. (Eventually I would make the dish into an event, offering it for two on the menu.)

While much of the inspiration came to me naturally, the execution was taxing, the most taxing work I'd done since much earlier in my career. Just as I'd worked nearly round the clock as a teenager in London, the focus these dishes demanded of me—not to mention the ongoing task of further refining them while also developing new ones—found me sleeping at Atlas most nights. I was so consumed with The Food and getting it right that I literally lived in the restaurant. I would work until two in the morning and be so tired that I'd curl up on a banquette in the dining room or under Table 1 right on the floor, and crash there. My alarm clock was the vacuum cleaner operated by the dishwasher in the morning. When I heard that, I'd stand up, reorient myself, go into the kitchen, wash up in the sink, and get right back to work. At the end of each week, I'd have grown a beard reminiscent of Paul McCartney's in his *Let It Be* days, then go home on Sunday, shave, and clean up for the week ahead.

That might sound crazy, but that's what it took. That's what was required to chip away at my menu while also dealing with the other issues that a chef has to manage, such as purveyors and the press. Nobody had heard of me in New York, nobody was out there waiting for me, but I knew that this was my chance to make an impression, to stake my claim. And the only way I knew to do it was to pour myself into it entirely. That's what it takes to be a chef. Your life needs to be constantly about The Food. It's not a switch you can turn on and off.

This devotion paid dividends as ideas began to lead one to the next like dominoes. As the last of the late-summer tomatoes came into season, I introduced a first course featuring *seven* different preparations of tomato— including a tomato sorbet topped with caviar; heirloom tomato petals with slices of burrata cheese with Maldon salt; and caramelized tomatillos and pureed baby heirloom tomatoes set on a puddle of tomato gelée, with cilantro and basil over the top. There was also a toasted baguette spread with tomato paste, a salad of pistachio and Parmesan with tomato *croquants*, and

Ayu with Red Wine, Huckleberry, and Spinach

Today I look at this dish, pictured on pages 158–159, a version of which I first served at Atlas, and think that I must've concocted it after a visit to Manhattan's Museum of Modern Art, because the visual composition is so undeniably inspired by Mark Rothko. The centerpiece of the dish is *ayu,* a sweet freshwater fish from Japan that, believe it or not, tastes like melon, a by-product of the fish's diet. It has a very fine texture. Traditionally it is grilled, but I find that technique overcooks the delicate flesh, so instead I roll it into a *ballotine* and poach it, having a bit of fun with its shape. The *ayu* is paired here with huckleberry "cannelloni" and garlicky spinach. The recipe for Red Wine "Cannelloni," from this dish, can be found on page 252.

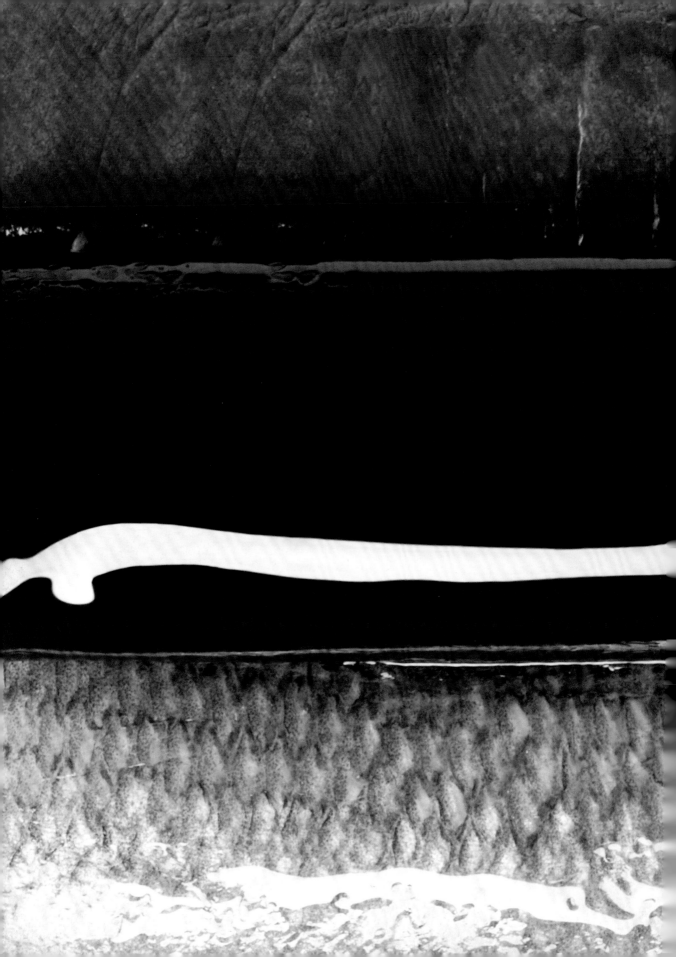

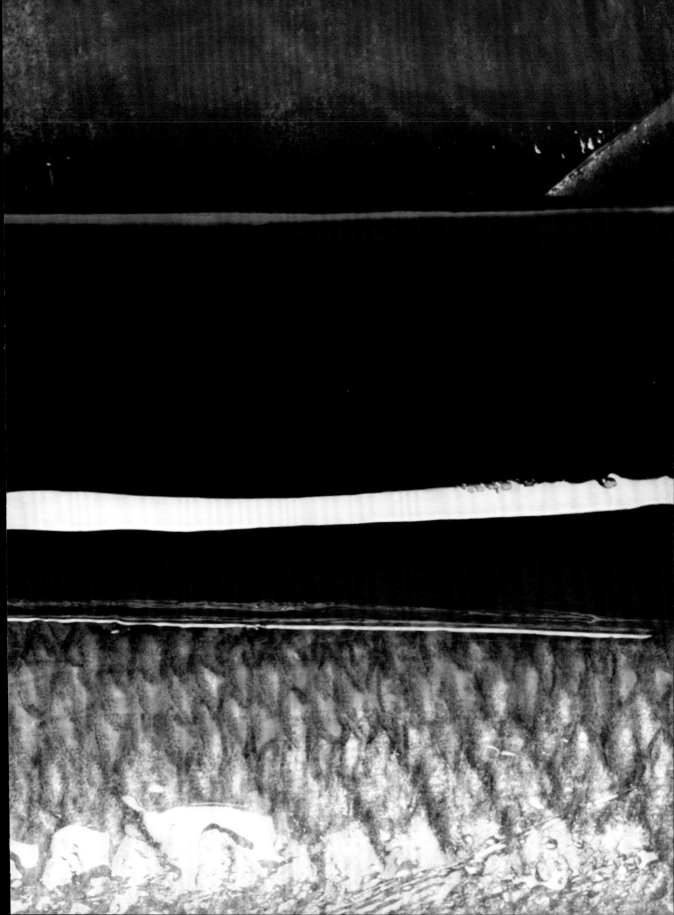

KINMEDAI/BLACK TRUFFLE/PEACH Don't know what to say. It works. Though pictured here with yellow peach, the less common white peach, with its blossomy quality, works beautifully with the earthy truffle and the fragrance of the *kinmedai*.

a tomato terrine. As September wore on, I added as a main course a cannon of lamb with braised artichokes in a coffee-cardamom fumet, and off I went into the autumn, invigorated by the possibilities of a new season.

Ironically, as my repertoire grew, my team shrunk. My menu, and what it took to achieve it, was a big challenge for a staff used to much less labor-intensive food. Within a week, two cooks walked. After another week, another two left. I was down to two guys. It was no fun being down so many staff members in the kitchen, but it was an opportunity to build up a team with guys of my choosing. Fortunately, one of the guys left was Jason Berthold, a young kid from Michigan who was just getting started in his career and had deft hands and a good work ethic. And one of the new chefs on board was Tom Rice, just back from a stint in Monaco working for Alain Ducasse, who was only too happy to come on board. I don't use words like *badass* to describe cooks, but if I did, Rice would be the reason I changed my policy.

It was tough to attract new talent because of the ongoing tension between the front of the house and the kitchen. The restaurant was run as a sort-of club for the regulars, so no reservation requests were denied, and the place was packed during prime time and downright empty on the fringes. Often, we'd go down in flames in the kitchen, drowning in tickets and the knowledge that customers were waiting an hour between courses. Adding insult to injury, I'd often spy the waitstaff in the corner drinking coffee and shooting the breeze—not an ounce of pride in our collective work.

In the midst of this chaos, a young cook named Jacob Proofer trailed with me for a night. He had been cooking in New York City since the age of nineteen and was looking for a new job. The night before he came to me, he had trailed in the kitchen of the legendary seafood restaurant Le Bernardin. Jacob had an interesting past: he had been discovered when he was nineteen and spent five years as a fashion model, traveling the world and living the life. But he couldn't stand it, and returned to his true love—food.

Jacob was a total pro, and I would have been delighted to have him. But the night he trailed with us was one of our disastrous nights, and after service I sat down with him and apologized. I was certain that there was no way he'd come to work at Atlas after what he'd seen at Le Bernardin the night before. He blew my mind when he looked at me and said, "I saw your food tonight, and I can see the potential of where it can go. I can see what you are trying to do, and I see that with the right people on board, this will be the best food in New York City."

I was humbled. "Thanks," I said.

"I want the job."

I could hardly believe it. I hired him.

That exchange was especially heartening because I was beginning to realize that one of the biggest challenges—at least to a cook with my depth of experience—wasn't the food. As the menu was taking shape, I was able, more able than I'd thought possible, to conceive and execute my own dishes. I had plenty to learn and years of development ahead of me, but the fundamentals were in place and I was happy with what I was turning out.

No, the bigger challenge was management. At least, that was the challenge here in America. I didn't realize until I was on my own, hiring cooks for the first time, how lucky I'd been to work in the rarefied air of those Michelin-starred kitchens in London and Paris, and even for Bouley here in New York. Those restaurants drew the most talented cooks like moths to a flame. Everybody who comes to work in those kitchens is up to the task, possessing a complete set of skills and knowledge of the fundamentals. In those kitchens, you showed up to work, got your instructions for the day, and could do whatever was asked of you.

But generally speaking, in a green kitchen like the one at Atlas, the cooks were more of a mixed bag and far more dependent on constant nurturing. I didn't appreciate this, so I had no idea how to hire properly. If somebody came from a kitchen like Daniel or Jean-Georges, my instinct was to consider them world-class material automatically. But those pedigrees didn't mean the same thing then as they might have back home: just because somebody had worked for the best didn't mean that they were the best or that they had the same motivations I did. It never occurred to me that somebody who had worked in top kitchens could be a slacker or simply not very good. And so I made some bad hires, and, to be honest, I didn't suffer them very well. If somebody sank rather than swam . . . well, let's just say that I wasn't standing ready with a life preserver; I was more likely to sack them on the spot. What can I tell you? I was young, and that was the example I'd been shown as a young cook.

But my attitude, to the food and to my staff, did pay off. Toward the end of September, the restaurant's publicist announced my arrival in an item that was picked up in the weekly "Chefs on the Move" roster in the *New York Times*:

> Paul Liebrandt has come to his new job as executive chef at Atlas on Central Park South from Bouley Bakery and, before that, from London (Restaurant Marco Pierre White and Pied-a-Terre).
> —Florence Fabricant, *New York Times*, September 20, 2000

Doesn't sound like much, does it? But it was the first time I'd seen my name in the *New York Times*, and it was exciting. Every moment was now tinged with pressure, because once you announce a new chef in the press, a restaurant is on high alert. Today there are more critics and bloggers than you can keep track of, but in those days there were just two reviewers we really, truly worried about: Hal Rubenstein from *New York* magazine and, above all, William Grimes from the *New York Times*.

Over the next month, I found my groove. Other dishes I introduced included a tempura of *rouget* and langoustines, paired with a pink grapefruit and seaweed salad; and a wild king salmon, with clams and a pumpkin curry. I didn't just lavish attention on first and main courses; I wanted every part of the meal to be memorable. For an *amuse-bouche* one night, I served a salsify soup topped with a slick of Belgian white beer and a thin slice of roasted quince—layer upon layer of flavor to welcome each guest to the restaurant.

My kitchen might not have been ready for the critics, but I was. I knew that the night one of them showed up, if the front of the house recognized them, that I'd do just what I'd done for my audition: go to town and improvise, shut out the rest of the world and cook for them. And sure enough, one night, about a week after the announcement in the *Times*, Jimmy came into the kitchen, looking stunned and confused.

"Oh my God," he said. "Hal Rubenstein just walked in the door."

His anxiety only amused me, because I was psyched. This was the moment I had waited almost a decade for, and I had a cockiness that only a twenty-four-year-old chef—blissfully unaware of the possibility of failure—could enjoy. It was my first time cooking for a critic, the moment of truth every young cook dreams of. I couldn't wait.

"Let's go!" I said. "Let's get him down, then!"

Rubenstein and his party sampled, among other dishes, the tempura and the lamb, as well as wild striped bass with a red pepper–saffron stew and the pasta I was serving at the time: tagliatelle with porcini mushrooms and truffle "perfume."

As if poor Jimmy wasn't nervous enough already, in the middle of Rubenstein's dinner, he staggered into the kitchen—this time looking as though he'd been shot through the heart, his face pale, his shirt drenched in sweat, the very personification of panic. As if the words meant impending Armageddon, he informed me that William Grimes had just shown up as a customer and been seated.

My reaction could not have been more different from his. *Bring it!* I thought, clapping my hands together. *Let's get it on.*

I shouldn't have done what I did next, but I decided to just improvise the food, supplementing and upgrading the dishes Grimes ordered. I rolled pasta *à la minute,* filled it with foie gras, shaped it into a tortellini, and topped it with foie gras consommé enlivened with a bit of lemon paste. It was a crazy thing to do, but I couldn't help myself.

I asked one of the waiters how Grimes was doing, and he told me that he couldn't tell, because he was reading the paper with one hand and manipulating his spoon with the other. So I waited for his bowl to come back, and when it did, it was as clean as it was when it came out of the dishwasher. We were doing great!

But my cooks seemed distracted, stealing glances in the same direction. I followed their gaze and saw that Jimmy was pacing around in the corner, positively flipping out under the pressure.

Something took over in me right then, the same sense of ownership, of leadership, that I'd seen displayed by any great chef I'd ever worked for. I knew that calm heads always prevail and that it's their responsibility to instill calmness in others, even if it has to be by intimidation. And so, I swooped in on him like a predator.

"Listen," I whispered. "If you can't calm down, leave the floor."

Jimmy pulled himself together, and we got through that night. Grimes came back with three guests the next time, and Rubenstein returned twice more. Even before the reviews ran, word was starting to get out around town, at least among foodies and cooks. The restaurant's business picked up. One night, I was out with Tom after work—we used to hang out at Blue Ribbon Sushi in Soho or at Whiskey Park just down the street from Atlas—and at the next table were another group of cooks.

"You hear about this guy Paul Liebrandt?" one of them said to his buds. "Guy's doing nine preparations of tomato. Insane shit." It was a compliment. I was so new on the scene that people knew my name but not my face. I was also realizing that being from London lent me an air of mystique here in New York, where—for reasons I don't quite understand—there are almost no high-profile British chefs. I felt like a mercenary.

Despite all the chatter about us in knowledgable food circles around town, we were only doing about sixty covers a night in a restaurant with sixty-four seats. *Maybe,* I thought, *what we're doing is too adventurous, not for everybody.* It wasn't even for all my cooks. One day, that October, Jason sat me down and told me that he just didn't connect with my food, that it wasn't for him. He was more interested in what Thomas Keller, whose *French Laundry Cookbook* had just debuted, was doing.

I wasn't very mature about that kind of difference in those days. "Just leave now, then," I told him in a huff. "I don't want your notice. Just go." He went on to work at Chanterelle for a number of years and then to The French Laundry, before becoming executive chef of Michael Mina's RN74 in San Francisco. About the same time, I brought in David Coleman, a sous-chef who had been the lieutenant to Rocco DiSpirito at Union Pacific.

Grimes reemerged for his third visit on Halloween night. I had a cook friend from Bouley who used to go hunting in Canada, and he had brought me some wild ducks from his latest outing. I had the birds in the walk-in, with the wings and feathers still intact because I didn't know what to do with them.

"Tell him we have a special of Wild Mallard Duck Cooked in a Salt Crust with Black Truffle and Red Currant Gelée," I said to Grimes's waiter. Grimes took the bait, ordered the special, and I was off to the races. I did a salt crust over the body of the duck, but left the wing intact, bending it back so it fanned out like a peacock. I tied the body to a brick to keep the wing back, and put it in the oven.

What followed was pure, instinctual cooking. Where did the idea for that duck come from, the combination of black truffle and red currant? I wish I could tell you, but I can't. It was the reward for sleeping in the restaurant, the way your brain starts to work when you devote more than a decade to The Food. It's not a linear thought process: it's creating a mind-set that breeds inspiration. When the duck was cooked, I put it on a silver tray and had the waiter present it to Grimes. I stood at the porthole and watched his face light up.

I felt great about that night and had a good enough vibe that I thought we had a chance at three stars. But in the next morning's *Times*, Alain Ducasse at the Essex House received three stars, and the air went out of my optimism. I felt, without hesitation, that Ducasse was operating a four-star restaurant. But by most people's estimations, he had made all the wrong public relations moves since his arrival in the States, and so was denied his four.

Wow, I thought. *If he's getting three, then there's no way we will. We are not Ducasse.*

Just before Thanksgiving, Hal Rubenstein reviewed us in *New York Magazine*. It was a very nice review, praising my "deftness with unexpectedly appealing combinations," but this was before the magazine had its own star system, so this didn't have the weight or clarity of a *Times* review.

Later that same week, I got a call from the photo desk of the *New York Times* . . . and that's the call you look for. The *Times* always took a photograph of the dining room to accompany the review, and usually took the picture late in the week prior to the week the review would run. But the *Times* rep threw me a curveball when he told me that they were also going to photograph my Green Apple–Wasabi Sorbet. A food shot as well as one of the dining room? I'd never heard of that.

"Let's just say that he really, really likes your restaurant," he said.

A photographer came by that Friday and took a picture of the sorbet as I drizzled a thin stream of olive oil over it.

On Monday, Grimes himself rang me up, his standard fact-checking call. How did I make the pig trotters, he wanted to know, and other technical bits. When he asked my age, I told him twenty-five, even though I was just twenty-four, because I thought the extra year might add some legitimacy to my chefdom. He didn't give anything away, so I got off the call as clueless about what to expect as when I'd answered the phone.

In those days, the *Times* critic made a weekly appearance on New York 1, a local cable news channel, on Tuesday night. With a cloud of winking

Tomato

I didn't devise some of the dishes on pages 168 and 169 until years after Atlas, but these three tomato preparations recall the tomato tastings I first began serving there. In addition to demonstrating my own development, they illustrate the incredible product available to a chef in New York City, where local tomatoes—such as those from nearby Eckerton Hill Farm—are as magnificent as any you will encounter anywhere. The dishes on the following pages include raw, partially cooked, and cooked tomato preparations, demonstrating the breadth of possibility with one ingredient. These are among the simpler dishes in the book; it's not easy to find perfect, or even near-perfect, tomatoes, and when I do I like to respect them, doing as little as possible to them, the ultimate example being the heirloom tomato offering on page 169.

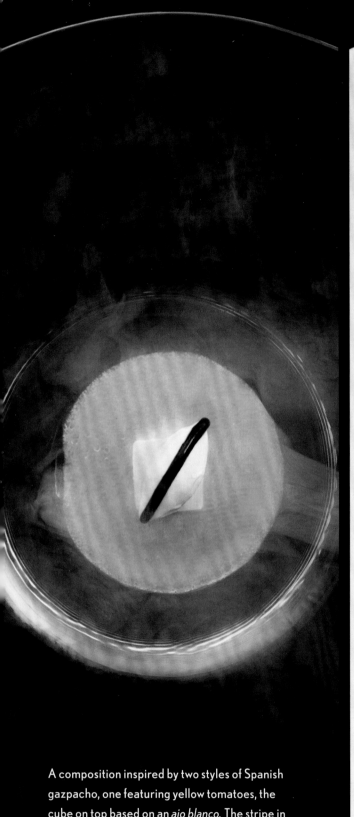

A composition inspired by two styles of Spanish gazpacho, one featuring yellow tomatoes, the cube on top based on an *ajo blanco*. The stripe in the center is a quenelle of burrata ice cream and black olive paste.

Black Prince tomatoes with albacore tuna confit, wrapped in smoked lardo and topped with a savory tomato financier.

Heirloom tomatoes with yellow plum extra-virgin
olive oil and smoked *fleur de sel.* (The recipe for
the oil is on page 253.)

electronic tiles obscuring his face and maintaining his anonymity, he would discuss the next day's review with the anchorperson, and the whole thing built up dramatically to the moment of truth: the revelation of the number of stars. That Tuesday, we all kept our eye on the little television in the back office. Shortly after eight o'clock, Grimes made his appearance. I could tell right off it was going to be a good review.

"There is a very interesting new place called Atlas," he said, "and a young chef named Paul Liebrandt who is redefining French food."

Grimes went on and on about the menu, describing the décor and the service and spending a great deal of time on lovingly detailed food descriptions. At some point, I stopped breathing. It sounded for all the world like a three-star review. But was that really possible?

"So how many stars?" asked the anchor.

"Three," said Grimes, and I ran into the dining room and took a victory lap, screaming, "We got three stars!"

The customers burst into applause. Arriving at the hostess podium, I saw that all six lines on the telephone were lit up, and not just for reservations. Other chefs from around town were ringing up to offer congratulations. (Amusingly, another hot young chef later called to congratulate me, when I'd already heard from mutual friends that he was royally enraged that I was right in with three.)

It was a great night. I took my cooks out for burgers and beers at the Corner Bistro, an old watering hole in the West Village, and we stayed out late into the evening, savoring our moment of triumph. Despite all the ups and downs, the comings and goings of the staff, the annoying cluster of insiders and their cottage cheese and special requests, we had pulled it off. And at just twenty-four, I was the youngest chef ever to attain three stars, even though the *Times* told the world that I was twenty-five. I only had myself to blame for that one—the one moment of professional doubt I'd had in months.

The power of the *Times* was instantaneous. We had done sixty covers on Tuesday but did one hundred on Wednesday. The next day, the celebration continued—calls and flowers from chefs and restaurateurs. The *Telegraph* called up from London. And the *Times* itself ran more than just a review: it was a love letter, with photographs of the food. Even Jason called to congratulate me, telling me I was right all along. Haughty young thing that I was, I wasn't very nice, but we both laugh about it when we run into each other today.

By the middle of the day on Wednesday, I had shifted gears. *All right,* I thought. *Now we go for four. Now it's time to work harder. Because now everybody's going to come in.*

The next few months were like a dream. Riding high on the strength of that review, and constantly revising the menu, I felt that I arrived. My little kitchen crew and I were like a rock band, working like maniacs every night and going out after hours for drinks or sushi. We didn't tear up the town like some of our colleagues, but we had a good time, and when we see each other today, it all comes rushing back in a torrent of happy memories.

If there was a disappointment during those months, it was that not everybody shared Grimes's enthusiasm for what I was trying to do at Atlas. The most violent dissenting view was expressed by Jonathan Gold, critic for *Gourmet* magazine at the time, who penned a scathing, downright personal evisceration, unprecedented in the pages of the publication.

The only thing that alleviated the sting of the *Gourmet* review was a letter I received from a fellow young chef, who expressed dismay at the attack and felt compelled to encourage me to continue trying to break new ground. He and I had never met, but he had recently left The French Laundry and was making a name for himself as chef at Trio restaurant in Chicago, where he was advancing his brand of so-called molecular gastronomy. That chef has gone on to be a brilliant success in his own right: Grant Achatz, who today presides over Alinea restaurant in Chicago.

Fortunately, that bad review was just a speed bump. My crew and I had a fantastic next six months, constantly changing the menu and welcoming the food cognoscenti of New York into our dining room. A highlight for me was that Thomas Keller and designer Adam Tihany dined at Atlas several times, studying blueprints between courses. (Little did I know they were planning the restaurant Per Se in the Time Warner Center just down the street.) I also had the honor of being treated like royalty at other restaurants. When I took my crew to Ducasse for lunch, the maestro himself prepared us a menu, then took us on a tour of his kitchen.

And yet, I must admit that I did make mistakes at Atlas, many of them. Though I wanted to be a chef, I was also exceedingly young to have become one. Most chefs spend years as a sous-chef to one or more mentors, developing under their auspices and tutelage before stepping into the spotlight on their own. Instead, I thrust myself out there after just a few months as a sous. And so, without the benefit of an editor, there were dishes that, looking back, I would not have served today: barbecued eel with chocolate glaze and watermelon comes to mind. But on the other hand, I look at dishes like phases in my life, and I had to go through those phases to get where I am today. I just wish that some of them might have been passed in private or in consultation with somebody who knew better. But what can you do? The past is the past.

It was also about this time that I began experimenting with the techniques being popularized by Ferran Adrià at El Bulli and by chefs who had worked for him, a new school that was moving away from Frenchified food and into a brave new world all their own. In particular, I was blown away by Albert Adrià's pastry book and the incredible effects on display there such as his use of flavor and texture within the realm of pastry, which broke from the French norm, treating desserts more like savory than sweet dishes with components such as caramelized avocado and bacon-caramel. The methods these chefs used are referred to worldwide by what I've come to think of as "the M word": molecular. It's a word I've come to detest because it sounds so scientific and unsensual. I much prefer the term *modernist cuisine,* although personally I refer to what I do as simply "open" cuisine, in that I'm open to new ideas, new techniques, and to melding them with the classics in my own way.

To be honest, I'm loathe to discuss this aspect of my food, because I think it pulls focus from what ought to be front and center: the flavor and the emotional impact. Suffice it to say that it was about this time that I began to experiment with such methods as spherifications and foams, and that much of my early experiments were bloody disasters, requiring me to hit the books and the kitchen and deepen my understanding.

Aspects of my personality were, in many ways, as underdeveloped as some of my food, and I had my missteps with the media. One night, Jimmy told me the editor of *People* magazine was in the house. As a prank, I donned a T-shirt that said "fucking fuck" across the chest and walked through the dining room to greet her. What was I thinking? Was it a rock 'n' roll gesture? A bid for some kind of bad boy street cred? I honestly don't know. I was twenty-four and that was that. I could also be a bit short with interviewers, a hostile witness if you will, no doubt trying to achieve an effect like the one Marco often did in his younger days. But times were different, and in the era of the media-darling chef in New York City, everybody was playing much nicer than that. As a result, I created an image for myself that's taken years to shake.

But things turned the following summer. When the restaurant experienced the normal downturn that almost every big-city establishment experiences in the dog days, anxiety set in among the management. Even the slightest dip in revenue incited a knee-jerk reaction. It was suggested to me that I shift gears and add "blue plate specials" to the menu, such as spaghetti and meatballs for the whole table to share.

I was incredulous. Spaghetti and meatballs? Served family style? Alongside the kind of food that was earning us rave reviews as one of the restaurants of the moment and that had been filling the place right up until Memorial Day? I refused.

And so began a long, hot summer between me and Jimmy, a summer in which I constantly trumpeted the need to keep integrity in "my kitchen" and he pointedly reminded me that it wasn't my kitchen, it was "the restaurant's kitchen." Technically, he was right, of course, but isn't the whole point of being a chef to have a personality, to be your own person, and cook your own food? I hate to validate the stereotypical image of a chef, but don't people expect that in restaurants of a certain caliber? Isn't that the whole point?

This cold war continued for a few months until, shortly before the September 11 terrorist attacks, the inevitable conclusion came, and I was sent off on a mandatory vacation. Knowing full well what was coming, I made my move, giving my notice after just more than a year, and moving on, a peripatetic cook once again.

Within five months, Atlas closed. Although things didn't end well there, I will always remember it as the place where I first became a real chef and the world first noticed me.

Sayori

This is a twisted way of eating sushi, with sea-salt-flavored cotton candy in place of the rice. The fish here, *sayori* (Japanese needlefish), is like a stealth submarine: fast, sleek, and undetectable. For the first part of this dish, we very gently nape the fillet with a chilled tofu crème seasoned with *myöga* (Japanese ginger) and lime confit, and finish it with nasturtium leaves. To produce the second part of the dish, we deep-fry the bone until it is completely crisp, wrap the belly around it, and season it with fresh wasabi. The belly is then placed inside a cocoon of sea-salt cotton candy, adorned with tiny pansy leaves and ice lettuce. To further the playfulness of this dish, we encourage our guests to eat it with their fingers.

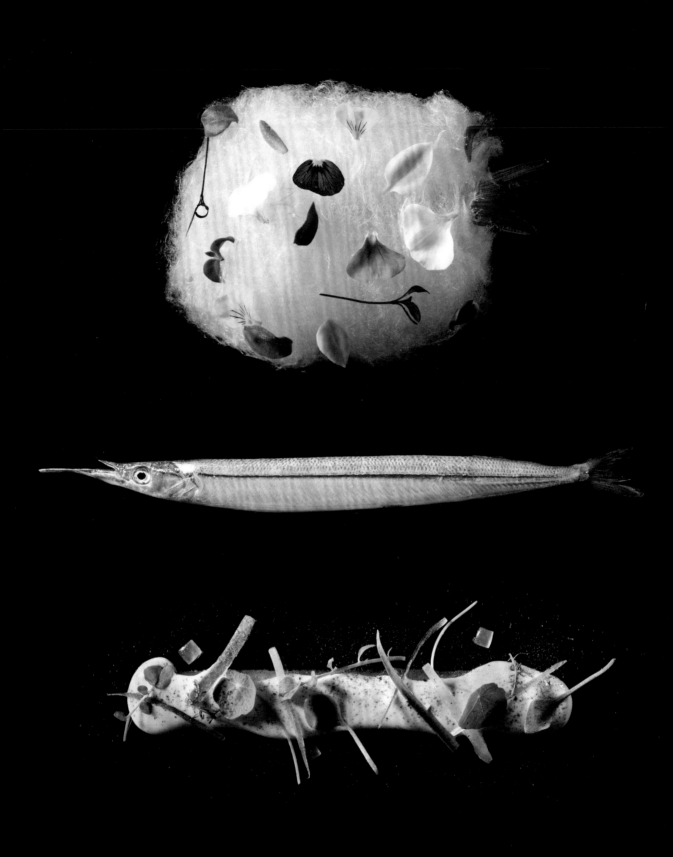

A PAUSE FOR REFRESHMENT

2001–2002

The economic walloping that was inflicted on New York City after the September 11 attacks spared nobody, and the restaurant industry was hit as hard as any, perhaps more so than many. None of the factors that induce people to go out for a fine-dining experience were in effect. People were unhappy, people were scared, people were angry, and people were broke.

My problems didn't amount to anything in that context, but I needed to keep working and to survive, so my next job was, incongruously, as chef of Papillon, a West Village bistro. It wasn't a place for me to expand my horizons. Instead, it was the chef equivalent of a successful actor returning to, say, Off Broadway, to his roots. Papillon was a chance for me to just *cook*, without pushing the envelope as I had at Atlas.

It turned out to be a sometimes enjoyable experience. The owners were good guys and gave me a bit more license than the ones back at Le Gans, although keeping within the necessarily restricted boundaries of a midlevel eatery. In the end, it was an opportunity to focus on craft and technique and get back to my base, to regain my bearings after my whirlwind first few years in New York. I still remember many of the dishes there rather fondly, such as

Sea Bass with Bay Leaf Butter, Barbecued Lentils, Sunchoke Puree, and a bone-in *côte de boeuf* for two that was rubbed with garlic, roasted in hay (a long-forgotten but very traditional cooking method), and served with oyster mushrooms and green mango.

Despite offerings like these, and what I considered an overall successful effort, the unfortunate truth is that all anybody remembers of Papillon are two dinners we prepared late in 2001—"sensory meals" in which we attempted to look at the effect of *all* the senses on the dining experience. My pastry chef cooked up the idea, and I went along with it, although I always knew we were playing with fire. (It wasn't something that grew organically out of my own background and predilections, and that's never the right road for a chef.)

That's not to say the dinners were without value. Some of the exercises we performed were intellectually and gastronomically interesting. For example, we served a loin of veal that was sliced paper thin, like a carpaccio. The slices were layered, pressed into a block, and frozen, then sliced like a steak and served with a spicy cilantro ketchup. The veal melted in the mouth, and, though raw, the chill made it taste like a piece of roasted veal. We blindfolded diners and had them rub silk and sandpaper between their fingers, then eat a langoustine tartare to confound their senses (many perceived a nonexistent crunch in the dish because of the sandpaper on their fingertips). Other elements of the evenings had no such intellectual value: we would abruptly march diners into a smoke-filled back room, then return them to their table to disrupt their sense of environment.

Does that sound silly? It was. I can't simply plead "youth" on this one, but it was a valuable lesson. I can now honestly say that this was the only time in my career as a chef that I did something that simply felt wrong, that wasn't *me*. I realized that there are two sides to being known in a place like New York City: it's not just earning a reputation that matters; you also have to nurture and protect it.

And yet, at the same time, there was a silver lining. The considerable press the evenings attracted were much-needed evidence for the caseworkers charged with evaluating my visa status and who would rule as to whether or not I deserved a green card in the highly scrutinized post-9/11 immigration environment. Those bureaucrats might not have been "foodies," but anybody with the tome of clippings I presented to them, they figured, must have *some* worth.

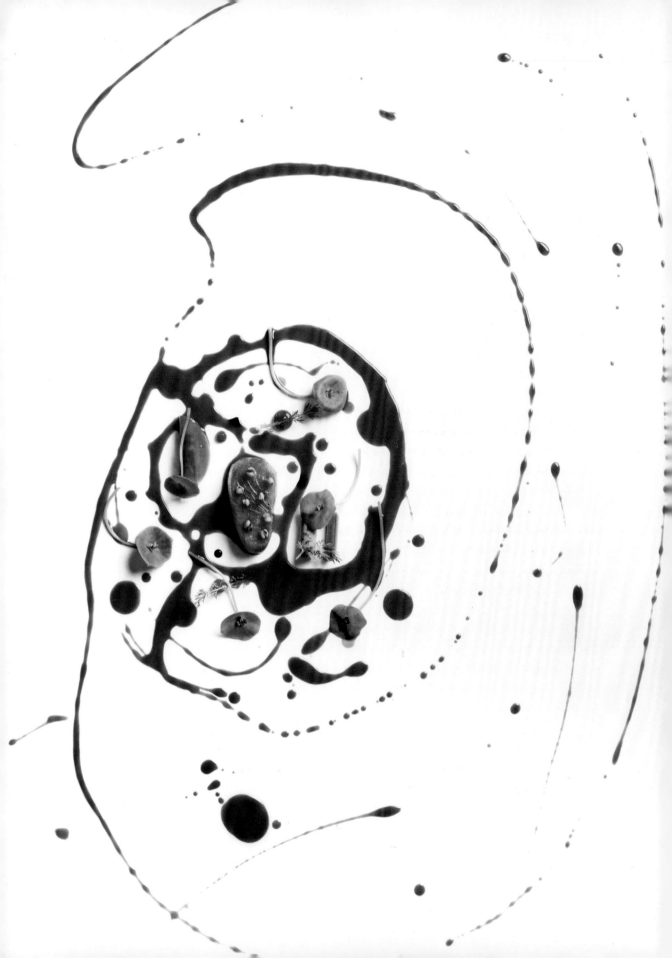

I was especially gratified that once those dinners had faded into the past, Papillon received a two-star review from William Grimes in the *New York Times*. (It was a step down from Atlas's three stars, but that was largely due to the more casual setting.) "If you believe in cuisine as an expressive language, then you have to applaud, or at least admire," he wrote of my menu. "Mr. Liebrandt is a big talent working, for the moment at least, on a small stage. He needs a bigger show."

There was another silver lining to my time at Papillon, and it was altogether surreal at the time. Sally Rowe, a documentary filmmaker whom I'd met while at Atlas (she was married to my wine director there), asked if she could begin trailing me for a film she had in mind. I agreed to work with her, and she and a small crew began making periodic visits to my kitchen and dining room, as well as to my apartment—even following me up and down the street as I walked to and from work.

It wasn't as glamorous as it might sound because of the sad state of my career. If I were going to choose a time to have a camera crew track my life, it wouldn't have been at that particular moment, but it was flattering nonetheless and a welcome counterbalance to the hardened atmosphere of the kitchen. Once in a while, Sally would interview me on camera, and, while this is a word that I would rarely use, it was a *therapeutic* exercise, a chance for me to open up and explore my feelings about where I was and what I wanted. Along the same lines, the mere presence of a camera cannot help but make one more self-aware of everything, from how you treat others to how you go about your day and, on a larger scale, whether you are getting closer to or further from your personal and professional goals.

She also captured moments—many of them—that anybody would have preferred to leave in the past, like girlfriends who were now part of posterity. There were fixed, Big-Brother-is-watching cameras in the kitchen that

---

WILD ALASKAN KING SALMON   There were two preparations of salmon I served at Papillon: one featuring the salmon confit, with white rhubarb and a red curry sauce made from the salmon bones; the other a *ballotine* of salmon belly with a chutney that's a play on piccalilli with broccoli instead of cauliflower. The recipe for Red Curry Jus (page 254) provides the delicious curry sauce from the former, also a perfect accompaniment to black cod.

my crew and I totally forgot about. The camera captured me going mental, berating and even hurling plates and pans at my cooks, then blaming *them* for my behavior. "Look what you made me do!" I screamed at one especially memorable moment. Fortunately, none of the worst bits made their way into the finished film. (As it turned out, Sally and her crew would follow me on and off for about nine and a half years, resulting in the film *A Matter of Taste: Serving Up Paul Liebrandt*. Even had the film never seen the light of day, it was a welcome addition to my life and something that helped me understand myself better.)

Despite Grimes's positive write-up, after about a year at Papillon, the owners—bowing to the financial pressures of the time—decided to change the concept into a more neighborhood-friendly eatery, with traditional bistro fare such as *croque monsieurs* and their American counterparts, most notably a hamburger that became our best seller. I went along for a few months, then decided that I just couldn't muster the necessary enthusiasm to stay in the job. I helped secure a new chef, stayed on to train him, then went on my way.

Having gone nonstop in professional kitchens for about a decade, I decided a break was in order. I spent two years working as a private chef to a few high-profile clients, including Lord Rothschild and HRH Prince Andrew in 2003 and 2004. I also took the time to travel, visiting Spain, Hong Kong, Southeast Asia, and Africa, finally getting to some of the places I'd imagined visiting as a child, when I envisioned a life in the military—only now, I was largely motivated by culinary interests. It was an eye-opening time. Having been professionally reared in an environment where workaholism was prized above all else, I quickly realized that intellectual and gustatory stimulation had great value as well. I stored up inspiration from restaurants and museums, from architecture and natural wonders, and came back to New York with my horizons broadened and an itch to put it all to work in new dishes.

When I was ready to get back to work in a restaurant, it took awhile to get started again after two years away. I might have been off the radar and out of the papers and food blogs for a bit, but I was a known chef in New York City, and there are few more fascinating times in life for such an organism than that spent in pursuit of the next restaurant. I wish I could tell you how many meetings I had with how many investors, for how many concepts—but now, years later, they all blur together into one long string of meals and drinks dates, coffees and site tours, business plans and audition menus. If every promise of imminent financing, lease signing, financial projections, and anticipated timing expressed to me during those years had come to fruition, I would be the most prolific and successful chef in all of New York City, perhaps in the world.

But every single one of the deals dangled before me went up in smoke. Would-be partners disappeared, never to be heard from again or with only parting meetings to let me down easy. Or another chef would swoop in and replace me in the business plan. This is nothing unusual in the restaurant business, which draws impresarios and would-be impresarios who dream big and often are well-meaning, but, where the money is concerned, are just as often either pathologically optimistic or downright delusional.

It was a soul-crushing period, my own version of *Groundhog Day*, an endless loop that, no matter how I came at it, dropped me back in the same place when I woke up the next morning.

GOING FOR BROKE

2005–2006

Finally, in 2005, everything fell into place and I was hired to be the opening chef of Gilt, in the former home of Sirio Maccioni's legendary restaurant Le Cirque in the New York Palace Hotel. The hotel was once owned by Harry Helmsley and operated by his wife, the notorious "Queen of Mean" Leona, but had recently been purchased by Prince Jefri, the brother of the Sultan of Brunei. The space, still under renovation when I first saw it, was surely going to be spectacular, with dishes that were to be paraded down a grand staircase from the kitchen to the dining room. It was going to build on the luxe trappings of Le Cirque, with the most elegant and expensive serveware, furniture, and artwork.

It was a setting that screamed out for fine dining and seemed the perfect place for me to make my return to that world. I was especially attracted to the project because the owners conveyed a desire to do something different from the traditional hotel restaurant. Having recently witnessed the decline of Peacock Alley in the Waldorf Astoria, as well as other comparable high-end establishments, the owners wanted to compete with the top three- and four-star freestanding restaurants in town. To that end, they had enlisted

Patrick Jouin, the designer responsible for, among other successes, Alain Ducasse's restaurant at the Plaza Athénée in Paris.

It seemed like an ideal scenario, but I was thrown a curveball after signing on to the project. Those same owners, seeking to hedge their bets, told me that they wanted to also serve what they referred to as "bistro food," by which they meant a menu of familiar hotel fare that might induce affluent Upper East Siders to dine there several times a week (never mind that we were not technically on the Upper East Side). In short, they wanted to have their cake and eat it, too.

Whereas in my younger years, I had to defend myself against the sabotage of fellow line cooks, the challenge at this stage of my career was to engage successfully with owners. I realized that there simply isn't room for two visions in one restaurant. But after close to two years of being out of a restaurant, I offered to meet them in the middle, with a menu divided into two cuisines, "Classic" and "Modern" (as we titled them on the physical document)—the former satisfying their desires, the latter satisfying mine.

The Classic dishes, as I presented them, would include, say, Dover sole with *pommes soufflé* and brown butter vinaigrette, rib eye for two with a cocotte of spring baby vegetables, and oysters on the half shell with caviar. The truth was, I was so eager to begin truly expressing myself again that, as I envisioned them, even the Classic dishes would be etched in my evolving style. For example, the oysters would be either served with lemon foam on top and a Comté cheese cracker on the side, or set in a gelée made of their own juices, topped with a quenelle of caviar, and accompanied by a spicy pecan brioche.

My pitch was accepted. I was hired and brought on some of my old boys, including Tom Rice—a crack team that brought a lot of different energies and experience to the table. I hit the jackpot when I called Francis Derby, who had worked for me at Atlas, asking him if he wanted to come on board. He brought with him a group of talented cooks who had been *stagiaires* together at Mugaritz in Spain: Amador Acosta, Johnny Mac, and Michael Santoro, as well as Juan Leon, who had worked at El Bulli. We were a great team and, to this day, remain good friends in close contact.

I proceeded to go to town on the Modern menu. There were so many ideas pent up in my brain, ideas I didn't even realize I had, ideas that were waiting patiently by the phone until The Food rang them up again. The passion and intensity with which I attacked that kitchen surprised me. I went for broke, pouring as much of myself and my amassed techniques as I could into each and every menu offering, especially with courses comprising a multitude of plates and preparations. I introduced dishes and concepts that remain with me to this day, such as first courses named for the season and presented as an array of small preparations and variations. "Flavors of Winter," for example, included roasted sweetbreads with blood orange, and a thimbleful of sea urchin suspended atop a chilled cucumber gelée. I also continued a pattern begun at Atlas with that array of tomato compositions, offering six preparations of langoustines as a first course.

At the same time, the exercise of cooking at Papillon left me with a new appreciation for simpler pleasures, expertly executed. So, alongside the above, I made room for a squash soup adorned with a pasta preparation that had haunted me since those L'Escargot days—langoustine tortellini. But most dishes were studies in unabashed excess. I wanted to really push the envelope at Gilt, to use the spectacular setting as permission to take each and every course as far as I could, to flex my muscles and show what I could do. A foie gras torchon, enveloped by a beet gelée, for instance, was etched as an arresting tribute to architect Frank Gehry.

If you wanted a simple roasted chicken, Gilt was not the place to find it. Our chicken was served as a dizzying array of dishes under the name Milk-Fed Poulard, Petit Farcie, Malt-Smoked Oyster Crust, and Crushed Black Truffle Jus. In it, the chicken leg was presented in a *ballotine* stuffed with truffle and chicken mousse; the wing was confited and served with smoked oyster butter; a hot chicken consommé was presented with squash fondant glazed with Szechuan pepper; and a cold jellied consommé was topped with crispy skin, black truffle, and garlic crème—all with other, smaller dishes served alongside.

At Gilt, I wanted each dish to be like Christmas morning for the table, the waitstaff showering the guests with as many beautiful packages as the square footage could contain.

There was another reason for my ambition at Gilt. In 2005 Michelin, the arbiter of culinary success in most of the world, launched a New York City guide, and I desperately wanted in and at the highest level. Thomas Keller's Per Se was awarded three Michelin stars, and, from day

Cod Cheek with Smoked Bone Marrow and Black Trumpet

I introduced this labor-intensive dish, pictured on pages 186–187, during my go-for-broke phase at Gilt and have tweaked it over the years. The cod is cooked very gently, and the bone marrow is poached in a cardamom-enhanced *escabèche.* Also here are octopus, cuttlefish, and grapefruit, all complemented with a viscous sauce made from cod bones. At the end of the day, this dish is all about texture, the protein in the marrow pulling the flavors together.

Red Abalone

with White Truffle and Gnudi

This is emblematic of the culinary wanderlust I experienced after Papillon and of the lengths to which I went in preparing food at Gilt. This dish offers my distinctly non-Italian take on Italian food, relocating white truffle and gnudi to an unfamiliar environment. For a seafood dish, this is remarkably meaty, owing to the toothsome abalone (we aged it for a few days almost as you would a piece of beef, to bring out the natural umami flavor) and the earthy truffle. One of the cardinal rules of Italian cooking is to not combine fish and cheese, but the ricotta in the gnudi marries perfectly with the other elements. The dish is put over the top, and belongs forever to Gilt, thanks to a caramelized abalone consommé—an almost oaky, surprisingly nonfishy broth added to the cup at the last second. The gnudi are elegant, made with no flour or semolina (although the finished gnudi are rolled in flour to form a skin on their exterior), consisting of just a touch of ricotta and some Parmesan cheese for the high note it adds. They are poached in a light white abalone *beurre monte*, truffle butter made with the trimming of the abalone in the dish. You can find the recipe for White Truffle Gnudi with Abalone Butter on page 256.

one, I wanted my work at Gilt to be a bid for similar enshrinement. That might seem foolhardy, but it remains my belief that if you don't challenge yourself, you simply can't grow as a chef.

When the *Times* reviewed Gilt, the new critic Frank Bruni wrote a mixed assessment, praising my technique and some dishes, but finding others too busy. "[Paul Liebrandt] is not a vacuously flamboyant bad boy, as his detractors have claimed," wrote Bruni. "He's an evolving young artist who needs to draw sharper distinctions between his greater and lesser ideas." There was encouragement and validity in that comment, but I was too crushed by the ultimate verdict—two stars, in one of the grandest rooms in town—to hear it. Even in the midst of Gilt's opulent dining room, I was at the low point of my career. In a moment that was mercifully not included in *A Matter of Taste*, I barked at Sally to "turn the camera off" as she captured my dismay and heartbreak.

The night of the review was a roller coaster. Of all the nights he could have picked for a visit, Alain Ducasse, a three-star deity in my eyes, dropped in for dinner that night and made it his mission to pick me up off the canvas.

"How old are you?" he asked, noting my obvious despair.

"Twenty-nine."

He waved his hand in the air. "You'll have many more reviews," he said. "Don't worry about it. You'll be fine."

But, as it turned out, for reasons unrelated to the food or the critics, I was doomed at Gilt. As any number of chefs can tell you, working with a union hotel crew can be a nightmare, and Gilt did nothing to reverse that conception. There was a sanctioned laziness by many hotel employees (not my own crack team in the kitchen) and also mysteriously high food costs

---

PORK SHOULDER WITH BABY RADISH, CONFIT TURNIP, AND TAMARIND
This is hearty elegance in an autumnal dish from Gilt. The pork shoulder is marinated in a brine-like mixture with a white beer base, then cooked very slowly *sous vide* and gently caramelized on the skin to produce a suckling pig–like texture. This is a very nice recipe that uses an economical cut of pork, with the beer imparting a yeasty flavor that marries well with the shoulder. It would be well-paired with tamarind, pumpkin puree, and artichokes that have been braised in apple cider. The recipe for Beer-Brined Pork Shoulder can be found on page 260.

Beet-Hibiscus-Glazed Foie Gras

with Trevise

This glazed foie gras, which I first made at Gilt, has its structural origins in L'Escargot's foie gras terrine with a Sauternes gelée, and offers yet another example of how influences from even one's earliest cooking days can find their way into dishes in later life. I'd go so far as to say that any dish that you make or observe on a regular basis stays with you, but especially memorable are those you came into contact with early in your career, because your repertoire and knowledge were so limited at the time you first spotted them.

I didn't prepare the terrine at L'Escargot myself. Upstairs, we served hot foie gras preparations. But downstairs, in the more casual restaurant, they served the terrine with small cubes of the translucent gelée alongside. Though expertly rendered, there was nothing especially new about that terrine, but whenever I passed by, my eye trained on it, much more than with the hot foie gras upstairs. I think it's because of the precision and order of a terrine. My first experiences with foie gras were so calamitous and messy; a terrine represented an ideal, a summit to be climbed. In the years since I became a chef, I began enrobing terrines with gelées, which makes for a lovely visual and also pairs each mouthful with what I consider the perfect amount of sweet complement.

But this dish didn't begin with my remembrance of L'Escargot or even of its foie gras terrine. Rather, it's my homage to the architecture of Frank Gehry, whose work I became enamored of on a trip to his Guggenheim building in Bilbao, Spain, in 2004. That admiration found its expression in this dish: the thought, abstract in nature, found grounding in the glazed foie gras. From there, I added a beet and hibiscus *croquant*, black olive *en croquant*, trevise, and a *shiso* leaf.

In flavor and appearance, this composition represents the way I'd always like to cook but am still striving to attain. One of my aspirations as a chef is to be able to give physical voice to a flicker of inspiration like this. I feel I attained it here, but it was a transcendent and fleeting accomplishment, an exhilarating moment in which I assembled a dish the way authors speak of merely following their characters as they take on a life of their own. Because of the graphic nature of my cuisine, I'm sometimes asked if I consider cooking an art or a craft. I reject the question. This dish is both lovely to look at and, if I say so myself, delicious to eat. Cooking does not exist in binary terms. Art or craft? It's both.

The recipe for Beet-Hibiscus-Glazed Foie Gras can be found on page 258.

that I began to investigate, demanding spreadsheets and other reports from the main office. Before I knew it, I was sacked, along with my entire team, including the pastry team. My Michelin hopes were, at least for the time being, quashed. I later learned that the costs were likely part of a shell game being run by one of the owner's representatives, who was accused of embezzling millions of the company's assets. But by the time this all came to light, it was too late. Gilt was no longer mine, and I was a free agent again, seeking my next restaurant, the next place to continue my evolution.

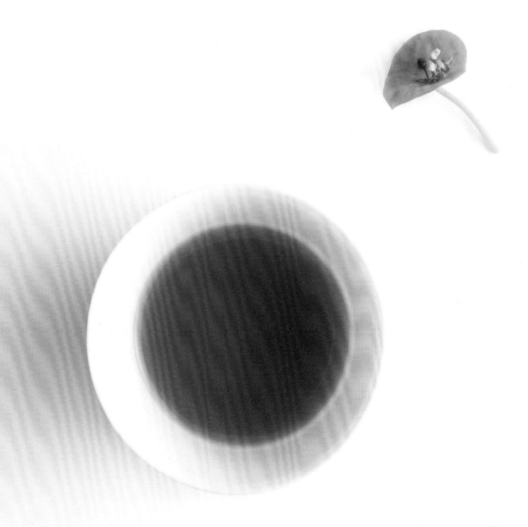

Beetroot-Blackberry Meringue

with Beetroot and Red Currant Sorbet

These vibrant, light-as-air meringues were part of the Flavors of Winter offering at Gilt, where they were paired with a tart-sweet beetroot and red currant sorbet. The meringue is simpler than it looks, made with beetroot juice, dried egg white powder, and gelatin; it's the shape that makes it appear complicated, the planetary curvature suggesting Mars. (My private joke at the time was that this composition was an expression of both my alienation and my anger toward the hotel and its staff.)

The meringues are prepared on acetate sheets in a food dehydrator, a once-obscure piece of equipment that is now readily available to home cooks; you can even buy one at Bed Bath & Beyond. I highly recommend them, not just for this recipe, but for creating a variety of snacks and garnishes.

The recipe for Beetroot-Blackberry Meringue can be found on page 261.

Ruby Red Shrimp
and Reindeer Lichen

The exceptional flavor of ruby red shrimp is the foundation of this light *ballotine,* glazed with pimiento pepper gelée, warmed, sliced, and served with reindeer lichen (sea moss), which has a nutty, almost mushroom-like quality. We present this at the table with light and creamy grits made with a consommé from the shrimp, an homage of sorts to a favorite of the American South: shrimp and grits.

FINDING MYSELF, FOR NOW

After Gilt, I spent a few years in the culinary wilderness, consulting for a variety of restaurateurs. While it was a period of relative professional stagnation, it was also a time of personal evolution. While at Gilt, I had met and fallen in love with a member of the service team, a captain named Arleene Oconitrillo, and our relationship had flowered into a full-fledged, long-term love affair. We decided to move in together, into an apartment in downtown Manhattan in 2006.

Relationships are never easy, and those between restaurant professionals can be especially trying. But for us, it was a perfect fit, each encouraging the other in our work, while forgiving each other our scarcity of leisure time (though we did our best to spend our Sundays together, a tradition we continue to this day). About a year after we moved in together, we adopted a dog, a "Hispanic Jack Russell" named Spencer who added immeasurably to our lives, bringing out a side of me I'd never seen before, an almost paternal instinct that made me want to be a better person.

Having been the chef at a number of restaurants, and being a little older, I finally had a chance to reflect on just what I wanted my food to be. It

From the Garden

This dish (shown on pages 202-203), our most celebrated upon Corton's opening, is my homage of sorts to Michel Bras, the French chef whose deft and artful touch with vegetables was legendary and inspirational, and whose restaurant I had once eaten at. The simplicity of this plate is deceptive because vegetables are so much more delicate than, say, a piece of beef: cooking them is all about feeling, almost intuiting, where they are in the process. For example, cooking a carrot *sous vide* means ensuring that all of the natural carotene remains inside. I remember saying to my cooks that I wanted the vegetables for this dish "not too cooked, not too raw." This ever-changing composition could include as many as thirty-eight types of vegetables on one plate and

was a powerful and productive time for self-reflection. Just as one matures through the years, so too does one's food. I came to a number of conclusions about what I wanted to do next. First and foremost, I wanted to continue to push myself and my cooks to execute at the absolute highest level. Second, I wanted to remain true to myself and my food, to continue to evolve and not take backward steps in order to feel more secure or stable. Third, I wanted to honor the other side of the equation, the pure pleasure of the guest, more than I might have done in my earlier years, to yoke my abilities and passion to the expectations and cravings of the diner. And fourth, I wanted to earn those Michelin stars.

In summary, I wanted to create a menu and a dining experience that were equal parts ambition and accessibility, and to, as they say here in America, knock it out of the park.

In 2007, a mutual friend arranged a coffee between me and Drew Nieporent—the garrulous restaurateur behind such successes as Nobu and Tribeca Grill—who was looking to do something with his space on West Broadway in TriBeCa, the original site of the long-shuttered Montrachet, a restaurant of great historical significance since it launched the careers of Drew and of David Bouley. For our future collaboration, we worked with designer Stephanie Goto to create a look that was sophisticated but under-stated—we wanted to create a kind of hushed dining temple, with a Zen-like serenity. For its name, we settled on Corton, borrowed from an area of Burgundy, linking the restaurant to its past as Montrachet.

With my new mission in mind, and with Arleene on board as our general manager, I began planning the menu, revisiting some successes from Gilt, simplifying them even in name, dropping the "Flavors of" from their titles and simply calling them "Early Spring" or "Winter." I also scaled down some dishes—the foie gras torchon would still be served with a beet and hibiscus glaze, but shed its accompaniments of foie gras royale and brioche and quail

---

SAFFRON VANILLA FUDGE Even though the acclaim for Corton meant New York had embraced me at last, this dish suggests that maybe I was homesick after all. It's a tribute to classical British fudge, flavored with green tea, saffron, and salted British butter, and is slow cooked for four hours.

The recipe for Saffron Vanilla Fudge, Banana Ganache, Matcha can be found on page 262.

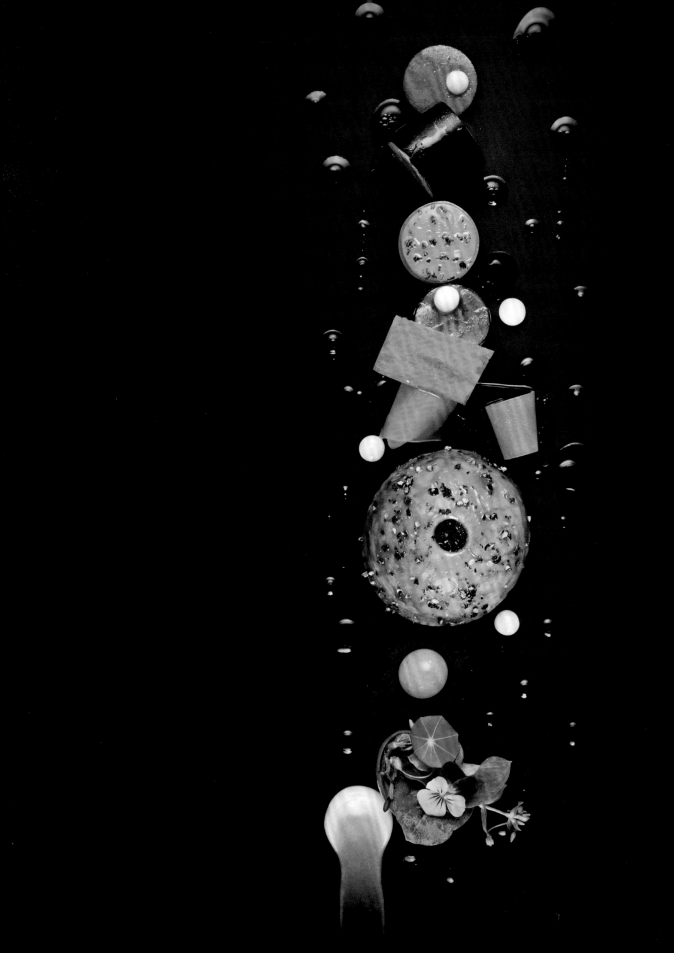

egg composition from Gilt. It was invaluable to have Arleene alongside for this period of my life, somebody who had only my best interests in mind and understood me, in some ways, better than I did myself. With her and her impeccable taste and instincts at the helm, I wouldn't have to second-guess decisions being made in the front of the house.

Even I could see that my food sparkled with a new clarity and focus. Balancing the thematic exercises such as the seasonal tributes were more conventional offerings, such as a velouté of Jerusalem artichokes served over peekytoe crab, and a squash soup paired with tempura porcini mushrooms and a porcini relish, a tribute to the coming fall.

The build out of the restaurant took ages, as is unfortunately commonplace in New York City. Finally, just before we were set to open, the financial crisis of 2008 hit, throwing the world in general, and the restaurant industry in particular, into a tailspin. But we decided to stay the course—what choice did we have?—and launched as planned on October 1, without adjusting our menu or our ambitions.

The dish that drew the most attention right out of the gate at Corton was From the Garden, an ever-changing selection of vegetable preparations, artfully arranged on one plate, and a visual knockout when it arrived at the table. It was a pure expression of my sensibility, but also something that food lovers of all stripes and levels of sophistication could embrace. My evolving approach and maturity were captured in a single offering. Every dish on the menu bore the mark of my palate and my graphic visual style, but in a more universally accessible package.

Despite the backdrop of financial calamity, we were an instant success, drawing food enthusiasts, writers, and bloggers in equal measure. The

---

DUCK/CARROT/MEYER LEMON An encapsulation of my mission at Corton is a variety of duck and carrot preparations. I challenged myself to devise as many iterations of those two primary ingredients as possible, such as a duck torte with salad, cold terrine of duck with carrot meringue, and duck sausage with carrot noodles. It was a revisiting of my entire career, from my young cook days, where I was schooled in never wasting any part of an ingredient, to where I had arrived in my own kitchen at last.

The recipe for Duck Leg Torte, a dish I originally served as part of a multi-preparation duck course, can be found on page 264.

reviews for Corton were rapturous: three stars from the *New York Times* (with an implication of possible four-stardom ahead) and four out of five stars from *New York* magazine. The James Beard Foundation nominated us as Best New Restaurant, and *Food & Wine* magazine proclaimed me one of the nation's Best New Chefs. The *Times* review was especially gratifying after the disappointment of Gilt; best of all was the headline, "Imagination, Say Hello to Discipline." I couldn't have written a better credo myself.

All of this attention was gratifying and—to be honest—a relief. The quips of dissenting critics, the misstep of those Papillon dinners, those years at sea between restaurants . . . I was finally able to let it all go, to do my work in a state of security and serenity, knowing that, at long last, New York considered me as much a part of it as I had always considered myself.

B y the following fall, there was one more critical hurdle looming on the horizon. That October, *The Michelin Guide* was to announce its class of 2010.

It had been a Michelin month for me leading up to this moment of reckoning. England's Heston Blumenthal and Spain's Juan Mari Arzak—both three-star gods—had each been in to dinner at Corton, and I had visited with them at the end of their meals. The visits quickly turned into mentoring sessions, with each of them offering me unfiltered advice, the kind of knowledge that could only be imparted by toques of their caliber. (The same thing happened when I was passing through Yountville, California, that season, and had breakfast with Thomas Keller.) Because I had been on the radar for almost a decade, ever since I first came on the New York scene at Atlas, there was a feeling around the culinary world that I had arrived, and Corton had become a mandatory stop for great chefs passing through New York.

There was a subtext to these impromptu meetings, a sense that I was being welcomed into the fold, that approval was being conferred upon me in

---

COLD SWORDFISH AND PERSIMMON TERRINE WITH RICOTTA A refreshing and whimsical dish from Corton, this is designed to tease and awaken the palate with its ceviche of fish, sweet fruit, and the ricotta's lactic quality.

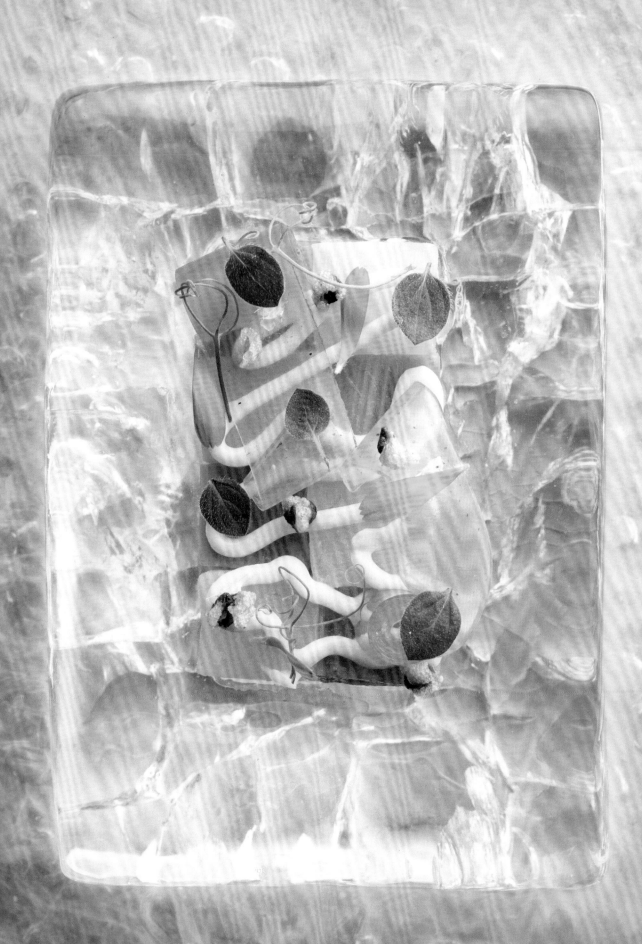

Smoked Caramel and Pomegranate

Just as I did when I was a young boy, I continue to go to the movies in my adopted home of New York City, sometimes on my own and sometimes with Arleene. There's only one thing missing for me here in America: Butterkist, the British concession stand favorite that I so enjoyed with my dad at the movies.

This smoked caramel and pomegranate dish runs that craving through the auteurist mind of a cinema-loving chef. I'm particularly proud of the interplay of textures and flavors in the mouth and with the pomegranate caramel, composed of pomegranate juice, isomalt, glucose, and a pinch of malic acid. After it's baked, it can be pulled into whatever shape you like. Its origins lay in childhood, but the connotations for my restaurant customers couldn't be more adult. Its regal combination of caramel and smoke might make you feel like you're sitting in a red leather armchair, perhaps in Scotland, sipping an aged Balvenie— a surprising but perfectly logical marriage of a childhood treat and a sophisticated adult indulgence.

a not-so-secret society. In accordance with this, it felt natural to ask advice, and much of what I got in return was essential to my career. A highlight of this period was when my muse, Pierre Gagnaire, came to dinner at Corton (alas, he didn't remember my working for him). In an English-French conversation that lasted about ninety minutes, he told me, "Be true to yourself." It was heartening and reaffirming. I'd always been true to myself, but it wasn't always easy. (Gagnaire's visit was also momentous for another reason: I'd never had a chance to tell him what an impact he'd had on me, and finally got to say the words, "You changed my life.")

This company and acceptance was all perfectly lovely, but it also had the quality of a dream. None of it would be real until I felt the sword of the Michelin Man on my shoulder, dubbing me into stardom. The Sunday prior to the announcements, I was out to dinner with Arleene, our mutual night off, and I was a wreck. Michelin had only been a part of the U.S. dining landscape since 2005. But for those of us who came up in Europe, *The Michelin Guide* had been around for more than a century and remained *the* final word on your success or failure. I had spent my early years in Michelin-focused Europe, and it would mean the world to me. I was so consumed with anticipation that I cannot even remember where we went or what I had for dinner that night.

The morning of the day the Michelin news was to be released, I was surprised at home with an early-morning cell phone call. It was *The Michelin Guide*'s director at the time, Jean-Luc Naret. On hearing his voice, I had a feeling that fortune was about to smile on me, because Naret was known for delivering exceptionally good news himself, phoning first-time star recipients and those moving up from one to two or two to three.

"Paul, I wanted to be the first to tell you," he said. "You're going right in with two."

I exhaled and released a pressure that had been steadily mounting since I first became a cook. I thanked Naret for the call and headed off to Corton,

---

"THE MARINE" From Corton, this dish of oyster, green apple, onion meringue, and shallot cream evokes one of my favorite scents, the essence of the ocean, so perfectly captured by the French term for sea foam, *écume de mer*. That faint oceanic smell never fails to take me back to my first days at St. Aubyns.

a little-boy grin on my face. On arrival at the restaurant, I looked over my kitchen, the cooks going about their work, same as they were in similar kitchens all over the world.

I called everybody to attention, had them get into formation along the line. I detected a collective shudder. They'd known that the Michelin verdict was imminent but had no idea if this was to be a celebration or a firing squad. I took a long pause, for effect, to own the news by myself for just a moment longer before sharing it.

"We got two," I said.

The celebration was muted. It had taken so much work to get there, and there had been so much anticipation, that it hardly seemed real. Everybody nodded and smiled. We took a break and had coffee together. And then we got back to work.

It was a funny day. The news wouldn't be officially released until a party planned for that evening, so although I knew what had transpired, few others did. The only plaudits that rolled in were from fellow inductees and multi-starred chefs. Daniel Boulud, a generous soul who was elevated from two stars to three that day, sent me a text saying, "If I were fourteen years old today, I'd want to come work for you."

But I have to be honest: Earning those stars offered me temporary satisfaction, which is the only form of satisfaction a chef can afford to indulge in. Within an hour, I felt a desire to harness our sudden momentum and push to the next level. Maybe it's because I'm the son of a military man or because I was professionally raised by perfectionists, but I found myself immediately restless, just as I was at Atlas after receiving three stars from the *Times*. I grabbed a menu and ushered my sous-chef, Ari Weiswasser, over to a banquette.

"This isn't three-star food," I told him. We took the whole menu apart and began thinking of ways to further refine each and every dish. That might

---

BEEF/CRAYFISH/ALMONDS/MORELS The dance and play of flavors in this springtime dish served at Corton remind me of cooking at Pierre Gagnaire, with its mingling of fifty-day-aged black Angus beef and crayfish. The cooking is very precise: the crayfish are cooked for exactly three minutes and forty seconds in a court bouillon, then brushed with almond oil.

sound severe, but the truth is that chefs—real, working chefs—don't think about "making it." Because the moment you do, you're finished. The nature of a chef's work is unique because we have to re-create our success from scratch every day. Yesterday's triumphant service doesn't mean anything to today's customer. And the experience of the happy loving couple at Table 12 has no bearing on the group of four at Table 16. You re-create and reaffirm your success with every plate that leaves the pass. Yesterday doesn't mean a thing. And neither does the first seating that just wrapped up five minutes ago. It's all about the next one. For all that's different in my profession since I started cooking, that's one thing that will never change.

This dish from Corton, pictured on pages 218-219, sums up my feelings about the intersection of life and food. Put aside for a moment the techniques required to create it, and appreciate everything it allows me to say: an expression of wonder at life moving all around, and yet, at the center of it all, the purple potato ice cream. I didn't conceive the dish with this in mind, but when I look at it, I recognize that I am that ice cream, surrounded by new influences and ingredients, new ideas and inspirations, trying to make sense of it all and to answer the question, Who Am I?

It's the query that keeps me looking forward and backward in time, drawing on the past even as I shape my future. Decades from now, when my work is done, I hope to have solved the Puzzle of Paul, at least on the plate. In the meantime, I will continue to revise and rewrite my menu—a biography expressed in a dozen or so dishes—until it's all clear to me, until everything I've learned and done comes together the way it was meant to.

I just hope there's time enough to get there.

EPILOGUE

I never did get the opportunity to push for that third Michelin star, at least not at Corton. In July of this year I left that restaurant and opened the Elm, a new restaurant in the white-hot neighborhood of Williamsburg in the borough of Brooklyn, New York. At the same time, a signature Paul Liebrandt restaurant in Manhattan is in the planning stages. Yet much remains the same. Every morning, around ten, I wave all the cooks in my kitchen to the pass for a meeting. It's one of the few moments before the dinner hour that we set our individual work aside and come together as a unit. As I brief them on menu changes and other news of the day, I can't help but marvel at the continuum in which we all participate. It often seems mere days ago that I was in their position, a young cook, standing amid a sea of blue aprons, eager to learn and to prove myself.

KAMPACHI/HUCKLEBERRY/ROSE/DAIKON Lightly cured *kindai madai* from Japan, mountain huckleberries, and a veil of pickled daikon. The use of rosebud powder as a sort of paint was inspired by the paintings of Cy Twombly.

Can it really have been twenty years since I first took knife in hand, since those formative days when I needed a Simon Davis to take me under his wing and show me the ropes? It hardly seems possible. I still remember my first day in a kitchen, my failed cooking experiments at home, my fledgling sense of mastery over the fundamentals. There are moments when I gaze over my cooks and—for a millisecond—forget what year it is. Am I back at Marco Pierre White's in London? Pierre Gagnaire's in Paris? Maybe it's because so much about so many kitchens is the same: The harsh lighting. The white tiles. The persistent Morse code of knives tapping on cutting boards. Baby-faced cooks in their aprons, learning on the job, simultaneously overwhelmed and exhilarated, and, in direct contrast, the hardened young veterans, swaggering about. It's like that in kitchens all over the world.

But the disorientation doesn't last long. I'm the chef now, responsible for the restaurant's vision, and for the kitchen's success or failure. But things have changed, and so have I. I'm a stern leader, and I expect a lot from my brigade, but I also try to be more supportive than most chefs were when I was coming up, to offer a more nurturing environment, to not simply throw newcomers to the wolves. Tough but fair would sum it up nicely.

The Food—*my* food—has been a constant evolution, a process of self-discovery carried out in public, on the plate, and evaluated by everybody from customers to critics to those who opine on the Internet and in the blogosphere. The evolution continues today. I'm not one to dwell or to wallow. My menu has always changed often, and I hope it always will. I don't seek or desire a set menu of signature dishes that I can lean on. Maybe it's because I'm such a fan of music, an ever-changing medium in which artists release new works with regularity, that I don't want my food to become stagnant, but rather to evolve on an almost daily basis. Even my most popu-

---

JAPANESE SARDINE WITH YUZU-RICOTTA WHEY AND FRESH CHICKPEA
Come to Scandinavia . . . via Japan. We call this dish "Smoke and Winter" on my menu, where we serve it during the dead of winter. The Japanese sardine, more gently flavored than its European counterpart, underscores the crispness of the season. The smokiness of the trout roe combats the sardine's chill, as does the warmth of the yuzu-ricotta whey and the grilled peanut oil that dresses the chickpea.

lar dishes are eventually retired or temporarily retired, even the From the Garden starter that drew such accolades when Corton opened. I could have served that until the end of my cooking days, but it's my fervent belief that once you start resting on your laurels as a chef, you have set yourself on the path to obsolescence.

It will be an evolution for me to have two venues under my leadership at one time, each offering its own singular style of cuisine and providing me an opportunity to give voice to different sides of my personality, to create menus and experiences that conjure distinct tones, moods, and points of view.

The Elm offers a less formal version of what we did at Corton or will likely do at the new Manhattan restaurant, with a focus on the building blocks of cooking, of letting the ingredients speak for themselves. We focus on fundamental techniques, emphasizing the nature of each dish's primary ingredient. (In some ways, I'm reminded of the two dining venues at L'Escargot, with a casual restaurant downstairs and smaller, more refined venue on the second floor.) Fine dining is a rewarding milieu in which to work, but it's not for everybody. The Elm offers Paul Liebrandt food in an environment that is more affordable. It's food that marks a return to my culinary roots and to the kind of food we chefs like to eat ourselves—truth be told, most of us keep it simple when we dine out.

Beyond the invigoration that comes from having new outlets for creativity, the new restaurants will afford me the chance to grow as a chef, to learn to trust my team in ways I've never had to before. At the same time, I still enjoy cooking, still crave the tactile pleasure of butchering fish or making fresh pasta, and still revel in the challenges and rhythms of a service—all the things that drew me to this business in the first place. As I continue to grow and develop, my goal will be to never lose sight of the young man who began washing dishes one summer and fell in love with cooking. It's that passion that has never waned and that will see me through the good and bad times ahead as I continue to define myself through The Food.

FOIE GRAS/CRAB/RED CABBAGE/ELDERFLOWER The red cabbage, purple mustard, and huckleberry set a mood, anchored by the foie gras, crab, and creamy mustard at the bottom—a study in food as tone.

A Note About the Recipes

Quantities of many of the ingredients in the following recipes are expressed in both volume and weight. For the best, most successful results, I encourage you to use a kitchen scale (inexpensive digital models are readily available to purchase online and in many kitchen supply stores), because weight is the only guarantee of precision. This is especially relevant in recipes that call on additives such as xanthan gum, Gellan, and Activa, where exactitude is a prerequisite for success. The volume measures are provided for your convenience, to give a sense of approximately how much of a given ingredient is required, but weights should be your guide as you prepare and cook these recipes.

"PAPA" Pierre Gagnaire, our culinary father

COMPOSITION POMMES DE TERRE

MAKES 6 SERVINGS

FOR THE POMMES MAXIM

2 large Yukon gold potatoes, preferably refrigerated for three weeks, peeled

½ pound (2 sticks, 227 grams) unsalted butter, melted and clarified (see Note)

1 tablespoon (25 grams) Crisp Film (see Sources, page 268)

FOR THE ALIGOT ESPUMA

6 large Yukon gold potatoes, preferably refrigerated for three weeks, peeled

¼ cup (50 grams) whole milk

¼ cup (75 grams) water

1½ cups (150 grams) Laguiole cheese (Comté may be substituted)

0.38 gram xanthan gum (see Sources, page 268)

Fleur de sel

Freshly ground black pepper

1 large (26.5 grams) organic egg white

FOR THE POTATO FONDANT

2 pounds (1 kilogram) large Yukon gold potatoes, peeled

1 teaspoon (5 grams) fleur de sel, plus more for serving

¼ pound (1 stick, 113 grams) unsalted butter

3 tablespoons (50 grams) duck fat (see Sources, page 268)

4 teaspoons (70 grams) Brown Chicken Stock (page 239)

2 teaspoons (10 grams) truffle juice (see Sources, page 268)

Freshly ground green peppercorns, to taste

MAKE THE POMMES MAXIM

Use a cylinder cutter to punch the potatoes into long cylinders. Use a paring knife to trim the cylinders to 1 inch long, then slice each cylinder on a mandoline into quarter-size circles. You should have at least 100 pieces.

Fill a large bowl halfway with ice water. Set aside.

Fill a medium, heavy pot with water and bring to a boil over high heat. Reduce the heat to medium, add the potato circles, and cook for 1 minute. Remove the circles from the water with a slotted spoon and transfer to the ice bath. Once the circles have cooled, drain them and spread them out on a paper towel–lined sheet tray. Place additional paper towels on top of the potatoes and gently pat dry, replacing towels as necessary until no excess water remains.

Preheat a convection oven to 300°F (149°C) with the fan set to 3. Combine the clarified butter and the Crisp Film in a medium bowl. Whisk together until fully incorporated. Transfer the butter mixture to a large, heavy pot and place over low heat. Add the dried potato circles.

Set a sheet tray upside down and top with a Silpat liner. Remove a small handful of potatoes from the butter, letting the excess butter drip off. Arrange 9 potatoes in an overlapping circle on the Silpat (each coin overlapping about 50 percent, with the 9th piece lifted to overlap the first). Add a 10th potato over the space in the center. Repeat with the remaining potato circles, arranging the rounds to fit all 10 completed circles on the tray.

Top the filled tray with another Silpat and place a very flat heavy metal tray on top (to press down on the potatoes). Transfer the tray to the oven and bake for 11 minutes. Rotate the tray and bake for another 11 minutes, until the potatoes are crisp all the way through and translucent with a very light sheen, but not browned. If more time is needed, keep rotating the pan and baking in 2-minute increments, until the potatoes are cooked.

(recipe continues)

Remove the tray from the oven and cool completely, keeping the potatoes covered with the second tray. Once they are cool, uncover the tray and carefully remove the potato pieces. Trim the potato rounds into perfect circles. Store the circles, layered on parchment paper, in an airtight container until needed. (The circles can be stored for up to two days in a dry, cool place. This recipe produces 4 more circles than you need; choose the most perfect ones for the dish and use the rest as a garnish.)

MAKE THE ALIGOT ESPUMA

Preheat the oven to 350°F (177°C). Wrap the potatoes in aluminum foil and place on a baking tray. Bake until the potatoes are cooked through and fork-tender, 45 to 60 minutes (cooking time will vary depending on potato size). Remove and set the potatoes aside to cool for 20 minutes. Unwrap the potatoes and cut each one in half lengthwise. Scoop about 1 cup (225 grams) of the flesh out of the skins. Discard the skins and any extra flesh, and press the flesh through a ricer.

In a Thermomix, combine the riced potatoes, the milk, and the water. While blending, bring the mixture to 167°F (75°C). Add the cheese and cook and blend the mixture until completely emulsified. Add the xanthan gum and season with fleur de sel and pepper. Turn off the heat and blend in the egg white. Strain the mixture into a small siphon canister and charge with one N_2O cartridge. Keep the mixture warm (around 140°F or 60°C) until needed.

MAKE THE POTATO FONDANT

Cut the potatoes into 1¼ × ¾-inch barrels. Put the potatoes, fleur de sel, and butter in a vacuum bag and seal at 100 percent vacuum. Bring a water bath in an immersion circulator to 194°F (90°C) and add the bag. Cook until the potatoes are just cooked through and tender but still retaining their shape, about 40 minutes.

Remove the potatoes from the bag and drain. Use a ¼-inch punch to punch through the center of each potato barrel lengthwise to form a hollow cylinder, discarding the center. Heat a large, heavy pan over low to medium heat and add the potato cylinders and the duck fat. Cook until the potatoes are lightly browned, then pour in the chicken stock. Cook until the stock forms a syrupy consistency, about 5 minutes. Add the truffle juice and peppercorns to the pan and stir to just combine. Spoon the glaze over the potatoes and cook for 1 more minute. The potatoes should retain their shape and be tender to the bite. Season to taste and remove the potatoes from the pan.

TO ASSEMBLE THE DISH

Pipe the warm espuma into the center of each fondant. Top each filled fondant with a pommes maxim, sprinkle with fleur de sel, and serve.

CLARIFIED BUTTER To clarify butter, put it in a small, heavy pot and patiently melt it over low heat, not allowing it to brown. As the butter melts, the milk solids will separate. Remove the pot from the heat, use a tablespoon to skim off those solids that have risen to the top, and carefully pour out the butter fat, taking care to leave any solids at the bottom of the pot behind.

WHITE ASPARAGUS

**SERVES 6 AS AN APPETIZER,
2 SPEARS PER SERVING**

My method for cooking asparagus. These may
be served on their own or dressed with the
Plum Extra-Virgin Olive Oil on page 253.

2 large spears white asparagus, peeled with a
  vegetable peeler

1 tablespoon plus 1½ teaspoons (20 grams)
  hazelnut oil

1 cup (10 grams) fresh orange peel, removed in
  strips with no pith attached

1 teaspoon (5 grams) fleur de sel

1 tablespoon (10 grams) freshly squeezed
  lemon juice

Put the asparagus, hazelnut oil, orange peel, fleur
de sel, and lemon juice in a large vacuum bag and
seal at 100 percent vacuum. Bring a water bath in
an immersion circulator to 185°F (85°C) and add
the bag. Cook until the asparagus is just cooked
through but still crisp and slightly firm to the touch,
15 to 20 minutes. (Pinch the asparagus through
the plastic to check for doneness.)

Fill a large bowl halfway with ice water. Use tongs
to remove the bag from the water bath and set
aside at room temperature for 15 minutes, then
further cool in the ice water until the spears are
34°F (1.1°C), 1½ to 2 hours.

Remove the bag from the ice bath and remove the
asparagus spears. Use a kitchen towel to dry the
spears and store the asparagus in the refrigerator
until ready to use. Serve cold.

STILTON-GREEN GARLIC CRÈME

MAKES 1 PINT (473 MILLILITERS)

1½ teaspoons (2.5 grams) unsalted butter

1 cup thinly sliced sweet onions, such as Vidalia
  (100 grams sliced)

¾ cup (150 grams) thinly sliced ramps plus
  3 tablespoons (28 grams) ramp greens
  (leaves)

Fleur de sel

Freshly ground black pepper

¾ cup (175 grams) skim milk

1 large (40 grams) egg, brought to room
  temperature

0.5 gram xanthan gum (see Sources,
  page 268)

1½ ounces (42.5 grams) Stilton cheese

2 tablespoons (40 grams) mascarpone cheese

Heat a large, heavy pan over medium-low heat.
Add the butter and let it melt to coat the pan. Add
the onions and ¾ cup ramps, and cook gently until
tender but not browned, about 4 minutes. Slice
the ramp greens into thin slivers.

Season the cooking vegetables with the fleur
de sel and pepper. Pour in the milk, cover with
a cartouche (see Note, page 234), and reduce
the heat to low. Cook for 25 minutes, or until the
vegetables have softened, then uncover the pan
and stir in the ramp greens. Remove the pan from
the heat and set aside to cool for 10 minutes.

Soft-poach the egg, by first heating a water bath
in an immersion circulator to 145°F (62.7°C).
Put the whole egg directly into the bath and cook
for 45 minutes. Remove with a slotted spoon and
crack to open.

Transfer the contents of the pan to a high-speed
blender and blend until a smooth puree forms,
about 2 minutes. With the motor running, sprinkle

(recipe continues)

in the xanthan gum, then add the poached egg, Stilton, and mascarpone. Blend until the mixture is completely emulsified, about 2 more minutes. Season with fleur de sel and pepper. Set a chinois or very fine-mesh strainer over a large bowl and strain the mixture. Set aside to cool.

When ready to use, warm the puree in a medium pot over low heat, but do not allow it to boil.

CARTOUCHE A cartouche is a parchment-paper lid that slows the reduction of liquids and helps prevent ingredients from over-browning. To make a cartouche, begin with a square piece of parchment paper slightly larger than the vessel the cartouche will cover. (Waxed paper may also be used.) Fold the square in half, then in half again. Keeping one open end as the "top" of the cartouche, fold the square diagonally into a triangle, and continue to fold the triangle over and over, keeping an open side as the top, until the bottom tip has narrowed to a point. Holding the tip of the cartouche over the very center of the pan, cut off any paper from the open back end that extends beyond the edge of the pan. Open the paper into a circle.

TAPIOCA CELERY JUS
MAKES 10 SERVINGS

Noble Sour vinegar is a crucial ingredient in this recipe. It can be difficult to find, but may be available from local specialty and gourmet shops.

1 cup (150 grams) small pearl tapioca

4 stalks celery, washed, 15 leaves reserved, washed, delicately dried, and cut into chiffonade

1½ cups (375 grams) White Chicken Stock (recipe follows)

¼ cup (100 grams) celery juice

1 teaspoon (5 grams) truffle juice (see Sources, page 268)

½ teaspoon (2.5 grams) Noble Sour vinegar, to taste

1 teaspoon (10 grams) minced fresh black truffle

1 teaspoon (10 grams) finely diced green mango

15 leaves cilantro, washed, delicately dried, and cut into chiffonade

Fleur de sel

Freshly ground black pepper

Put the tapioca in a medium bowl, cover with cold water, cover loosely with plastic wrap, and refrigerate overnight.

When you're ready to proceed, strain the soaked tapioca through a fine-mesh strainer set over the sink. Heat a medium, heavy pot over low heat. Add the tapioca and celery to the pot, then pour in the chicken stock to cover the tapioca. Bring to a simmer and lower the heat to maintain a simmer without allowing the stock to boil. Cook, stirring continuously, until the tapioca is translucent and thickened, about 20 minutes. Stir in the celery juice and cook over low heat for 5 minutes.

Remove the pot from the heat and set a chinois or very fine-mesh strainer over a medium bowl. Pass the mixture through the strainer, pressing on the solids with a spatula, to extract as much flavorful jus as possible. Discard the solids and set the liquid aside to cool. (The jus can be stored in an airtight container in the refrigerator for up to three days.)

When ready to serve, stir the truffle juice and vinegar into the jus, then gently stir in the black truffle, green mango, celery leaves, and cilantro leaves. Reheat gently in a small pot, season with fleur de sel and pepper, and stir to incorporate.

WHITE CHICKEN STOCK
MAKES 2 GALLONS (8 LITERS)

2.6 gallons (10 liters) cold water

8 pounds (3.6 kilograms) whole chickens (hearts, gizzard, and neck, if present, removed and discarded or saved for another use)

4 stalks lemongrass, smashed and thinly sliced

2 carrots, peeled and thinly sliced

4 Spanish onions, very thinly sliced

2 heads garlic, smashed and peeled

½ bunch lemon thyme (regular thyme may be substituted)

5 bay leaves, preferably fresh

20 whole black peppercorns

Heat a very large, heavy stockpot over medium heat and add the water, chickens, lemongrass, carrots, onions, garlic, lemon thyme, bay leaves, and peppercorns. Bring to a simmer and cook for 2 hours. Adjust the heat as necessary to keep the liquid from boiling. Use a tablespoon to skim off any fat and impurities that rise to the surface.

Remove the pot from the heat and set aside at room temperature for 10 minutes. Skim off any remaining fat that rises to the surface. Strain the mixture through a cheesecloth-lined strainer to remove any stray particles. (The stock can be refrigerated in an airtight container for up to one week, or divided into smaller airtight containers and refrigerated for up to one month.)

BLOWFISH WITH VADOUVAN SPICE AND BURNT LAUREL

MAKES 6 SERVINGS, 2 PIECES PER SERVING

Make this dish with East Coast blowfish, not the notorious Japanese fugu, which can be toxic. (You will likely need to ask your fishmonger to special order the fish in advance.)

¼ cup (30 grams) fleur de sel

5 cups (1,000 grams) cold water

12 pieces blowfish loin, about 3 ounces (85 grams) each

3 tablespoons (30 grams) vadouvan spice (see Sources, page 268)

2 tablespoons (15 grams) extra-virgin olive oil

24 pieces laurel leaf (aka fresh bay leaf)

Make a salt brine by combining the fleur de sel and the water in a medium, heavy pot. Bring to a boil over high heat and allow the salt to fully dissolve. Remove the pot from the heat, let the liquid cool, transfer to an airtight container, and refrigerate overnight.

Arrange the blowfish loin pieces in a glass baking dish or other shallow vessel in a single layer, and pour the salt brine over the pieces to submerge them. Cover loosely with plastic wrap and refrigerate for 1 hour.

Remove the blowfish and rinse under cold running water for 10 seconds. Thoroughly pat the blowfish dry with a paper towel. Line a baking tray with a kitchen towel and top with the blowfish pieces. Place another towel on top and put the tray in the refrigerator to dry the blowfish for 2 hours.

Put the vadouvan spice and oil in a medium mixing bowl and stir together with a spoon until incorporated. Remove the blowfish from the refrigerator and dress each piece with the spiced oil, turning to coat evenly. Cover the bowl with plastic wrap and refrigerate overnight to cure the blowfish.

Preheat the broiler to high. Line a sheet tray with a Silpat and place the blowfish on the tray. Arrange 2 laurel leaves over each piece of fish. Place the tray under the broiler and broil, until the outside of the blowfish is lightly caramelized and the leaves are just lightly smoldering, not blackened, 4 to 6 minutes. The blowfish should register an internal temperature of 118°F (48°C) on a digital thermometer. Remove the tray from the broiler and set aside to rest for 5 minutes before serving.

VADOUVAN SPICE Vadouvan is a variation on garam masala that combines onions, shallots, and garlic with spices found in Indian curry. There are many different blends; ours features cardamom, cumin, black pepper, dry orange, fennel seed, and anise.

BRAISED LAMB NECK

SERVES 6

Here I share the recipe for the neck preparation that is pictured on page 75. Note that the marinade needs to be refrigerated for three days and that the lamb itself must be patiently cooked for seven hours, then refrigerated overnight to set its shape. But it is worth the effort. This dish is made with lamb neck, which has a perfect balance of meat and fat. It's a muscle that has a phenomenal flavor—not as gamy as leg and not as mild as a loin of lamb. For the best flavor and marbling, make this with a cut from a young spring lamb. This dish would pair well with Moroccan elements such as couscous with candied almonds, raisins, and feta.

FOR THE LAMB NECK MARINADE

15 pods (3.75 grams) green cardamom

2 heads garlic, separated into cloves, peeled, halved lengthwise, germ removed (100 grams peeled cloves)

2 medium shallots, thinly sliced (50 grams sliced)

3 sprigs thyme, stems only

1 teaspoon (15 grams) whole coffee beans, preferably Arabica

1½ pounds (700 grams) lamb neck, off bone (ask your butcher to debone the neck before weighing out the meat), cut into 4-inch segments

FOR THE BRAISING LIQUID

½ sprig flat-leaf parsley

½ star anise

2½ teaspoons (12.5 grams) fennel seeds

⅛ teaspoon (0.16 gram) whole black peppercorns

⅛ teaspoon (0.16 gram) whole cumin seeds

Kosher salt

Freshly ground black pepper

1 tablespoon (5 grams) lamb fat or duck fat (both available on request from many butchers)

2 medium cloves garlic, peeled, halved lengthwise, germ removed (12 grams peeled cloves)

½ medium shallot, thinly sliced (25 grams sliced)

1 stalk lemongrass, smashed with the edge of a chef's knife and thinly sliced (100 grams sliced)

1 tablespoon fresh ginger, peeled and thinly sliced (6.25 grams sliced)

1½ cups (200 grams) robust red wine such as Shiraz

¼ cup (25 grams) red wine vinegar

½ cup (75 grams) nut brown ale such as Newcastle Brown Ale

4 cups (800 grams) Brown Chicken Stock (recipe follows)

MAKE THE LAMB NECK MARINADE

Heat a medium, heavy pan over medium heat. Add the cardamom pods to the pan and toast them, shaking the pan to prevent browning or scorching, until they are fragrant, 3 to 5 minutes. Set the pan aside and let the pods cool, then transfer them to a spice grinder and grind them.

Put the garlic, shallots, thyme, coffee beans, and ground cardamom in the bowl of a food processor fitted with the steel blade. Pulse until a paste forms. Put the lamb pieces in a baking dish in a single layer and rub the marinade over the meat, thoroughly coating all sides. Cover with plastic wrap and refrigerate for three days.

(recipe continues)

MAKE THE BRAISING LIQUID

Preheat the oven to 250°F (121°C). Put the parsley, star anise, fennel seeds, peppercorns, and cumin seeds in the center of a 6-inch-square piece of cheesecloth. Gather up the cheesecloth by the corners and tie it closed with kitchen twine to make a sachet. Remove the lamb from the marinade and brush off any excess solids. Season the lamb with salt and pepper.

Heat a large, heavy Dutch oven or other wide, deep pot over medium-high heat. Add the lamb or duck fat and let it melt, coating the bottom of the pan. Add the lamb pieces and sear, using a pair of tongs to turn the lamb as it lightly browns, about 2 minutes per side. Once the lamb is evenly browned, remove it from the pot and set it aside.

Turn the heat down to low and add the garlic, shallot, lemongrass, and ginger to the Dutch oven. Cook, stirring with a wooden spoon, until the vegetables are browned, about 5 minutes. Pour in the red wine, red wine vinegar, and the ale and add the sachet. Use the spoon to scrape off any flavorful bits stuck to the bottom of the Dutch oven. Bring the liquids to a boil, then lower the heat so the liquid is simmering and continue to simmer until the liquid has reduced by half, about 8 minutes.

Set a small wire rack in the Dutch oven, atop the reduced vegetable mixture. Arrange the seared lamb on top of the rack so that the lamb and other solids are separated, and pour in the chicken stock to cover by ¼ inch. Cover with a cartouche (see page 234), then cover the Dutch oven with aluminum foil and place in the oven. Braise until the lamb neck is very tender, about 7 hours.

Remove the Dutch oven from the oven and set aside to let the lamb cool. Once cool, remove the lamb and arrange it in a small, shallow pan, making sure there is no space between the pieces. Cover the pan with plastic wrap and top with a pan of equal size, pressing down to help shape the lamb into even blocks. Move the pans to the refrigerator and let sit overnight.

Strain the braising liquid through a chinois or very fine-mesh strainer, discarding the solids. Refrigerate the liquid in an airtight container.

Remove the lamb from the refrigerator and use a sharp knife to trim it into 1 × 1-inch blocks. Rewrap the lamb with the plastic wrap and refrigerate until ready to serve it.

When ready to serve, pour the braising liquid into a large pot and bring to a simmer over low heat. Simmer until the sauce reaches a syrup-like consistency. Add the lamb to the pot and very gently reheat (the lamb will be very tender), glazing it with the reduced braising liquid until the lamb is glazed and lightly warmed through, but still retaining its shape, about 4 minutes. The lamb can be stored in airtight containers, covered in plastic, and reserved in the refrigerator for up to three days.

BROWN CHICKEN STOCK

MAKES 4.2 QUARTS (4 LITERS)

This rich stock, an enhancement of my standard White Chicken Stock, makes a good base for braising liquids, meat-style jus, or a sauce base for meaty fish such as monkfish.

1 cup (200 grams) peanut oil

5 pounds (2.3 kilograms) chicken wings, each cut into four 1-inch pieces

1 pound (4 sticks, 453.5 grams) unsalted butter

4 medium Spanish onions, sliced thinly on a mandoline

2 medium heads garlic, separated into cloves, peeled, halved lengthwise, germ removed

½ bunch thyme

5 bay leaves, preferably fresh

20 whole black peppercorns

10 pounds (4.5 kilograms) chicken carcasses (necks and backs)

1 bottle (750 milliliters) robust red wine such as Shiraz

About 8.4 quarts (8 liters) White Chicken Stock (page 235)

Preheat the oven to 375°F (191°C). Heat a large, heavy pot over medium heat and add the peanut oil and chicken wings. Cook, stirring, until the wings are golden brown all over, about 8 minutes. Turn the heat down to medium-low and add the butter. Cook, stirring, until the butter is nut brown in color and fragrant. Add the onions, garlic, thyme, bay leaves, and peppercorns and cook, stirring occasionally, until the onions are lightly brown, 8 to 10 minutes. Remove from the heat and set aside.

Put the chicken necks and backs on a sheet tray and roast in the oven until the chicken is cooked through and nut brown all over, 35 to 50 minutes. Transfer the necks and backs to a large chinois or very fine-mesh strainer and hold suspended over a bowl for 2 minutes to allow the fat to drip off.

Return the pot with the wings and vegetables to medium heat and pour in the wine. Use a wooden spoon to scrape off any flavorful bits stuck to the bottom of the pot and cook until the mixture is syrupy. Add the necks and backs to the pot and pour in enough chicken stock to cover the solids. Simmer the mixture very gently over low heat for 2 hours, continuously skimming fat off the surface.

Remove the pot from the heat and set aside at room temperature for 10 minutes. Use a tablespoon to skim off any remaining fat that rises to the surface. Strain the mixture through a cheesecloth-lined strainer to remove any stray particles. (The stock can be stored, covered, in the refrigerator for one week or frozen for up to four weeks.)

RABBIT-CUTTLEFISH RILLETTES

MAKES 15 RILLETTES

This recipe uses Activa, a popular brand of the additive transglutaminase, which binds proteins. I use it because it seamlessly achieves a binding effect that traditionally called for the use of an ingredient such as egg whites, which added a flavor of their own. These rillettes may be served as stand-alone canapés; extra confit may be refrigerated and tossed in a simple salad dressed with a sherry vinaigrette.

You may need to plan ahead and ask your fishmonger to special order the cuttlefish.

FOR THE RABBIT CONFIT

5 strips of lemon peel, no pith attached

5 strips of orange peel, no pith attached

10 pods green cardamom

10 whole black peppercorns

1 cup (120 grams) fleur de sel

½ cup (100 grams) granulated sugar

6 pieces (1½ pounds, or 700 grams, total) rabbit shoulder

1½ cups (300 grams) duck fat (see Sources, page 268)

FOR THE GREEN BREAD CRUMBS

1½ cups (180 grams) panko (Japanese bread crumbs)

7 cups (280 grams) loosely packed flat-leaf parsley, coarsely chopped

1 teaspoon (20 grams) extra-virgin olive oil

1 tablespoon (10 grams) matcha green tea powder (see Note)

FOR THE RABBIT-CUTTLEFISH RILLETTES

1 tablespoon (5 grams) duck fat (see Sources, page 268)

2 medium cloves garlic, peeled, germ removed, and finely diced (5 grams diced)

1 tablespoon (15 grams) capers, salt- or brine-packed, rinsed and patted dry

3 ounces raw cuttlefish, cleaned and finely diced (85 grams diced)

1 teaspoon (2.5 grams) piment d'espelette (see Sources, page 268)

7 ounces (200 grams) Rabbit Confit (from recipe above)

1 gram Activa RM (see Sources, page 268)

Fleur de sel

Freshly ground black pepper

1 tablespoon (20 grams) Dijon mustard

MAKE THE RABBIT CONFIT

Put the lemon peel, orange peel, cardamom pods, peppercorns, fleur de sel, and sugar in a large bowl and stir to incorporate. Add the rabbit pieces and toss to coat thoroughly. Line a baking tray with plastic wrap and arrange the pieces on the tray without crowding. Refrigerate for 6 hours to allow the mixture to penetrate the meat.

Remove the rabbit from the refrigerator and rinse under cold running water to wash off the cure. Pat the rabbit dry with paper towels and place in a 12 × 12-inch vacuum bag with the duck fat. Seal the bag at 100 percent vacuum. Bring a water bath in an immersion circulator to 154°F (67.5°C) and add the bag. Cook for 12 hours in the water bath.

Remove the bag from the water, then allow the bags to sit at room temperature for 20 minutes. Fill a large bowl with ice water. Put the room-temperature bags in the ice water and chill for 30 minutes. Drain the ice water and return the bags to the now empty bowl. Cover them completely with ice until the internal temperature of the meat registers 34°F (1.1°C), 1 to 2 hours.

Remove the bags from the ice and cut them open at the top. Remove the rabbit from the bags and pull off all of the meat from the shoulder bones. Discard the bones and use two forks to finely shred the meat. Place the meat in a covered container until ready to use. (The meat can be stored in a container in the refrigerator for up to three days.)

MAKE THE GREEN BREAD CRUMBS

Put the panko, parsley, olive oil, and green tea powder in the bowl of a food processor fitted with the steel blade. Blend on high speed until coarse green bread crumbs form; you should have about 2 cups bread crumbs. Wrap the bread crumbs in plastic wrap. (They can be stored, refrigerated, for up to two days.)

MAKE THE RABBIT-CUTTLEFISH RILLETTE

Heat a medium, heavy skillet over medium heat and add the duck fat, tipping the pan to coat it completely. Add the garlic and capers and cook, stirring, until the garlic is tender but not browned, about 5 minutes. Turn the heat down to low and add the cuttlefish. Cook for 3 minutes, stirring frequently with a spatula to make sure the cuttlefish doesn't brown. Add the piment d'espelette and cook for 1 minute, stirring, to toast the powder.

Remove the pan from the heat, use the spatula to scrape the mixture out into a small, stainless steel vessel, and set aside to cool. Fill a large bowl with ice and set the bowl with the cooled cuttlefish mixture on top. Add the rabbit confit and fold together to incorporate. Dust the mixture with the Activa and fold to incorporate. Season with fleur de sel and pepper to taste.

Spread out a 6 × 6-inch piece of plastic wrap on your work surface and spoon heaping teaspoons of the cuttlefish mixture into the center. Bring all four corners up to meet and twist together to form a tight ball. Repeat until all the mixture is used (you should have about 15 plastic-wrapped balls). Place the prepared balls on a sheet tray and refrigerate for 3 hours to set their shapes.

Remove the balls from the refrigerator and set aside to temper at room temperature for 30 minutes. Bring a water bath in an immersion circulator to 140°F (60°C). Add the plastic-wrapped balls to the water bath and cook for 8 minutes until set. Use a slotted spoon or spider to remove the balls and carefully unwrap them.

Place the balls on a warm baking tray and brush each ball with the Dijon mustard. Place the green bread crumbs in a shallow dish and gently roll the rillettes in the bread crumbs, taking care not to crush them, and evenly coat them. Serve warm. (The rillettes can be stored raw and wrapped in the refrigerator for up to one day.)

Matcha green tea powder is a finely ground Japanese green tea. It can be found in health food stores; see Sources, page 268.

Piment d'espelette is a mild pepper popular in Basque cooking.

SQUID-LEMONGRASS VELOUTÉ
MAKES 1 PINT (473 MILLILITERS)

1 tablespoon (12.5 grams) unsalted butter

12 stalks lemongrass, smashed and thinly
    sliced (600 grams sliced)

2 medium shallots, sliced (50 grams sliced)

1 pinch plus 1 teaspoon (2.5 grams) kosher salt

1 medium clove (7.5 grams) garlic

1 tablespoon grated fresh ginger (7.5 grams
    grated)

2 tablespoons (50 grams) Chartreuse
    (see Sources, page 268)

1 cup (500 grams) White Chicken Stock
    (page 235)

½ cup (250 grams) heavy cream

3.5 ounces (99 grams) squid (body and
    tentacles)

6 stems (5 grams) cilantro, with leaves, plus
    40 leaves (5 grams) cilantro

1 tablespoon (20 grams) mascarpone

3.5 grams soy lecithin powder (see Sources,
    page 268)

0.5 gram xanthan gum (see Sources,
    page 268)

1 tablespoon (22.5 grams) fish sauce

1 tablespoon (25 grams) fresh lemongrass
    juice

Heat a large, heavy pot over medium-low heat.
Add the butter and let melt to coat the pan. Add
½ cup (100 grams) of the lemongrass and cook
for 5 minutes, stirring frequently and making sure
the lemongrass doesn't brown. Add the shallots
and a pinch of salt. (The salt will help draw out the
moisture and prevent browning.) Cook the shallot
mixture for 5 minutes, then add the garlic and the
ginger and continue to cook for 5 more minutes,
stirring frequently so the mixture does not brown.

Pour in the Chartreuse and use a wooden spoon
to scrape off any bits stuck to the bottom of the
pan. Cook until the mixture is dry. Pour in the
chicken stock and cream and raise the heat to
medium. Bring the mixture to a boil, then add the
squid and the remaining lemongrass. Lower the
heat, cover the pot, and simmer for 10 minutes.
Remove the pan from the heat. Add the cilantro
stems and leaves, cover the pot, and set aside for
30 minutes.

Strain the mixture through a fine-mesh strainer
and discard the solids. Transfer the mixture to a
high-speed blender and add the mascarpone,
lecithin, and the xanthan gum. Blend on high
speed for 1 minute to combine. While the mixture
is blending, add the 1 teaspoon salt, the fish sauce,
and lemongrass juice. Set a fine-mesh strainer
over a pot and pour the mixture through the
strainer. Season to taste and keep the velouté
warm to serve. (The velouté can be refrigerated
in an airtight container for up to two days. Reheat
gently before serving.)

TÊTE DE COCHON

MAKES 60 SERVINGS, 2 PIECES PER SERVING

In terms of flavor, this is a very traditional French pig head terrine, but rather than presenting it as an overwhelmingly rich slab of meat, it's etched as a boudin (sausage). One might serve this with a sucrine lettuce salad dressed with sherry vinaigrette, topped with shaved aged gouda cheese, and accompanied by warm toasted brioche.

FOR THE TÊTE DE COCHON

¼ cup (30 grams) fleur de sel

1 teaspoon (10 grams) pink curing salt (sodium nitrite; see Sources, page 268)

10 cups (2,000 grams) cold water

One 5-pound (2.3 kilograms) medium pig head, deboned (special order from your butcher; ask for it to be deboned so you have skin, jowl, and face; reserve everything else for pork stock or soup for another dish)

FOR THE FARCE AND ASSEMBLY

1 large head garlic, separated into cloves, skin intact (50 grams of cloves)

Extra-virgin olive oil

9 ounces (255 grams) pig cheek/neck meat (from recipe above)

1 tablespoon (12.5 grams) thyme leaves

4 ounces (113 grams) brioche bread, crusts removed, soaked for 15 minutes in whole milk, drained, and squeezed out

Fleur de sel

Freshly ground black pepper

1 teaspoon (3 grams) Activa RM (see Sources, page 268)

MAKE THE TÊTE DE COCHON

Put the fleur de sel, the pink salt, and the water in a container large enough to hold the pig head pieces. Add the pieces and refrigerate for 48 hours. (The skin will soften during this time.)

Remove the brined head pieces and discard the liquid. Dry the meat and skin pieces thoroughly by sandwiching them between paper towels and refrigerating them for 6 hours. Slice the pig skin into 8 × 2-inch strips (you should have 15 pieces). Butterfly the strips.

MAKE THE FARCE

Heat a medium, heavy pot over low heat. Add the garlic and pour in just enough olive oil to cover. Cook the garlic at a simmer (never a boil), until the garlic is soft and fork-tender, about 2 hours. Remove the pot from the heat and set aside to cool to room temperature. Remove the garlic from the oil. (The garlic-infused oil can be refrigerated in an airtight container for up to four weeks.) Remove and discard the garlic skins and add the garlic to a blender. Puree until a paste forms (you should have about ½ cup) and set aside until needed.

Fill a large bowl with ice water and set a medium bowl on top. Grind the pig cheek and neck meat through a grinder fitted with a small disc and place the ground meat in the bowl set over the ice bath. Add the garlic confit, thyme, and brioche and use a spatula to fold the mixture together until just incorporated (do not overmix).

Form a small amount of the mixture into a test patty and add the patty to a small, heavy pan set over medium heat. Cook for 1 minute on each side. Check for seasoning and texture; it should be firm yet tender to the bite, like a good sausage. Based on the flavor of the test patty, season the remaining raw mixture with fleur de sel and pepper as needed (this technique is to avoid tasting raw pork, and is necessary due to variations in fat and other factors in different breeds), and transfer it to a large plastic piping bag. Refrigerate until ready to use.

(recipe continues)

TO ASSEMBLE THE DISH

Put the pig strips on a baking tray and pipe a very small amount of the farce in a thin line down the center of each strip. Lightly dust the farce with the Activa. Fold the pig strips over the farce to form a cylinder and use a sharp knife to trim the edges. Lightly roll each cylinder to form a tight boudin and wrap it tightly in plastic wrap, securing the wrap at each end by twisting the plastic tightly. Place on a baking tray and refrigerate overnight.

Remove the chilled boudins from the refrigerator and set them out at room temperature to temper for 30 minutes. Bring a water bath in an immersion circulator to 178°F (81°C). Put the cylinders in a vacuum bag and seal at 100 percent vacuum. Add the cylinders to the water bath and cook for 8 hours.

Remove the cooked boudins and allow them to sit at room temperature for 20 minutes in the bag. Fill a large bowl with ice water and add the boudins to the ice water for 30 minutes. Drain the ice water and cover the boudins fully with ice until the internal temperature registers 34°F (1.1°C), 1 to 2 hours. Remove the boudins from the bag and wrap tightly with fresh plastic wrap. Refrigerate for 2 hours, then slice into 1½-inch discs and serve as desired.

SCALLOP "PASTA"

MAKES 4 BAGS (16 RAVIOLI PER BAG)

This is the "pasta" pictured in the dish on page 110. Another fine use for it would be to cut the pasta into larger pieces and layer it with sautéed porcini mushrooms, like a rustic lasagna.

7 ounces (200 grams) diver scallops

Pinch of fleur de sel

1 gram Activa RM (see Sources, page 268)

Fill a large bowl halfway with ice water. Briefly refrigerate the bowl and blade of a food processor to chill, then set up the processor. Put the scallops and fleur de sel in the bowl of the food processor and process on high until they form a smooth paste but are not liquefied, 10 to 15 seconds, sprinkling in the Activa during that time.

Transfer the mixture to a medium stainless steel bowl and set over the ice bath, stirring until the mixture cools. Divide the mixture evenly among 4 vacuum bags. Without sealing the bags, vacuum each bag three times to remove any air from the mixture. While the mixture is still in the bag, press it into a thin, 9-inch square and seal in the machine at 100 percent vacuum.

Fill a large bowl with ice water.

Bring a water bath in an immersion circulator to 135°F (57°C) and add the bags. Cook for 7 minutes, then remove the bags from the water and place in the ice water bath to chill for 30 minutes. Remove the bags from the ice water and cut open the bags. Use a sharp knife to carefully cut each large square of scallop into 16 squares, each 2 × 2-inches. Fold each square into a 1 × 1-inch ravioli, handling the scallops gently as they are extremely fragile. Serve immediately.

"THE GOLD BAR"

SERVES 12

FOR THE PRESSE

½ cup (50 grams) feuilletine (see Sources, page 268)

1½ cups (150 grams) sucre (or nut-free) crumbs

2½ ounces (70 grams) white chocolate

½ teaspoon (2.5 grams) fleur de sel

FOR THE CARAMEL

3 tablespoons (40 grams) granulated sugar

½ teaspoon (10 grams) glucose syrup (see Sources, page 268)

Pinch of fleur de sel

2 teaspoons (4 grams) cocoa butter

¼ cup (50 grams) heavy cream

1 ounce (28 grams) Jivara 40% chocolate (see Sources, page 268)

1 tablespoon (12.5 grams) unsalted butter

FOR THE CRÉMEUX

2 sheets (5 grams) gelatin

4 large (80 grams) egg yolks

3 tablespoons (40 grams) granulated sugar

1 cup (200 grams) heavy cream

1 cup (200 grams) whole milk

10 ounces (280 grams) Caribe 64% chocolate (see Sources, page 268)

FOR THE GLAÇAGE

2 sheets (5 grams) gelatin

1 cup (180 grams) granulated sugar

¼ cup (60 grams) black cocoa powder (see Sources, page 268)

¼ cup (120 grams) heavy cream

¾ cup (150 grams) water

5 ounces (142 grams) Caribe 64% chocolate (see Sources, page 268)

12 small pieces gold leaf (see Sources, page 268)

MAKE THE PRESSE

Put the feuilletine and sucre crumbs in a food processor fitted with the steel blade and blend on high speed until the mixture is a fine consistency. Transfer the mixture to a bowl and set aside.

Bring a medium pot of water to a simmer over medium heat. Set a heatproof bowl over it to create a double boiler. Add the white chocolate to the bowl and melt the chocolate. Use a rubber spatula to fold the crumb mixture into the chocolate, then fold in the fleur de sel. Remove the bowl from the double boiler.

Lay a large sheet of parchment or waxed paper on a work surface and transfer the mixture to the paper. Top with another piece of parchment or waxed paper, and use a rolling pin to spread the mixture into a 3-millimeter-thick layer. Transfer the sheet to a baking tray and refrigerate until set, about 3 hours.

Place an 8 × 8 × 1-inch mold on top of the sheet and use a sharp knife to cut around the mold. Gently remove the paper and place the presse base into the mold. Refrigerate the mold uncovered. (This can be made and formed one day in advance.)

(recipe continues)

MAKE THE CARAMEL

Heat a medium, heavy pot over medium-low heat. Add the sugar and glucose syrup and cook, stirring, until a light caramel forms, 5 to 10 minutes. Use a rubber spatula to stir in the fleur de sel, cocoa butter, and cream, to help the ingredients emulsify. Reduce the heat to low and add the chocolate and the butter. Continue to stir until the chocolate and butter are melted and the mixture is emulsified. Pour the caramel over the prepared presse to evenly coat it, and continue to chill the mold in the refrigerator until the caramel sets, about 3 hours.

MAKE THE CRÉMEUX

Fill a small bowl with ice water. Add the gelatin and set aside to bloom for 5 minutes.

Bring a medium pot of water to a simmer over medium heat. Set a heatproof bowl over it to create a double boiler. Add the egg yolks, sugar, cream, and milk to the bowl. Whisk to incorporate, then cook the crémeux, stirring with a spatula, until the temperature reaches 187°F (86°C) on a digital thermometer.

Remove the gelatin from the water and use your hands to squeeze the liquid out. Add the gelatin to the crémeux and stir to melt the gelatin completely. Remove the bowl from the double boiler and add the chocolate to the mixture, stirring until the mixture is fully emulsified. Pour the crémeux into the mold on top of the caramel and allow the layers to set in the refrigerator for 4 hours. Once the layers are completely set, remove the mold and cut the bar into 1 × 4-inch pieces.

MAKE THE GLAÇAGE

Fill a small bowl with ice water. Add the gelatin and set aside to bloom for 5 minutes. Sift together the sugar and the black cocoa through a fine-mesh sieve into a medium bowl.

Heat a medium, heavy pot over medium heat. Whisk in the cream and water and bring to a boil. Whisk in the sugar-cocoa mixture until fully incorporated. Continue to boil until the sugar is dissolved. Remove the gelatin from the water and use your hands to squeeze the liquid out. Add the gelatin to the mixture and stir to combine. Once the gelatin has melted, remove the pot from the heat and stir in the chocolate, mixing with a rubber spatula until the glaçage is emulsified.

Fill a large bowl with ice water. Place a medium bowl on top, and top with a very fine-mesh strainer. Strain the glaçage through the strainer and cool down, stirring frequently, until the temperature reaches 104°F (40°C) on a digital thermometer.

Place a wire rack over a baking tray and arrange the sliced gold bars on the rack. Spoon the warm glaçage over the bars, evenly coating the bars and letting the excess drip through the wire rack. Place the coated bars in the refrigerator, uncovered, until fully set, about 2 hours.

Use an offset spatula to remove each gold bar from the wire rack. Use kitchen shears or a sharp paring knife to trim any excess glaçage off the base. Decorate the top of each bar with pieces of gold leaf and serve.

RED CABBAGE GELÉE

MAKES ABOUT 15 SERVINGS

FOR THE RED CABBAGE PUREE

½ stick cinnamon

10 pieces (12.5 grams) star anise

20 whole pods (5 grams) green cardamom

1 teaspoon (1.25 grams) Szechuan peppercorns

1½ pounds red cabbage, cut into chiffonade (680 grams chiffonade)

One bottle (750 milliliters) robust red wine

1 cup (250 grams) tawny port

1 teaspoon (12.5 grams) fresh thyme leaves

1 fresh bay leaf

3 large cloves garlic, halved lengthwise, germ removed (22 grams peeled cloves)

2 ounces (57 grams) bacon

0.25 gram xanthan gum (see Sources, page 268)

2 tablespoons (25 grams) duck fat (see Sources, page 268)

FOR THE RED CABBAGE GELÉE

2 cups (450 grams) braising liquid (from recipe above)

1 cup (150 grams) red cabbage, braised (from recipe above)

0.72 gram High Acyl Gellan (Gellan LT; see Sources, page 268)

1.13 grams Low Acyl Gellan (Gellan F; see Sources, page 268)

0.10 gram sodium hexametaphosphate (see Sources, page 268)

MAKE THE RED CABBAGE PUREE

Heat a medium, heavy pan over medium heat. Toast the spices in the pan until fragrant, about 1 minute. Set the pan aside and let cool.

Put the cabbage, wine, and port in a large bowl. Put the spice mixture, thyme, bay leaf, and garlic in the center of a large square of cheesecloth. Tie the sachet closed with kitchen twine. Add the sachet and the bacon to the bowl with the cabbage and cover the bowl tightly with plastic wrap. Refrigerate for 48 hours.

Transfer the chilled mixture to a large, heavy pot. Cover the pot with a cartouche (see page 234) and set over medium heat. Bring to a simmer, then reduce the heat to low and cook until the cabbage is tender, 3 to 4 hours. Remove and discard the sachet and bacon, and set the mixture aside to cool. Once cooled, reserve 2 cups (450 grams) of the braising liquid and 1 cup of the braised cabbage for the gelée.

Transfer the remaining liquid and cabbage to a high-speed blender. Add the xanthan gum and duck fat and puree until smooth, about 2 minutes. Fill a large bowl with ice. Place a medium bowl on top of the ice-filled bowl and set a chinois or fine-mesh strainer over the bowl. Strain the puree into the bowl and set aside to cool. Once cooled, transfer to a plastic container, cover tightly, and refrigerate until ready to use. (You should have 1 pint of puree, which can be stored for up to three days.)

MAKE THE RED CABBAGE GELÉE

Heat a medium, heavy pot over medium heat. Add the reserved braising liquid and 1 cup of the cabbage puree and heat until the temperature registers at 194°F (90°C) on a digital thermometer. Add the Gellan LT, Gellan F, and sodium hexametaphosphate. Remove the pot from the heat. Blend with an immersion blender until the mixture is fully emulsified.

Return the pan to the heat and bring the temperature back up to 194°F (90°C). Strain the mixture into a sauce gun. Dispense the mixture on a 7 × 5 × 1-inch tray and refrigerate until the gelée is set, about 1 hour. Once the gelée is set, cut it into 1 × 1-inch cubes. Cover the tray tightly in plastic wrap and refrigerate until ready to use. (The gelée can be stored in the refrigerator for up to three days.)

HALIBUT JAMÓN

MAKES APPROXIMATELY 60 SLICES
Note that this preparation, while not terribly
complicated, requires 48 hours.

2 pounds (1 kilogram) skinless halibut fillet,
    cleaned by your fishmonger

1 cup (200 grams) sel gris (see Sources,
    page 268)

½ cup (100 grams) granulated sugar

7 tablespoons (75 grams) vadouvan spice
    (see Sources, page 268)

1 tablespoon (20 grams) Dijon mustard

Wrap the fillet in cheesecloth, using just enough
cheesecloth to surround the fillet one time.

Put the sel gris, sugar, and 3 teaspoons of the
vadouvan spice in a medium mixing bowl and
stir together until well incorporated. Divide the
mixture in half or simply transfer approximately
¾ cup into a measuring cup.

Sprinkle half of the salt mixture onto a baking tray,
roughly the size of the fillet. Lay the cheesecloth-
wrapped halibut down on top of the salt. Sprinkle
the remaining mixture evenly over the top of
the fillet. Cover loosely with plastic wrap and
refrigerate for 24 hours.

Remove the fillet from the refrigerator and brush
off the salt mix. Unwrap the fillet, discard the
cheesecloth, and brush the tray clean of the salt
mix. Line the tray with parchment paper and set
the fish on the paper. Let dry unwrapped in the
refrigerator for 12 hours.

Use a pastry brush to paint the skinned side of the
fish with a thin layer of Dijon mustard. Sprinkle
the remaining ¼ cup of vadouvan evenly over the
mustard to coat it. Remove from the tray and place
on a wire rack. Place the rack in the refrigerator
and let the halibut dry for 12 more hours.

To serve, remove the tray from the refrigerator
and, with a sharp slicing knife, cut the fish on a
slight bias into paper-thin pieces. (The jamón will
keep, wrapped in plastic wrap and refrigerated,
for up to five days.)

"THE BAGEL"

MAKES 25 SMALL BAGELS

Note that you will need 25 small bagel- or doughnut-shaped molds, which you can find online or in specialty kitchen stores. The egg yolk bagels must be served the same day they are made.

FOR THE POTATO BAGEL

Kosher salt

4 large Yukon gold potatoes

2 large (80 grams) eggs, separated

2 teaspoons (10 grams) active dried yeast

¼ cup (70 grams) soy milk

¼ cup (70 grams) wheat flour

¼ cup (25 grams) all-purpose flour

2 teaspoons (2 grams) finely grated orange zest

Pinch of fleur de sel

Freshly ground black pepper

FOR THE EGG YOLK CRÈME

8 large (160 grams) egg yolks (reserve the whites for another recipe)

2 drops fresh lemon juice

Pinch of piment d'espelette (see Note, page 241, and Sources, page 268)

Fleur de sel

Several pieces gold leaf (see Sources, page 268)

MAKE THE POTATO BAGEL

Preheat the oven to 350°F (177°C). Make a thick bed of kosher salt on a baking tray and arrange the potatoes in a single layer. Bake the potatoes for 90 minutes. Remove from the oven and let cool. When the potatoes are cool enough to handle, peel them, discard the skins, and pass them through a potato ricer, reserving 2 cups (150 grams) in a large mixing bowl.

Lower the oven to 95°F (35°C). Stir together the egg yolks, yeast, soy milk, both flours, and orange zest in a large stainless steel mixing bowl. Season with fleur de sel and pepper and mix just to combine. Cover tautly with plastic wrap, place the bowl in the oven, and let proof for 40 minutes.

Remove the egg yolk mixture from the oven and add to the potatoes. Put the egg whites in a separate large bowl and whisk until they are light and fluffy but not stiff. Use a spatula to gently fold the egg whites into the potato mixture just until combined. Cover the bowl with plastic wrap and refrigerate for 24 hours.

Preheat a convection oven to 375°F (191°C). Remove the potato mixture from the refrigerator and use a spoon to portion the dough out into 1½-inch round, bagel-shaped silicone molds. Place the molds on a baking tray and place in the oven (making sure the fan is turned off). Bake for 9 minutes, then turn the pan 180 degrees and bake until the bagels are set, another 9 to 10 minutes. Remove from the oven and set the bagels aside to cool for 5 minutes in their molds. Gently unmold the bagels and transfer to a wire rack to cool. Trim around the edges with kitchen shears or a paring knife if necessary.

MAKE THE EGG YOLK CRÈME

Put the egg yolks in a large vacuum bag and seal at 100 percent vacuum. Bring a water bath in an immersion circulator to 149°F (65°C) and add the bag. Cook for 1 hour. Remove the bag from the water and cut it open. While the egg yolks are still warm, pass them through a fine tamis (drum sieve) into a medium bowl. Add the lemon juice and piment d'espelette and fold the mixture together until incorporated. You should have just under 2 cups. Use a vacuum to remove the air from the crème and transfer the crème to a plastic piping bag. Keep the crème warm, but make sure the temperature does not rise above 149°F or 65°C.

To serve, pipe a spiral of the egg yolk crème into the center of each bagel. Finish with a pinch of fleur de sel and garnish with a touch of gold leaf. Serve warm.

BLACK OLIVE GNOCCHI

MAKES 45 PIECES, ENOUGH TO SERVE 6

These may be served on their own or dressed with a black olive tapenade that has been thinned with olive oil and topped with freshly grated aged gouda.

FOR THE OLIVE PUREE

1 teaspoon (20 grams) extra-virgin olive oil, plus more for serving

1 cup black olives, such as Niçoise, washed and pitted (25 grams pitted)

¾ cup thinly sliced shallots (87.5 grams sliced)

¼ cup (75 grams) ruby port

½ cup (100 grams) water

2½ teaspoons (12.5 grams) truffle juice (see Sources, page 268)

1 teaspoon (20 grams) squid ink (available at specialty and gourmet shops and many fish stores)

1½ teaspoons (10 grams) balsamic vinegar

1½ teaspoons (20 grams) soy sauce

0.5 gram xanthan gum (see Sources, page 268)

FOR THE GNOCCHI:

6 large Yukon gold potatoes, scrubbed and pricked with a fork

½ large (25 grams) egg

¼ cup (35 grams) finely grated Parmesan

¼ cup (35 grams) 00 flour (see Sources, page 268)

1 teaspoon (5 grams) kosher salt, plus more to salt the pasta's cooking water

MAKE THE OLIVE PUREE

Heat a medium, heavy pot over low heat. Add the olive oil, olives, and shallots and cook, stirring with a wooden spoon, for 8 minutes, until the shallots are softened but not browned. Pour in the port and scrape off any bits stuck to the bottom of the pan. Raise the heat to medium and bring the port to a simmer. Continue to cook until the port is reduced by half, about 5 minutes. Pour in the water and truffle juice, return to a simmer, and continue to simmer until the olives are softened, about 10 minutes. Stir in the squid ink, balsamic vinegar, and soy sauce.

Transfer the mixture to a blender and blend on high for 1 minute. With the blender running, add the xanthan gum and blend until incorporated.

Fill a large bowl with ice. Set a medium bowl over the ice and set a fine-mesh strainer over the bowl. Strain the mixture through the fine-mesh strainer. You should have 2 cups of puree. Transfer the bowl to the refrigerator and chill overnight. (You only need 50 grams, or 2 teaspoons, of puree for the gnocchi; the puree may be refrigerated for up to five days and used to make more gnocchi, or thinned with warm water and used as a sauce for the gnocchi.)

MAKE THE GNOCCHI

Preheat the oven to 350°F (177°C). Wrap the potatoes in aluminum foil and place on a baking tray. Bake until the potatoes are cooked through and fork-tender (cooking time will vary depending on potato size). Remove the tray from the oven and set the potatoes aside to cool for 20 minutes. Unwrap and cut each potato in half lengthwise. Scoop 8½ ounces (241 grams) of the flesh out of the skins into a large bowl. Discard the skins and press the flesh through a ricer. Keep warm.

Put 2 teaspoons (50 grams) of the black olive puree and the egg in a small bowl and mix together with a rubber spatula until completely incorporated. Gently fold the puree mixture into the potatoes. Put the Parmesan, flour, and salt in a separate bowl and mix to incorporate. Gently fold the Parmesan mixture into the potatoes until a cohesive dough just forms (do not overwork).

Lightly flour a work surface and roll the dough into 1 × ¼-inch batons. Place the batons on a floured, parchment-lined baking tray and chill in the refrigerator for 3 hours.

Fill a medium pot about two-thirds full with water and salt liberally. Bring to a boil over high heat, then lower the heat so the liquid is simmering. Remove the batons from the refrigerator and add to the water. Blanch the batons until they float to the surface, about 1½ minutes. (The potatoes release tiny gas bubbles in the water, allowing the gnocchi to float as they start to cook. However, the middle of the gnocchi still remains uncooked. Floating the gnocchi for 30 seconds more allows for thorough cooking.)

Use a slotted spoon or a spider to remove the gnocchi from the water and place on a warm sheet tray. Drizzle the gnocchi with olive oil and serve immediately.

GREEN APPLE–WASABI SORBET
MAKES ABOUT 2 CUPS

I've always served this as a savory offering, but you can employ it as anything from an intermezzo to a dessert. If serving as a dessert, it would pair especially well with white chocolate, in either a crème or a ganache.

2¼ cups (500 grams) fresh Granny Smith apple juice (pressed fresh or bottled)

¾ cup (100 grams) liquid glucose (see Sources, page 268)

5 grams Low Acyl Gellan (Gellan F; see Sources, page 268)

0.5 gram malic acid (see Sources, page 268)

1 teaspoon (20 grams) fresh wasabi

Put the apple juice and the liquid glucose in a Thermomix and begin blending on low. Heat the mixture to 194°F (90°C). Sprinkle in the Gellan and blend on high for 30 seconds until fully incorporated. Turn off the heat and keep blending while adding the malic acid and the wasabi. Blend for 30 seconds more until incorporated. Remove the mixture and transfer to Pacojet containers. Freeze the green apple–wasabi sorbet until solid, then spin in the Pacojet container two times.

To serve, scoop teaspoon-size quenelles, placing them in small, chilled serving bowls. Serve with demitasse spoons.

RED WINE "CANNELLONI"

MAKES ABOUT 16 CANNELLONI; SERVES 8
This recipe produces the cannelloni in the dish on pages 158–159, which features a pleasing interplay between the acidity of the red wine and the floral quality of the huckleberry. These are a delicious accompaniment to foie gras, game terrine, and any kind of smoked fish.

FOR THE RED WINE GELÉE

¾ cup (350 grams) fresh beet juice

1 cup (200 grams) robust red wine such as Shiraz

1.6 grams Low Acyl Gellan (Gellan F; see Sources, page 268)

0.16 gram High Acyl Gellan (Gellan LT; see Sources, page 268)

FOR THE HUCKLEBERRY GELÉE

1½ cups (300 grams) water

5 grams Low Acyl Gellan (Gellan F; see Sources, page 268)

1½ cups (200 grams) fresh huckleberries

0.5 gram malic acid (see Sources, page 268)

MAKE THE RED WINE GELÉE

Pour the beet juice into a heavy pan and bring to a boil over medium heat. Cook for 5 minutes, skimming off any impurities that rise to the surface. Remove the pan from the heat and strain the juice through a cheesecloth-lined strainer into a bowl. Wipe out the pan and return the clarified beet juice to it. Bring to a boil over medium heat and let cook until the liquid is reduced to about ¼ cup. Remove the pan from the heat and let cool completely. Reserve until ready to use.

Heat a large, heavy pot over high heat and pour in the red wine and beet juice reduction. Heat until the temperature registers 194°F (90°C) on a digital thermometer. Add the Gellan F and Gellan LT and remove the pot from the heat. Use an immersion blender to blend the mixture until smooth, about 2 minutes.

Set the pot back over high heat and, whisking constantly, return the temperature of the mixture to 194°F (90°C). Skim off any excess foam. Remove the pot from the heat and strain the mixture through a chinois or very fine-mesh strainer into a sauce gun. Quickly dispense the mixture evenly onto 4 flat (7 × 5 × 1-inch) trays to form thin sheets, coating the bottom of the trays. Cover the trays tightly with plastic wrap and refrigerate for at least 2 hours to set.

When ready to use the gelée, cut it into a minimum of 16 strips measuring 4 × 2.5 inches (10 × 6 centimeters). Remove them from the tray and set aside.

MAKE THE HUCKLEBERRY GELÉE

Set a large heavy pot over high heat and pour in the water. Heat until the temperature registers 194°F (90°C) on a digital thermometer. Add the Gellan F and remove the pot from the heat. Use an immersion blender to blend until fully emulsified. Add the huckleberries and the malic acid, return the pot to the heat, and bring to a boil. Remove the pot from the heat.

Fill a large bowl with ice. Transfer the huckleberry mixture to a medium bowl and place it over the ice bath to set into a firm block, about 30 minutes. Once the gelée is set, cut it into small pieces. Add the pieces to a high-speed blender and blend for 30 seconds to form a fluid gel, being careful not to heat the mixture. Fill a large bowl with ice. Transfer the mixture to a medium bowl and set over the ice for 2 minutes, stirring gently with a rubber spatula without aerating it to cool the mixture completely. Pass through a chinois or very fine-mesh strainer into a bowl. Keep covered in the refrigerator. (The mixture can be stored for up to three days.)

Transfer the huckleberry gelée to a piping bag or plastic pantry bag fitted with a Number 3 plain tip. Pipe a thin line of the huckleberry gelée down the center of each red wine gelée strip. Gently fold the strips around the huckleberry gelée to form cannelloni. Refrigerate for at least 20 minutes to set. You may store the cannelloni in the refrigerator until ready to serve, but they should be served the same day as prepared.

PLUM EXTRA-VIRGIN OLIVE OIL

MAKES ABOUT 1 CUP

This recipe produces the plum olive oil used to dress the heirloom tomato preparation on page 169. Accordingly, it would make a fine dressing for any tomatoes. Its fruity, green freshness also recommends it as a summer dressing for white beans, onions, or vegetables. For a twist on Caesar salad, use it to dress romaine lettuce. It's also wonderful drizzled over scallops and lobster.

8 yellow plums, halved and pitted (335 grams pitted)

½ cup (170 grams) fresh pineapple juice

5 kaffir lime leaves (see Sources, page 268)

1½ tablespoons (15 grams) freshly squeezed lime juice

1 gram xanthan gum (see Sources, page 268)

¼ cup (30 grams) extra-virgin olive oil

1 teaspoon (5 grams) fleur de sel

Put the plums, pineapple juice, and kaffir leaves in a medium, heavy pot. Top the pot with a cartouche (see Note, page 234) and set over low heat. Cook until the plums are tender and broken down, and their skin is soft, but still retain their yellow color with no browning, about 45 minutes. (Do not allow the liquid to simmer or boil; if it does, lower the heat immediately.) Remove the pot from the heat, remove the cartouche, and set the plums aside to cool for 30 minutes.

Set a fine-mesh strainer over a medium bowl and pass the plums through the strainer, pressing on the plums with a spatula. Discard the pulp and the leaves. Cool the plum juice infusion completely, then add the lime juice and stir together to incorporate. (You should have 2 cups of plum juice infusion.)

Transfer ¾ cup (150 grams) of the mixture to a high-speed blender and add the xanthan gum. (Save the remaining plum mixture to make another batch or two of the oil; it may be refrigerated in an airtight container for up to two days.) Blend until the mixture thickens. With the motor running, slowly add the olive oil in a steady stream until fully emulsified. Add the fleur de sel. Set a chinois or very fine-mesh strainer over a container set over ice, and strain the dressing through the strainer. (The oil may be used right away, or refrigerated in an airtight container for up to two days.)

RED CURRY JUS
MAKES 1 QUART (1 LITER)

1½ tablespoons (40 grams) grapeseed oil

13 ounces (750 grams) salmon bones, very dry, cut to 2.5 × 1.5-inch (6 × 4 centimeters) pieces (your fishmonger can provide these for you, or save the bones from another recipe)

½ cup (200 grams) Red Curry Paste (recipe follows)

3 tablespoons (50 grams) rice wine vinegar

3 cups (650 grams) Brown Chicken Stock (page 239)

1 tablespoon (15 grams) red curry powder

0.5 gram xanthan gum (see Sources, page 268)

1 tablespoon (10 grams) freshly squeezed lime juice

2 teaspoons (10 grams) fleur de sel

Heat a large skillet over high heat and add the grapeseed oil. Heat until the oil is shimmering and almost smoking. Add the salmon bones and sauté until the bones are just golden brown on both sides, about 1½ minutes on each side. Remove the pan from the heat and transfer the bones to a large plate. Discard the oil from the pan and place over medium-low heat. Add the curry paste and stir constantly until the paste is toasted, about 2 minutes. (Do not allow the paste to scorch, which can happen easily.)

Pour in the rice wine vinegar and use a wooden spoon to scrape off any bits stuck to the bottom of the pan. Cook until the pan is dry. Return the browned bones to the pan and pour in the chicken stock. Bring the mixture to a gentle simmer, then reduce the heat to low. Simmer until the liquid is reduced by one-third, using a tablespoon to skim off the excess fat from the surface of the jus. Remove the pan from the heat and stir in the red curry powder. Cover the pan and set aside for 30 minutes to hydrate the curry powder.

Line a fine-mesh strainer with cheesecloth and set over a large bowl. Strain the jus through the cheesecloth-lined strainer and discard the salmon bones. Add the xanthan gum and use an immersion blender to blend the mixture until smooth. Set a fine-mesh strainer over a medium saucepot and strain the mixture into the saucepot. Stir in the lime juice and season to taste with fleur de sel. Let cool completely. (The jus can be covered and stored in the refrigerator for up to one week.)

RED CURRY PASTE

MAKES 2 CUPS

This is not a classic Thai red curry paste, but rather my interpretation of one. It's a wonderful marinade for chicken, beef, or pork, and can also be used to marinate beetroot prior to roasting. For a green curry paste (a perfect finishing element for delicate spring salmon), add ramp tops to the recipe.

2 tablespoons (10 grams) whole coriander seeds

2 medium red shallots, small dice (50 grams diced)

2 cloves garlic, peeled, halved lengthwise, germ removed, minced (15 grams minced)

½ stalk lemongrass, tough outer layer removed and discarded, flesh finely chopped (50 grams chopped)

1 tablespoon plus 1½ teaspoons (20 grams) fleur de sel

1.5 ounces galangal, seeded and finely chopped (42.5 grams chopped)

1 tablespoon plus 1½ teaspoons (20 grams) palm sugar (see Sources, page 268)

2 limes, zested

2 tablespoons (50 grams) shrimp paste (see Sources, page 268)

12 cilantro stems with no leaves, finely chopped

6 red bird's eye chiles, seeds removed

8 Holland red chiles, seeded and finely chopped

1 small combava (dried kaffir lime), grated on a microplane

Heat a medium, heavy pan over medium heat. Add the coriander seeds to the pan and toast them, shaking the pan to prevent scorching, until they are fragrant, 3 minutes. Set the pan aside and let the seeds cool.

Use a mortar and pestle to grind together the shallots, garlic, and lemongrass until a fine paste forms. Add the fleur de sel, galanga, palm sugar, lime zest, and shrimp paste. Continue to grind the mixture in the mortar and pestle until a fine, cohesive paste forms. Add the coriander seeds, cilantro, chiles, and combava. Continue to grind the mixture until a very fine paste forms. (You should have 2 cups of paste.)

Place the paste in a sealed plastic container and refrigerate for at least 24 hours to allow the flavors to mature. Use the red curry paste as needed. (The paste can be stored covered in the refrigerator for up to five days.)

WHITE TRUFFLE GNUDI WITH ABALONE BUTTER

MAKES 60 GNUDI, ENOUGH TO SERVE 6 TO 8

These gnudi can be served alongside proteins such as Dover sole.

FOR THE ABALONE BUTTER

1 cup (200 grams) crisp white wine

½ cup (100 grams) white wine vinegar

5 medium shallots, thinly sliced (125 grams sliced)

5 stalks parsley, stripped of their leaves

4 ounces (113 grams) abalone, sliced into thin strips

2 stalks lemongrass, smashed and cut into fine chiffonade (100 grams chiffonade)

¼ cup (100 grams) heavy cream

½ pound (2 sticks, 227 grams) cold unsalted butter, diced

Fleur de sel

Freshly ground black pepper

FOR THE GNUDI

1½ cups (250 grams) ricotta cheese

½ cup (50 grams) finely grated Parmesan cheese

1 large egg yolk (20 grams)

3.75 grams Activa YG (see Sources, page 268)

00 pasta flour (see Sources, page 268)

1 cup (150 grams) Abalone Butter

2 teaspoons (5 grams) minced fresh white truffle (see Sources, page 268)

Smoked fleur de sel (see Sources, page 268)

Freshly ground black pepper

MAKE THE ABALONE BUTTER

Heat a medium, heavy pot over medium heat. Add the wine, vinegar, shallots, parsley, abalone, and lemongrass and bring to a simmer. Continue to simmer until the liquid is reduced by one-third, 5 to 8 minutes. Pour in the cream, bring to a simmer, and continue to cook until the liquid is reduced by one-quarter, about 4 minutes. Add the butter a few pieces at a time, whisking to emulsify while the mixture simmers. As soon as all the butter is incorporated, remove the pot from the heat and season with the fleur de sel and pepper. Strain the mixture through a chinois or very fine-mesh strainer into a saucepan. Keep covered and warm until ready to use.

MAKE THE GNUDI

Line a fine-mesh strainer with a piece of cheese-cloth. Set the strainer over a medium bowl and add the ricotta. Place in the refrigerator and drain for 12 hours, to remove all the moisture from the ricotta.

Combine the strained ricotta, Parmesan, egg yolk, and Activa in a large bowl (discard the strained liquid). Cover the bowl tightly with plastic wrap and refrigerate for 1 hour. Remove the mixture from the refrigerator and use a scale to weigh out 5-gram pieces (roughly 1 rounded teaspoon each) of the ricotta mixture. Dust your hands with the flour and roll the ricotta pieces gently between your palms to form small balls, ½ inch (1.3 centimeters) in diameter. Place the balls on a lightly floured baking tray and repeat until all the mixture is used (you should have about 60 balls). Lightly dust the formed ricotta balls with additional flour and cover the pan with plastic wrap. Refrigerate until the ricotta balls are firm, about 1 hour.

Remove the balls from the refrigerator and repeat the rolling and dusting process to form them into perfect spheres. Cover the balls with plastic wrap and refrigerate overnight. (During this resting period, the flour will be absorbed and a light skin will form around the balls.)

Remove the balls from the refrigerator, and
dust and roll the balls once again with flour. (It is
essential that the mixture be kept cold to maintain
the spherical shape, so keep the tray in the
refrigerator as you cook each batch.)

To serve, melt some of the abalone butter in
a medium, heavy pan over low heat. Add the
gnudi and very gently swirl them in the pan, 1 to
2 minutes without allowing the butter to boil.
Add the truffle to the pan, swirling to coat the
gnudi, and spoon the gnudi and butter into dishes.
Season with fleur de sel and black pepper. Serve
at once.

BEET-HIBISCUS-GLAZED FOIE GRAS

MAKES 40 BALLS

Over the years, I've glazed foie gras with everything from almond milk to spiced apple juice to black truffle, and this version is one that I keep coming back to. In addition to being served on its own as a cold dish, foie gras makes an apt pairing with Rossini-style beef.

You will need forty 1-inch spherical silicone molds (see Sources, page 268). Be sure to wear insulated or cryogenic gloves to protect your hands when working with liquid nitrogen.

FOR THE FOIE GRAS

9 ounces (255 grams) grade A foie gras

1⅓ cups (250 grams) whole milk

1⅓ cups (250 grams) water

0.5 gram pink curing salt (sodium nitrite; see Sources, page 268)

1 teaspoon (5 grams) fleur de sel

0.5 gram freshly ground white peppercorns

FOR THE BEET-HIBISCUS GLAZE AND ASSEMBLY

2½ cups (500 grams) fresh beet juice (juice your own or purchase from a juice bar)

7.5 grams agar-agar (see Sources, page 268)

1 cup (20 grams) hibiscus flowers (see Sources, page 268)

½ cup (5 grams) fresh orange peel strips, no pith attached

4 sheets (10 grams) gelatin

Liquid nitrogen (check your Yellow Pages for a local supplier)

MAKE THE FOIE GRAS

Put the foie gras in a large bowl, and pour the milk and the water over the top. Cover the bowl with plastic wrap and refrigerate overnight.

Remove the soaked foie gras from the liquid and thoroughly pat it dry with a paper towel. (Discard the liquid.) Put the foie gras on a baking tray and cover with plastic wrap. Set it aside to come to room temperature. Use tweezers to carefully remove the veins and the blood spots.

Combine the pink salt, fleur de sel, and peppercorns in a small bowl. Place the foie gras on a sheet of plastic wrap and season it with the pink salt mixture. Cover with an additional sheet of plastic wrap and set aside to cure in the refrigerator for 8 hours or overnight.

Transfer the foie gras to a vacuum bag and seal at 100 percent vacuum. Bring a water bath in an immersion circulator to 131°F (55°C) and add the bag. Cook until the internal temperature of the foie gras reads 131°F (55°C) on a thermometer, about 15 minutes.

Fill a large bowl with ice. Set a medium bowl over the ice. Remove the foie gras from the water bath, cut open the bag, and pour it into the medium bowl. Blend the foie gras with an immersion blender until it is fully emulsified, about 15 seconds. Stir gently with a rubber spatula to release any air bubbles, and continue stirring until the foie gras is chilled to 104°F (40°C), and thickened (be careful not to break the emulsion).

Use a spatula to gently transfer the foie gras into a large plastic piping bag. Cut the tip of the bag with a scissors and pipe the foie gras into forty 1-inch spherical silicone molds. Gently tap the molds on your work surface to release any air bubbles. Place the molds in the refrigerator to set overnight.

MAKE THE BEET-HIBISCUS GLAZE

Pour the beet juice into a medium, heavy saucepan and bring to a boil over medium heat. Cook for 5 minutes, using a tablespoon to skim off any impurities that rise to the surface. Remove the pan from the heat and strain through a cheesecloth-lined strainer to remove any stray particles.

Carefully wipe out the pan. Pour the clarified beet juice into it, and bring it back to a boil over medium heat. Continue to boil until reduced by approximately one-third (you will have about 2¼ cups). Remove the pan from the heat and let the reduction cool completely. Cover and refrigerate.

Heat a heavy, medium pot over medium-low heat. Pour in 2 cups of the beet juice and sprinkle in the agar-agar. Bring the mixture to a simmer and cook, whisking constantly, for 5 minutes to fully hydrate the agar-agar (it will dissolve into the liquid). Use a tablespoon to skim off any impurities that rise to the surface, and remove the pot from the heat. Set aside for 5 minutes, then add the hibiscus flowers, the orange peel, and the gelatin sheets. Whisk until the gelatin is completely dissolved, and set aside for 7 minutes to allow the hibiscus and orange to infuse the liquid. Strain the mixture through a chinois or very fine-mesh strainer over a medium, heavy pot. (You should have 2 cups.) Set the pot over very low heat and keep the glaze at 122°F (50°C).

Remove the foie gras balls from the molds and gently thread onto metal skewers. Pour the liquid nitrogen into an insulated bowl (see Sources, page 268). Working with 1 skewer at a time, and holding it by one end, dip the balls into the liquid nitrogen for 5 seconds, then remove the skewer and dip it into the warm beet-hibiscus glaze for 1 second, and remove it. Hover the foie gras ball above the liquid nitrogen for 3 seconds. Dip once more into the glaze for 1 second, and hover again above the nitrogen for 3 seconds. Gently remove the skewer from the ball, taking care to not break the glaze, and place on a metal tray. Repeat with the remaining balls, cover the tray with plastic wrap, and refrigerate for at least 2 hours, or up to 24 hours.

Let rest at room temperature for 5 to 10 minutes before serving.

BEER-BRINED PORK SHOULDER
MAKES 8 SERVINGS

6 cups (1,500 grams) water

1 cup (115 grams) kosher salt

1 teaspoon (10 grams) pink curing salt (sodium nitrite; see Sources, page 268)

4 cups (1,000 grams) white beer (preferably Japanese Hitachino white ale)

4 pounds (1.8 kilograms) Berkshire pork shoulder, off the bone (ask your butcher to prepare this for you)

½ teaspoon (2.5 grams) fleur de sel

½ teaspoon (8 grams) ground green peppercorns

Make a brine by adding the water, kosher salt, and pink salt to a large pot and bringing it to a boil over high heat. When the salt has fully dissolved, remove the pot from the heat. Let cool and refrigerate overnight in an airtight container.

The next day, remove the brine from the refrigerator and stir in the beer.

Cut the pork shoulder into 4 large, equal pieces and put them in a large bowl. Pour the brine over the pork shoulder. Cover the bowl tightly with plastic wrap and refrigerate for 36 hours.

Remove the pork shoulder pieces from the brine and use paper towels to dry the pieces fully. Discard the brine mixture. Divide the pieces into 4 vacuum bags and seal at 100 percent vacuum. Bring a water bath in an immersion circulator to 153°F (67°C). Add the bags and cook the pork for 24 hours. Remove the bags and allow them to sit at room temperature for 20 minutes. Fill a large bowl with ice water and add the bags to the water for 30 minutes. Drain the ice water and cover the bags fully with ice until the internal temperature of the pork registers 34°F (1.1°C), which may take 1 to 2 hours. Remove the bags from the ice and place on a baking tray. Press a weight atop the pork to set a flat shape and refrigerate overnight.

Remove the pork from the bags and use a sharp knife to cut the pieces into 1½ × 1½-inch cubes. Heat a large, heavy skillet over low heat and add the pork, skin side down. Cook until the pork is caramelized and thoroughly heated through, about 6 minutes. Remove the pan from the heat and transfer the pork to a wire cooling rack. Rest for 2 minutes, then season with the fleur de sel and peppercorns.

BEETROOT-BLACKBERRY MERINGUE

MAKES 20 TO 25 SMALL
OR 10 TO 12 LARGE MERINGUES
Serve these with red-fruit sorbets or caviar.

2½ cups (500 grams) beet juice (juice your own or purchase from a juice bar)

FOR THE SIMPLE SYRUP

½ cup (100 grams) water

½ cup (100 grams) granulated sugar

FOR THE MERINGUES

5 sheets (12 grams) gelatin

1 ¾ cups (430 grams) reduced clarified beet juice (as prepared)

½ cup (15 grams) freeze-dried blackberries (see Sources, page 268)

2 teaspoons (10 grams) cassis liqueur

3 tablespoons (24 grams) egg white powder (see Sources, page 268)

1.2 grams xanthan gum (see Sources, page 268)

¼ cup Simple Syrup

Pour the beet juice into a medium, heavy pan and bring to a boil over medium heat. Cook for 5 minutes, using a tablespoon to skim off any impurities. Remove the pan from the heat and strain through a cheesecloth-lined strainer into a bowl to remove any stray particles.

Carefully wipe out the pan, pour the clarified beet juice into it, and bring to a boil over medium heat. Continue to boil until reduced by approximately half (you will have about 1¾ cups, or 430 grams). Remove the pan from the heat, and let the reduction cool completely. Reserve until ready to use.

MAKE THE SIMPLE SYRUP
Combine the water and sugar in a small, heavy pot and bring to a boil. Remove the pot from the heat, cool, and reserve. (You should have 1 cup simple syrup. Note that the meringue recipe only uses ¼ cup; refrigerate the rest in an airtight container for another use.)

MAKE THE MERINGUES
Fill a small bowl halfway with ice water. Add the gelatin and let it bloom for 5 minutes.

Put the clarified beet juice, blackberries, cassis, egg white powder, and xanthan gum in a medium bowl and blend with an immersion blender until fully combined and emulsified. Cover and refrigerate.

Squeeze the gelatin to release any excess liquid and place in a medium, heavy pan. Add the simple syrup and warm over low heat, stirring occasionally, until the gelatin is completely dissolved, about 1 minute. Pour the mixture into a medium heatproof bowl and let cool to room temperature.

Pour the cold beet mixture into the bowl of a stand mixer fitted with the whisk attachment and whip on high speed until soft peaks form, about 2 minutes. With the mixer still on, slowly stream in the syrup-gelatin mixture, making sure that everything is incorporated, and whip until stiff peaks are achieved, 2 to 3 minutes.

Transfer the meringue mix to a piping bag fitted with a Number 3 plain tip, or a disposable piping bag, snipping off the tip. Pipe a quarter-size beet meringue on acetate and place in a dehydrator set at 115°F (46°C) for 24 hours. Keep the meringues in the dehydrator until needed, but no longer than three days. Gently remove from the acetate when ready to serve.

SAFFRON VANILLA FUDGE, BANANA GANACHE, MATCHA

MAKES 6 SERVINGS, 2 PIECES
PER SERVING

FOR THE SAFFRON FUDGE

½ cup (100 grams) granulated sugar

1 tablespoon (12.5 grams) water

1 tablespoon (31.25 grams) liquid glucose
   (see Sources, page 268)

¼ cup (115 grams) heavy cream

½ piece vanilla bean, split and scraped

2½ ounces (71 grams) salted butter, cut into
   cubes and at room temperature

0.25 gram saffron threads

1 tablespoon (15 grams) fleur de sel

FOR THE VANILLA SABAYON

¾ sheet (2 grams) gelatin

1¼ cups (250 grams) heavy cream

½ vanilla bean, split and scraped

2 large (50 grams) egg whites

¼ cup (45 grams) granulated sugar

FOR THE BANANA GANACHE

¾ sheet (2 grams) gelatin

¼ cup (62.5 grams) pureed banana

1.25 grams freeze-dried banana powder
   (see Sources, page 268)

2.7 ounces (76.5 grams) white chocolate,
   coarsely chopped

2 teaspoons (10 grams) unsalted butter, at
   room temperature

FOR THE MATCHA SABLÉ AND ASSEMBLY

2.8 ounces (79 grams) unsalted butter, cubed
   and at room temperature

⅓ cup (80 grams) sugar

2 large (40 grams) egg yolks

1 cup (100 grams) all-purpose flour, plus more
   for rolling out the dough

2 tablespoons (7.5 grams) baking powder

1 teaspoon (5 grams) matcha green tea
   powder (see Note, page 241)

Fleur de sel

Extra-virgin olive oil

MAKE THE SAFFRON FUDGE

Heat a medium, heavy pot over medium heat. Add the sugar, water, and glucose and heat until the temperature reaches 320°F (160°C) on a digital thermometer. Deglaze the mixture with the cream in two stages: first, add half of the cream, stirring until the mixture is fully emulsified; then pour in the remaining cream and stir to dissolve the sugars. Reduce the heat to low and add the vanilla bean pod. Cook the mixture very slowly for four hours, stirring frequently, until the temperature reaches 246°F (119°C). Remove the cream mixture from the heat and slowly add the butter, stirring constantly. Once the butter is completely emulsified, stir in the saffron, fleur de sel, and vanilla bean seeds.

Line a sheet tray with a Silpat nonstick mat and place two 1-inch-high caramel rulers (see Sources, page 268) spaced about 12 inches apart on it. Remove the vanilla pod and pour the fudge mixture onto the sheet tray, gently tapping the tray to release any air bubbles. (The mixture should be about ¾ inch high.) Place the sheet tray in the refrigerator and chill until the mixture is set, about 2 hours. Remove the fudge from the Silpat and use a sharp knife to cut the fudge into 1½ × 1½-inch squares. Place the squares on a Silpat-lined sheet tray and refrigerate. Remove the fudge from the refrigerator 10 minutes before serving to temper.

MAKE THE VANILLA SABAYON

Fill a small bowl with ice water. Add the gelatin and set aside to bloom for 5 minutes. Heat a heavy, medium pot over low heat and add the cream and vanilla bean pod. Bring to a simmer. Remove the pot from the heat, cover, and set aside to infuse for 1 hour.

In a large bowl, whisk together the egg whites and sugar until they are light and fluffy but not stiff. Strain the cream mixture through a chinois or very fine-mesh strainer. Add a small amount of the whipped egg whites to the cream and use a spatula to fold them together. Add the rest of the egg whites and gently fold until just incorporated. Add the mixture to a double boiler and heat over low heat until the mixture reaches 176°F (80°C) on a digital thermometer. Remove from the heat and stir in the bloomed gelatin and vanilla bean seeds. Stir until the gelatin is completely dissolved and incorporated.

Fill a large bowl with ice water and place a medium bowl on top. Set a chinois or very fine-mesh strainer over the bowl and strain the sabayon mixture through it, stirring to chill evenly. (You should have 2 cups.) Refrigerate the sabayon until ready to use.

MAKE THE BANANA GANACHE

Fill a small bowl with ice water. Add the gelatin and set aside to bloom for 5 minutes. Put the banana puree and banana powder in a medium, heavy pot. Use an immersion blender to blend until smooth, then place the pot over low heat. Bring the mixture to a simmer, then remove the pan from the heat. Cover the pan with a lid and set aside to infuse for 20 minutes.

Melt the white chocolate in the upper pot of a double boiler set over simmering water. Add the butter and stir to incorporate and emulsify completely. Add the bloomed gelatin and the banana mixture to the chocolate mixture, and keep stirring until completely emulsified. While the mixture is still warm, strain it through a chinois or very fine-mesh strainer into a bowl (you should have just over ½ cup). Set aside to cool,

uncovered, in the refrigerator. Once the mixture is cooled, transfer to a piping bag fitted with a small tip.

MAKE THE MATCHA SABLÉ

Add the butter and sugar to the bowl of a stand mixer fitted with the paddle attachment. Cream together until the mixture is lightened and fluffy. Add the egg yolks and mix to incorporate. Sift the flour, baking powder, and 1 teaspoon of the matcha through a fine-mesh sieve into a medium bowl and whisk to incorporate. Slowly sift the flour mixture into the butter mixture and mix until incorporated and a dough forms. Remove the dough from the mixer and wrap in plastic wrap. Refrigerate it overnight.

Preheat the oven to 320°F (160°C). Remove the dough from the refrigerator, unwrap, and place on a lightly floured work surface. Roll the dough into a circle 3 millimeters thick. Use a 1½-inch round cutter to punch out 12 discs and transfer the discs to a Silpat-lined sheet tray. Bake the sablés for 6 minutes, until they are set but not browned. Remove from the oven and let cool completely.

TO FINISH THE DISH

Spoon the vanilla sabayon into a mixing bowl. Whisk until medium peaks form, then transfer the sabayon to a piping bag fitted with a medium tip. Pipe a firm dollop, about 1 inch in diameter, on the center of a plate. Gently place a matcha sablé directly on top. Layer the saffron fudge on top of the sablé. Season with fleur de sel. Pipe the banana ganache over the fudge, draping the ganache over the edge. Drizzle with olive oil and fleur de sel. Dust with the remaining ½ teaspoon matcha powder and serve.

DUCK LEG TORTE

MAKES 4 TORTES

Though I serve this as part of a multi-preparation duck course (see page 207), this torte may also be served alongside a simple salad.

FOR THE FOIE GRAS

1 lobe grade A foie gras

2½ cups (500 grams) whole milk

2½ cups (500 grams) water

FOR THE FILLING

4 cups (1,000 grams) water

¼ cup (45 grams) kosher salt

½ teaspoon (5 grams) pink curing salt (sodium nitrite; see Sources, page 268)

½ cup (100 grams) granulated sugar

2 stalks lemongrass, thinly sliced (100 grams sliced)

10 whole juniper berries

1 small knob fresh ginger, thinly sliced (about 1 teaspoon, or 10 grams sliced)

2 fresh bay leaves

1 tablespoon (12 grams) whole mustard seeds

1 tablespoon (5 grams) whole coriander seeds

1 pound (453.5 grams) duck leg (2 large legs), deboned, fat side scored with a sharp knife

1 ounce (28 grams) Activa RM (see Sources, page 268)

2 ounces (57 grams) foie gras (as prepared)

FOR THE SAVORY TORTE DOUGH

½ pound (2 sticks, 227 grams) salted butter

4 cups (500 grams) all-purpose flour, sifted, plus extra for dusting

2 tablespoons (15 grams) fleur de sel, sifted

1 tablespoon (15 grams) granulated sugar, sifted

½ cup (170 grams) whole milk, warmed slightly

4 duck foie gras fillings (see below)

1 large egg yolk (20 grams)

1 teaspoon (5 grams) cocoa nibs, crushed

MAKE THE FOIE GRAS

Put the foie gras, milk, and water in a large bowl and cover with plastic wrap. Refrigerate overnight. Remove the foie gras from the bowl and pat dry with paper towels. Use a warm, sharp knife to cut it into 2 × 1-inch slices. Pat the slices dry again with paper towels and use a tweezers to remove any veins or blood spots. Put the foie gras on a baking tray and cover tightly with plastic wrap. Refrigerate until ready to use.

MAKE THE FILLING

Heat a medium, heavy pot over medium heat and add the water, kosher salt, pink salt, sugar, lemongrass, juniper berries, ginger, bay leaves, mustard seeds, and coriander seeds. Bring the mixture to a simmer and cook until the salts and sugar dissolve. Remove the pot from the heat and let cool, uncovered, in the refrigerator overnight.

Set a chinois or very fine-mesh strainer over a large bowl and strain the brine mixture through it. Add the duck to the mixture and cover with a lid or plastic wrap. Refrigerate overnight.

Remove the duck from the brine and pat dry with paper towels. Discard the brine. Lay a piece of plastic wrap down on a cool work surface and set 1 duck leg on top, fat side down. Lightly dust the flesh side of the duck with the Activa.

Lay the next duck leg, fat side down, and repeat the same process until there are three layers of Activa coating (the final layer of coating is on the outside). Put the duck in a large vacuum bag and seal at 100 percent vacuum. Bring a water bath in an immersion circulator to 162°F (72°C) and add the duck. Cook for 18 hours.

Remove the bag from the water bath and allow it to sit at room temperature for 20 minutes in the vacuum bag. Fill a large bowl with ice water and add the bag to the water for 30 minutes. Drain the ice water and cover the bag fully with ice until the internal temperature registers 34°F (1.1°C), 1 to 2 hours. Remove the bag from the ice and place the duck on a sheet tray. Press a weight atop the duck to set a flat shape and refrigerate overnight.

Remove the pressed duck from the bag, and cut the meat into four 2 × 1-inch cubes. Place a slice of the prepared foie gras atop the duck. Place the duck foie gras on a chilled tray and refrigerate for at least 3 hours to chill and set the shape. (The duck component must be cold when you finally assemble the torte.)

MAKE THE TORTE DOUGH

Cube the butter and allow it to come up to room temperature. Put the flour, fleur de sel, and sugar in the bowl of a stand mixer fitted with the paddle attachment and paddle together on medium speed, then add the butter and mix until incorporated. With the motor running, stream in the milk until a cohesive dough is formed, about 90 seconds. Turn out and knead on a lightly floured surface until the dough is very smooth, about 5 minutes. With floured hands, shape the dough into a ball, wrap in plastic, and let rest overnight in the refrigerator.

Dust a clean work surface with flour and roll the dough out to a 1/8-inch-thick sheet. (Do this quickly, as the dough must be very cold while rolling out.) Place it on a floured, parchment-lined sheet tray, wrap in plastic wrap, and chill in the refrigerator for 3 hours.

Unwrap the chilled dough and punch out 6-inch rounds. Lay one round of dough onto a 3-inch demi-sphere mold (see Sources, page 268) lined with plastic wrap. Place the duck foie gras filling in the mold with the foie gras side down.

Take another 6-inch round of dough and brush one side with egg yolk. Lay the second round atop the torte, egg yolk side down, to form a ravioli. Repeat three more times for three more molds. Turn the molds upside down onto a floured, parchment-lined sheet tray. Take a ring that is 1/2 inch larger than the demi-sphere mold and punch down around the mold to remove excess dough. Press a flour-dusted fork around the edge of dough to crimp and seal. Carefully remove the mold and plastic.

Punch a 1/8-inch hole at the top of the dome to allow steam to release while the torte is baking. Place in the refrigerator for 3 hours. Very lightly brush the tortes with egg yolk and season with cocoa nibs.

Preheat a convection oven to 350°F (177°C). Place the prepared tortes on a Silpat-lined baking tray and bake (low fan) for 13 minutes, or until evenly golden brown. Use a spatula to transfer the tortes to a cooling rack. Let rest for 5 minutes prior to serving. (The finished tortes may be refrigerated overnight on a plastic-wrapped tray.)

SPAGHETTI WITH LAMB BOLOGNESE

MAKES 1 QUART (1 LITER) OF SAUCE; SERVES 4

This popular staff, or family, meal at Corton offers a clever honoring of the kitchen tradition of not wasting any part of an ingredient. Italian Bolognese is traditionally made with a combination of beef, veal, and pork. But in my kitchen at Corton, we've made it a lusty, unabashedly flavorful way to use the parts of a lamb that are left after the butchering. This also is my personal attempt at keeping my kitchen happy. I remember all too well the paltry staff meals—or lack of meals entirely—at the kitchens that I came up in, and how desperately hungry and exhausted we were during service.

¼ cup extra-virgin olive oil plus extra for drizzling

1 pound (453.5 grams) lamb rump (ground by your butcher)

½ pound (227 grams) lamb neck pieces (ground by your butcher)

½ medium onion, minced

2½ medium cloves garlic, minced

1 small carrot, peeled and finely diced

3 whole star anise

1½ (12.5 grams) jalapeño chile peppers, seeded, rib removed, and finely diced

¾ cup (150 grams) Jack Daniel's Tennessee Whiskey

1 tablespoon plus 1½ teaspoons tomato paste

½ cup (125 grams) whole milk

¼ cup (125 grams) lamb cooking jus (from recipe on page 237) or lamb stock

1 green bell pepper, seeded

Kosher salt

Freshly ground black pepper

½ pound (227 grams) dried spaghetti

1 cylinder of the Finishing Butter (recipe follows)

Heat a large, heavy pan over high heat. Pour in the oil and heat until it is shimmering and almost smoking. Add the lamb rump and neck and brown the meat, stirring often to ensure even cooking, until well and evenly caramelized, about 10 minutes. Use a slotted spoon to transfer the meat to a plate and set it aside.

Lower the heat to medium-low and add the onion, garlic, carrot, star anise, and two-thirds of the diced jalapeños. Cook, stirring until the vegetables are caramelized, about 8 minutes. Pour in the whiskey and add the tomato paste. Stir with a rubber spatula to coat the vegetables with the paste, and continue to cook and stir until the whiskey is reduced by half, about 4 minutes.

Return the meat to the pan. Pour in the milk and jus. Cover with a cartouche (see Note, page 234) and slowly braise on the stove top for 8 hours, stirring occasionally to keep the meat and sauce from sticking to the bottom of the pan.

Remove the pan from the heat, let cool to room temperature, then cool in the refrigerator overnight, with the cartouche in place.

Preheat the oven to 325°F (163°C). To roast the bell pepper, impale it on a long kitchen fork and cook it in the flame of a gas jet, turning it, until the skin is blackened all over. When cool enough to handle, peel off the skin, drizzle olive oil over it, and season it with salt and pepper. Put the bell pepper in a small baking vessel, cover it with foil, and bake for 25 minutes. Remove and let the pepper cool, and dice it.

When ready to serve, bring a large pot of salted water to a boil over high heat. Add the spaghetti to the boiling salted water and cook until al dente, about 9 minutes.

Remove the cartouche from the Bolognese and use a slotted spoon to fish out and discard the star anise. Rewarm the Bolognese over medium-low heat. Stir the remaining one-third diced jalapeños and the diced bell pepper into the sauce. Dice the finishing butter and stir it into the sauce, a few pieces at a time, to thicken it.

Drain the pasta, shaking out the excess water, and transfer it to the pan with the Bolognese, tossing well. Divide the pasta and sauce among 4 plates or wide, shallow bowls, and serve.

FINISHING BUTTER
MAKES TWO 10-INCH CYLINDERS
This compound, or flavored, butter is a potent finishing agent for the Bolognese and a fine way to augment any lamb sauce. For a dramatic and different take on garlic bread, spread it over toasted bread.

- ½ pound (2 sticks, 227 grams) unsalted butter, softened at room temperature
- ¼ cup (40 grams) Madras curry powder
- 2 teaspoons (10 grams) ground star anise
- 4 small limes, finely zested and juiced
- 2 tablespoons (10 grams) Tabasco Green Sauce
- 2 tablespoons (10 grams) Jack Daniel's Tennessee Whiskey
- 2 tablespoons (10 grams) ketchup
- 1½ teaspoons (10 grams) freshly, finely grated Parmigiano-Reggiano cheese
- 1 tablespoon (5 grams) Worcestershire sauce

Put all the ingredients in the bowl of a stand mixer fitted with the paddle attachment. Mix on low speed until the ingredients come together into a smooth mixture, about 3 minutes.

Use a rubber spatula to scrape the butter out of the bowl and onto a clean, dry work surface. Divide it in half and shape each half into a 10-inch-long cylinder. Wrap each cylinder tautly in plastic wrap and refrigerate until ready to use. (The butter will keep for up to two weeks.)

SOURCES

AMAZON
www.amazon.com
FOR: 00 flour, demi-sphere molds, egg white powder, feuilletine, freeze-dried banana powder, freeze-dried blackberries, Low Acyl Gellan (Gellan F), High Acyl Gellan (Gellan LT), gold leaf, glucose syrup, liquid glucose, palm sugar, shrimp paste, specialty chocolates

D'ARTAGNAN
www.dartagnan.com; 800-327-8246
FOR: duck fat, foie gras

THE INGREDIENT FINDER
www.theingredientfinder.com
FOR: smoked fleur de sel, *vadouvan* spice

JB PRINCE
www.jbprince.com
FOR: caramel rulers, silicone molds, *sous vide* equipment and supplies

KALUSTYAN'S
www.kalustyans.com; 800-352-3451
FOR: hibiscus flowers, kaffir lime leaves, matcha green tea powder, piment d'espelette, pink curing salt (sodium nitrite), sel gris, *vadouvan* spice

THE MODERNIST PANTRY
www.modernistpantry.com;
469-443-6634
FOR: Activa RM, Activa YG, agar-agar, N_2O chargers, Crisp Film, iSi Soda Siphon, malic acid, sodium hexametaphosphate, soy lecithin powder, xanthan gum

PLANTIN
www.plantin-truffle.com
FOR: truffles, truffle juice, and other truffle products

SHERRY-LEHMANN
www.sherry-lehmann.com; 212-838-7500
FOR: Chartreuse

TESTEK INSTRUMENTS
www.testek.ca
FOR: insulated bowl (liquid nitrogen cooking bowl)

ACKNOWLEDGMENTS

I would like to offer my heartfelt appreciation to the following colleagues for their contributions to this project:

Andrew Friedman, for his brilliant words

Evan Sung, for his brilliant photography

Heston Blumenthal, for his exceedingly generous and humbling foreword, and for being a good countryman

Pam Krauss, publisher of Clarkson Potter, for her longtime support and encouragement

A huge thank-you to all my team, past and present: Michelle Quintana, Mazen Mustafa, Victoria Blamey, Ari Weiswasser, and Tom Rice, to name a few

My agent, David Black, for his shepherding of this project from its inception

My editor, Jessica Freeman-Slade, and the entire design and marketing teams at Clarkson Potter: Stephanie Huntwork, James Massey, Jane Treuhaft, Amy Boorstein, Kate Tyler, and Maha Khalil

And to Arleene: Simply, thank you . . . with all my heart

INDEX

Note: Page numbers in *italics* refer to photographs and captions.